Advance praise for *How Digital Is Your Business?*

"Slywotzky and Morrison deliver a strategic and practical roadmap that helps you to separate your best digital opportunities from the quicksand of technology for its own sake. Through powerful examples, they remind us that the most successful digital businesses are those founded on a bulletproof business model."

> —*Michael J. Hagan,*
> COO and co-founder, VerticalNet, Inc.

"This is the first of the 'digital' books that really gets it. Though the digital age changes the playing field, Slywotzky and Morrison prove that the fundamental rules of business are still in force."

> —*Dr. Klaus Wucherer,*
> senior vice president, Siemens AG

"Through excellent case studies, this book offers insights into the art and science of positioning businesses for digital transformation. *How Digital Is Your Business?* is about more than techniques for selling widgets online; it's an illuminating glimpse of a new digital landscape."

> —*Bob Lambert,*
> senior vice president, New Technology and Development, The Walt Disney Company

"Like risk, change is not optional. *How Digital Is Your Business?* is a must-read for executives from traditional bricks-and-mortar companies facing the challenges of the digital economy. Its real-world case studies prove that it's possible for any company to transform itself into a customer-centric digital business design. Slywotzky and Morrison offer a roadmap to creating new value for both our customers and our shareowners."

> —*Earnest W. Deavenport, Jr.,*
> chairman and chief executive officer, Eastman Chemical Company

"Only a few players currently excel in the digital world. Slywotzky and Morrison describe concrete approaches that hold real promise for the companies—whether traditional or new economy—that are willing to take up the challenge."

> —*Roxanne J. Decyk,*
> vice president of Corporate Strategy, Royal Dutch/Shell Group

"Using digital technology to forge powerful customer relationships based on new and unique value propositions is e-business's next frontier. At American Airlines, we find the customer-centric principles outlined in *How Digital Is Your Business?* right on target."

> —*Mike Gunn,*
> executive vice president, Marketing and Planning, American Airlines

"Slywotzky and Morrison show you how digital technology, strategically applied, can remake any industry—from concrete to financial services. The book is filled with relevant examples, and the workbook style helps you immediately apply the concepts to your own industry. If you want to challenge your thinking and create true value, read this book."

> —*Rich Noll,*
> corporate vice president, Sara Lee Corporation

"The concept of Digital Business Design is both enlightening and insightful, but more importantly, actionable. Embrace it now—before your competitors do."

> —*Mark J. Lotke,*
> managing director, Internet Capital Group

"A clear and compelling articulation of why companies need to redesign their businesses around the customer and digital technologies."

> —*Deryck Maughan*
> vice chairman, Citigroup

How
DIGITAL
Is Your
BUSINESS?

Also by Adrian J. Slywotzky and David J. Morrison

The Profit Zone
Profit Patterns

Also by Adrian J. Slywotzky

Value Migration

How
DIGITAL
Is Your
BUSINESS?

ADRIAN J. SLYWOTZKY
DAVID J. MORRISON

WITH KARL WEBER

CROWN
BUSINESS
NEW YORK

Published by Crown Business, New York, New York. Member of the Crown Publishing Group.

Random House, Inc. New York, Toronto, London, Sydney, Auckland

www.randomhouse.com

Crown Business and colophon are trademarks of Random House, Inc.

Printed in the United States of America

Library of Congress Cataloging-in-Publication Data

Slywotzky, Adrian J.
    How digital is your business? / Adrian J. Slywotzky, David J. Morrison; with Karl Weber—1st ed.
    Includes index.
    1. Electronic commerce—Management.   I. Morrison, David J.   II. Weber, Karl, III. Title.
    HF5548.32.S59 2000
    658.8′00285—dc21

                                                                    00-057020

ISBN 0-609-60770-7

10 9 8 7 6 5 4 3 2 1

First Edition

CONTENTS

How
DIGITAL
Is Your
BUSINESS?

INTRODUCTION

WHY THIS BOOK? And why now? After all (you may be thinking), this isn't the first book on e-commerce and the Internet. It may not even be among the first *hundred* books on these topics, as a casual glance at any bookstore's shelves makes clear. What can this book say that's new and different?

That casual impression is correct in one sense, wrong in another. Correct because the digital revolution *has* been under way for years and has spawned hundreds of books, including several excellent ones. Wrong because *How Digital Is Your Business?* is not a book on e-commerce or the Internet. It's a book on *digital business*. And that means it could not have been written even eighteen months ago.

We define a digital business as one in which strategic options have been transformed—and significantly broadened—by the use of digital technologies. Under this definition, it's not enough to have a great Web site or a wired workforce or neat software that helps to run a factory. A digital business uses digital technologies to devise entirely new value propositions for customers and for the company's own talent; to invent new methods of creating and capturing profits; and, ultimately, to pursue the true goal of strategic differentiation: *uniqueness.*

Digital business, so defined, is a phenomenon that has emerged only since 1996. It gathered momentum in the last two years of the twentieth century.

☐ Not until 1998 did Dell Computer's on-line configurator—one of the first Choiceboards, a powerful new tool for digital business—appear in anything like its current form.

☐ Not until May of the same year did it become apparent that what we call 10X Productivity—order-of-magnitude improvement in

3

cost, capital requirements, and cycle time—could be and in fact was being realized through the use of digital technologies.

☐ Not until early in 1999 did it become clear that AOL, Yahoo!, and eBay had all developed viable business models for doing business on the Internet.

☐ And not until the early months of 2000 did it become clear that GE, one of the business world's great incumbent companies, was moving forcefully to bring about the first successful large-scale transition from a nondigital to a digital business model.

Add to these facts the reality that the creation of a fully developed digital business design takes four to five years to complete, and it's apparent that what we now know about digital business was *impossible* to know, except in vague outline form, prior to 2000. Thus, we'd argue, this is the *first* book about digital business. It won't be the last.

Having been exposed to the hype and furor that digital technologies have aroused, we have no desire to contribute to them. But we believe that digital business represents a fundamental change from past business models. By comparison, other business movements, like the quality movement of the 1980s or the reengineering movement of the 1990s, will prove to be significantly narrower and more technical, and will have less impact.

The breadth and depth of the digital revolution are so important that no one in business can afford *not* to make digital business a leading priority during the next half-decade. The situation of today's business leaders—those responsible for decisions that affect customers and determine how talent, money, and other resources are deployed—is comparable to that of any professional whose field is being altered forever by the emergence of a new and better way of working.

Think of an architect during the early years of the twentieth century, when steel-girder construction and the invention of the elevator were making skyscrapers possible; or imagine a physician in the middle of the nineteenth century, when the discoveries of anesthesia (in the 1840s) and of sterile technique (in the 1860s) were transforming surgery from a torturous horror into a life-saving miracle. No responsible professional would want to ignore such developments. It's now clear—far clearer than

Introduction

it was even two years ago—that the changes made possible by new digital ways of doing business will be equally radical, beneficial, and liberating.

The history of digital business is just emerging from the discovery stage. But early developments have already revealed some important lessons for those who would lead—or join—the second wave of business digitization. This book makes available to anyone in business the economic and organizational implications of the success stories (as well as the struggles and setbacks) of companies that are showing the way toward the Digital Business Designs of the future.

These companies are the digital pioneers, and several chapters in this book tell their stories: Dell Computer (Chapter 4), Cemex (Chapter 5), Charles Schwab (Chapter 7), and Cisco Systems (Chapter 9). Taken together, these chapters illustrate the extraordinary outcomes that Digital Business Design makes possible, and they suggest the qualitative changes in business culture and values that accompany digitization. The stories of these four companies offer profiles of the digital businesses of the future.

Chapters 12 and 13 present a different kind of case study: the current experiences of two large and powerful incumbents, GE and IBM, as they transform themselves into digital businesses. These chapters sketch out what it takes to change a traditional enterprise into a digital business, and some of the problems and obstacles that must be overcome.

Chapter 14 tells yet another type of business story: the success of the few large-scale Internet-based businesses that have developed viable (and profitable) digital business designs. AOL, Yahoo!, and eBay are examples of what it takes to *start* in a digital space and build an effective business model. Legions of struggling dot-com companies have begun to learn some of the hard but necessary lessons.

Other chapters focus on specific aspects of digital business design: the Choiceboard, a powerful but little-known digital tool; 10X Productivity, one of the remarkable benefits that digitization offers; and the organizational effects of going digital. Each element of the digital business picture provides ideas and methods that can help every company that is crafting a transition from a conventional to a Digital Business Design. The chapter sequence allows the ideas, information, and stories to be mutually reinforcing and cumulative in their effect.

We hope that, after reading this book, the importance and urgency of digitization for *all* businesses today will be clear. The current business climate of relative prosperity (and the record-setting bull market) can dampen the sense of urgency about fundamental business reinvention. "We're doing fine," is the feeling, "so why rush into something we don't really understand?" That reaction is human, understandable, and very dangerous.

Consider the people for whom you're responsible: your customers, your employees, your partners. Within the next three years, it simply won't be possible to do a world-class job of serving them, and the other stakeholders who rely on you, without becoming digital. But if you begin today the process of transforming your company through Digital Business Design, you'll be able to offer them benefits no other company can match—the unique value propositions that are the ultimate reward of digitization.

The time is now, and the starting gate is right here.

HOW DIGITAL IS
YOUR BUSINESS?

THE DIGITAL DIFFERENCE

At various moments during the past two decades, companies and the individuals who lead them have become aware of *digitization* as a disruptive, creative force that is revolutionizing how people work, play, communicate, buy, sell, and live. The moments of recognition came at different times and were driven by specific phenomena: the advent of the personal computer . . . the proliferation of E-mail . . . the growth of ERP (enterprise resource planning) systems . . . the popularity of the Internet. As a result, most people either identify *digital business* with one or more of these phenomena or consider it simply the sum total of the high-tech innovations multiplying around us.

That view is fatally incomplete. Digital business—especially Digital Business Design (DBD), the approach we advocate and explain in this book—is not about any of these phenomena. Nor is it about wiring everybody in the company, providing all your salespeople with laptops, converting your R&D and manufacturing facilities to CAD/CAM, selling your products through your Web site, or allowing employees to telecommute from their homes.

> *Digital Business Design* is the art and science of using digital technologies to expand a company's strategic options. DBD is not about technology for its own sake; it's about serving customers, creating unique value propositions, leveraging talent, radically improving productivity, and increasing profits. It's about using digital options to craft a business model that is not only superior, but *unique.*

In terms of the benefits it offers customers, the rate of growth it sustains, its ability to develop talent, and the financial results it attains, a digital business accomplishes what would have been considered impossible just a few years ago.

Dell Computer and Compaq are in the same industry and produce similar products. Yet Dell is a digital business; Compaq is not. What's the difference? Dell is *unique* in the following ways:

☐ The degree to which it knows its customers and gives them exactly what they want.

☐ The outstanding financial results it achieves in an industry that verges on unprofitability.

☐ The unparalleled level of strategic control it has attained in its business.

Like other PC companies, Compaq relies almost exclusively on retail outlets to sell its products. It *guesses* what demand will be, produces the number of machines it thinks customers might buy, and then tries to sell them to customers through its distributors. By contrast, Dell manufactures a PC only after receiving an order from a customer who has paid Dell in full. (The customer designs her own computer using an online tool called the configurator, and she pays via credit card with a few clicks of the mouse.) Thus, Dell uses the customer's money to finance production. Compaq relies on traditional methods of financing. It produces machines and ships them to its distribution channels, hoping that retailers will pay for them—eventually.

Guesswork about customers is prevalent not only in industries that operate by the seat of the pants but also in those that spend millions on state-of-the-art market research. In industry after industry, reliance on guesswork has unfortunate results. In a visit to any car dealer in autumn, customers can expect to be offered rebates, markdowns, and financing schemes that are unprofitable for the producer—all in an effort to get rid of unsold inventory and make room for next year's models.

The fallout from the way almost every company has been forced to operate yields a litany of woes: asset intensity, high levels of risk, precarious levels of profitability, little in the way of strategic control, and customers with little loyalty.

What if there were a better way? What if you could reverse the way business is done? What if you knew exactly what your customers wanted, and produced only those products? What if you could do away with the guesswork and the waste of unsold inventory? What if you could enjoy order-of-magnitude (ten-fold) increases in productivity?

What if you could become a digital business?

Digital Business Design enables companies to achieve goals that were long considered unattainable. Businesses accept, at least in theory, the premise that it is a sin to waste the time and talents of employees. Yet most companies commit this sin by making it necessary for their workforce to spend far too much time doing the low-value work of reinventing the wheel by replicating solutions to problems that have already been solved. This sin is committed not only by industrial-age businesses (e.g., manufacturing firms) but by "knowledge companies"—professional service and consulting firms, and media companies. This book explains how DBD offers a way out.

Another economic sin businesses recognize is asset intensity. Businesspeople want to make the most of every dollar invested. Yet, in the real world, the bigger a business grows, the more its capital is tied up in real estate, buildings, machinery, inventory, and support systems. Companies come to believe that this is the only way to provide timely service to customers. After all, they reason, without a warehouse full of products and a growing fleet of delivery trucks, they might get caught short during the next holiday season. But the results are shrinking rates of return and such a dead weight of assets that adjusting nimbly when the current business model becomes obsolete is almost impossible. DBD can help solve this once-intractable dilemma.

MIGRATING TO THE NORTHEAST QUADRANT

Until recently, the probability that any organization would enjoy long-term success was determined by a single factor: *the quality of its business design*. Today, the multiplication of digital technologies has introduced a second crucial competitive factor: *the degree of its relevant digitization*. In this chapter, we'll show you how to determine where you stand, compared with other companies that are implementing the science of Digital Business Design (DBD). We'll also introduce the eight-point DBD Benefits Scale, which will help you understand what DBD can do for your company, your customers, and your talent, and will get you started on developing an action plan for realizing those benefits.

In today's economy, any organization can be mapped onto a field based on its level of digitization and its business design. (See Figure 1–1.) We call it the DBD matrix. The kinds of companies that may be identified are:

- ☐ Low digitization, bad business design (Southwest quadrant).
- ☐ High digitization, bad business design (Northwest quadrant).
- ☐ Low digitization, great business design (Southeast quadrant).
- ☐ High digitization, great business design (Northeast quadrant).

Most businesses are in the Southwest quadrant. They have a weak business design, a business design that is fundamentally flawed, or a business design that is obviously vulnerable to changes that are already happening. These companies have poor answers or no answers to the basic business design questions: What customers do I choose to serve? Why do they buy from me? Why do people work here? How do I make money? How do I protect my profits? and so on.

FIGURE 1–1   The Digital Business Design Matrix

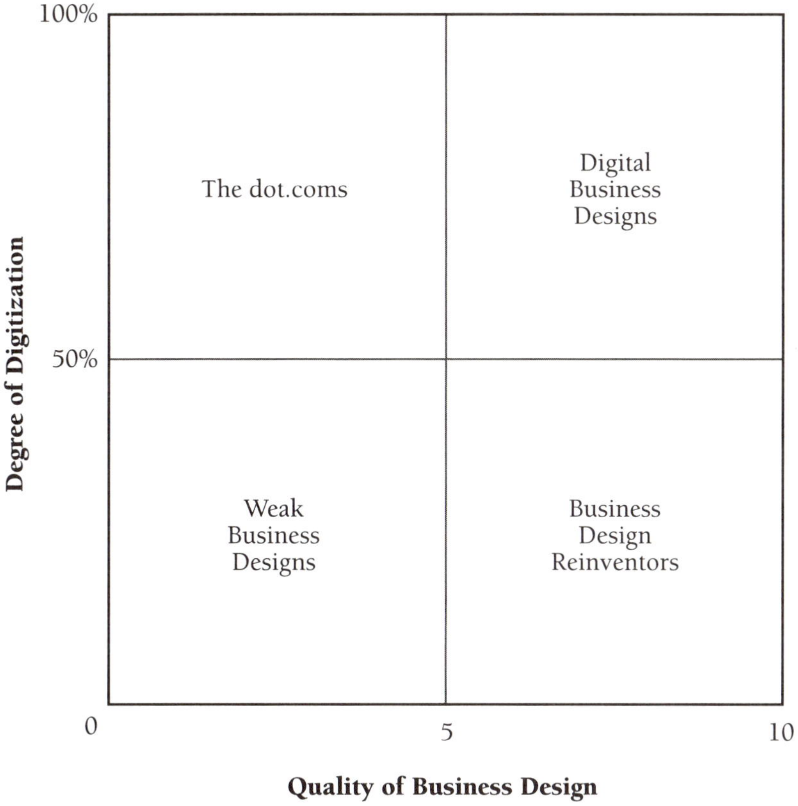

```
100% ┌──────────────────┬──────────────────┐
     │                  │                  │
     │                  │     Digital      │
     │  The dot.coms    │     Business     │
     │                  │     Designs      │
     │                  │                  │
 50% ├──────────────────┼──────────────────┤
     │                  │                  │
     │     Weak         │     Business     │
     │   Business       │     Design       │
     │    Designs       │   Reinventors    │
     │                  │                  │
   0 └──────────────────┴──────────────────┘
     0                  5                 10
```

Degree of Digitization (vertical axis)

Quality of Business Design

Northwest quadrant companies have high degrees of digitization but are still disadvantaged by a flawed or incomplete business design. Most dot-com companies are in the Northwest quadrant.

The Southeast quadrant contains businesses with relatively low digitization and great business design, like GE or Swatch. In our earlier book, *The Profit Zone,* we dubbed these companies "the Reinventors." All have been phenomenally successful because of the brilliance and courage of their leadership teams. They crafted business designs that captured and controlled large and growing segments of the value chain, and then, as necessary, reinvented those designs to keep pace with changes in customer priorities, technology, social and economic conditions, and competitive forces.

However, the following truth has now become clear.

> Tomorrow's most spectacular business success stories will be found in the Northeast quadrant, home to the minority of companies that will have made the transition to Digital Business Design.

Unsurprisingly, several of the best-run businesses in the Southeast quadrant are already hard at work adapting to the digital age. The approaches they are developing will enable them to take full advantage of the benefits of digitization faster than their competitors. In effect, these companies are on the march toward the Northeast quadrant. (As we'll discuss later, GE is well advanced in this process.)

We'll use the four-quadrant map as a guide throughout this book. The Northeast quadrant is our reference area for the powerful combination of great business design and smart digitization that we call Digital Business Design (DBD).

THE FINANCIAL IMPLICATIONS

At a recent conference, we asked 300 executives to rate their own businesses on the business design scale (0 to 10) and the digitization scale (0 to 100 percent). The average response was:

- ☐ Business design: 4.6
- ☐ Digitization: 15 percent

What amount of untapped value could be realized by moving the average company significantly upward along both of these scales? For example, suppose you could shift your own company as follows:

- ☐ Business design: 4.6 → 9.0
- ☐ Digitization: 15 percent → 80 percent

What kinds of business results could be achieved as a result of such a shift? In the course of this book, we'll answer this question by looking closely at four pioneering companies that have already migrated into the Northeast quadrant: Dell Computer, Cemex, Charles Schwab, and Cisco Systems. We'll examine how these companies have used Digital Business Design to acquire commanding positions in their industries, and we'll glance at other companies that have begun to emulate them. Table 1–1 compares the key financial results obtained by the digital reinventors and by their leading nondigital competitors in the same fields.

From 1997 through 1999, Dell's pretax profit margins averaged 11 percent. Its major competitors such as Compaq, HP, and IBM (which sold PCs primarily through various retail and wholesale channels rather than directly to customers, as Dell does) essentially had breakeven businesses. During the same period, Cemex's pretax margins were 22 percent compared to an average of 11 percent for the world's other top cement producers (Lafarge, Holderbank, Heidelberger, and Blue Circle).

Schwab's pretax profit margins averaged 18 percent. Those of the top competing brokerage houses, Merrill Lynch and PaineWebber, averaged 10 percent. Cisco's pretax profit margin during this period was 28 percent.

TABLE 1–1 Digital Reinventors vs. Nondigital Competitors

Three-Year Average Pretax Profit Margins (1997–1999)

	Digital Leaders	Top Competitors
Dell Computer	11%	1%*
Cemex	22	11
Charles Schwab	18	10
Cisco Systems	28	7

*Estimated average margin in competing PC businesses.

Three-Year Average Revenue Growth Rates (1997–1999)

	Digital Leaders	Top Competitors
Dell Computer	48%	21%†
Cemex	11	10
Charles Schwab	27	12
Cisco Systems	44	10

†Estimated average growth rate in competing PC businesses.

Its top competitors (Cabletron, 3Com, and Bay Networks) averaged only 7 percent.

The differences in growth rates were as striking as the differences in profitability. Dell and Cisco grew 30 percent faster than their competitors; Schwab grew 15 percent faster than its competitors.

Companies that have shifted to Digital Business Design by integrating a smart business model with business-driven exploitation of digital options can produce profit margins and growth rates that are significantly higher than their best competition. These differences are simply not achievable without DBD. Furthermore, these differences may *grow* over time, as the early advantages now being gained by the digital innovators are consolidated and used for creating even greater investment and performance improvements in the next cycle.

Digital Business Design can enhance your business's financial results in a host of specific ways. No matter what measure you choose—profits, revenues, return on assets, sales per employee, rate of growth, P/E ratio, market valuation—Digital Business Design can improve it significantly, and not by squeezing value out of customers and suppliers. DBD creates entirely new sources of value and enhances customer satisfaction and supplier performance.

YOUR PLACE ON THE MAP

For a moment, shed your identity. Step outside your skin. Imagine that you are a Digital Business Design specialist hired to analyze your business and advise your company on its next moves:

- ☐ What is your assessment of your company's current situation?
- ☐ Where would you place your company in the DBD matrix (Figure 1–1)? On a scale of 0 to 10, how would you rate your company's business design? (Your answer will locate your company on the east–west axis of the map.)
- ☐ On a scale from 0 to 100 percent, how digital are you? (Your answer will locate your company on the map's north–south axis.) If

you're not immediately certain how to rate your degree of digitization, the next section of this chapter will help.

☐ Where would you place your chief competitors on the four-quadrant map? In which direction are they moving? How quickly? Are there any new players on the horizon? If so, where are they likely to appear on the map?

☐ What strategic opportunities does the above analysis suggest for your company? How can you begin to address them?

YOUR DIGITAL RATIO

One important aspect of moving from a conventional to a Digital Business Design—that is, toward the Northeast quadrant—involves shifting many of your company's key activities from paper-based processes to digital (usually on-line) processes. To obtain at least a partial measure of how digital your business is, complete a simple two-minute exercise we refer to as *estimating your Digital Ratio.* Use it before you launch the process of moving to DBD and it will provide a baseline reading; at any stage in the transition, use it to measure your progress. It will also help you to place your company accurately on the four-quadrant map.

Working quickly, check off your company's digital percentages in Figure 1–2. How much of your company's selling is done on-line? For many companies, the answer may be zero, or less than 10 percent. By contrast, customers of discount broker Charles Schwab make over 50 percent of their trades on-line, up from single digits as recently as 1996, while networking company Cisco Systems sells more than 90 percent of its gear on-line. Similarly, ask how much delivery of products, services, or information your company does on-line? How much supply-chain management? Customer service? Billing? And so on.

The resulting pattern of checkmarks provides a rapid digital profile of your company. If most of your checkmarks are on the left side of the table, expanding your use of digital options may create tremendous opportunities for you to improve the customer relevance, talent leverage, and economic efficiencies of your business.

FIGURE 1–2   Your Digital Ratio

	0%	10%	20%	30%	40%	50%	60%	70%	80%	90%	100%
Selling											
Delivery											
Supply Chain											
Customer Service											
Billing											
Buying											
Recruiting											
Training											
Finance											
R&D											
Manufacturing											
Marketing											

Suppose your competitors and other companies in the same and related industries were filling out Figure 1–2. How would your profile compare to that of your strongest direct competitor? Would it match that of the company with the best business design in your industry? How do you anticipate that the comparison will change during the next twelve months?

Moving from the left side to the right side of Figure 1–2 is *not* an end in itself. Any decision to move a particular activity toward the right, and how far, depends on your key business issues, what is required to improve your value proposition for your customers and employees, and the capital and process economics of your business.

In many cases, 100 percent digital is *not* what your customers want. Take selling, for example. The corporate customers of a large Wall Street law firm demand face-to-face contact with a partner; on-line selling would be inappropriate and ineffective. But the same customers might value on-line billing and even on-line delivery of a part of the product (for example, electronic transmission of draft proxy statements for rapid review and correction by the client). The goal is not (necessarily) to be 100 percent digital, but rather to offer the right solutions for your customers. The ideal formula will probably change over time; so should your company's profile.

One executive from a chemical manufacturing firm reacted to his own company's Digital Ratio this way:

> Our scores are low across the board. But I think the biggest mistake we could make would be to try to digitize across the board. Our *first* issue is to figure out—soon—which of these dimensions are the three or four that are most critical to our business from a customer and profitability perspective.

He's right, of course. The digital innovators—Dell, Cemex, Schwab, and Cisco—have all moved aggressively from left to right in almost every part of their business profile, but they've done so only *after* articulating the business issues they needed to address. They knew that digitizing an irrelevant or low-value process is worse than not digitizing at all. However, their experience shows that digitization that is customer-centric and profit-driven leads to previously unattainable results. If your company's profile falls consistently on the left side of the Digital Ratio table, it's a warning sign (and a sign of opportunity). Competitors that have migrated further to the right are likely to be establishing advantages that will enable them to take customers and profits away from you.

THE REAL BENEFITS OF DBD

Figuring your Digital Ratio is a useful exercise; for many companies, it will be a sobering one. ("Good grief, haven't we moved any further to the right than *that*? . . .") But it only scratches the surface of what DBD really means.

> On the surface, Digital Business Design is about how many of your business processes are conducted on-line. At a deeper level, it's about whether you've transformed the way you do business by taking advantage of the new strategic options enabled by digital technologies.

The experience of the digital innovators shows that DBD can fundamentally change the way you do business. It enables you to make a dramatic, positive shift toward realizing the following benefits of DBD:

1. The basis of your business decision-making shifts from *guessing* to *knowing*.
2. The value proposition you offer to your customers shifts from a *mismatch* (great or small) to a *perfect fit*.
3. Information flow within your company shifts from *lag time* to *real time*.
4. Your customer service model shifts from *supplier service* to *customer self-service*.
5. The use of your employees' time shifts from predominantly *low-value-added work* to *maximum talent leverage*.
6. Your processes shift from a focus on *fixing* errors to *preventing* them.
7. Your productivity growth pattern shifts from a norm of *10 percent improvement* to *10X productivity improvement*.
8. Your organization shifts from a collection of *separate silos* to an *integrated system* in which information, ideas, and solutions are shared.

Because these shifts in the way you do business are customer-focused, talent-focused, and profit-focused, they are the real payoff of DBD. Digitizing a significant fraction of your business processes is a necessary and important step, but it is not the endpoint. The eight scales of business transformation measure not only how digital your processes are but also how fully your customers, your talent, and your investors are *benefiting* from the shift. Thus, movement along these scales is a more accurate reflection of movement toward the Northeast quadrant.

Measure your own business against the DBD Benefits Scale in Figure 1–3. As with the Digital Ratio, work fairly quickly. You may find that it takes a little longer to complete this table. But a set of rapid, intuitive responses is likely to be 90 percent accurate.

How does your business's profile appear on this scale? Do the characteristics of your business fall mainly on the left side or the right side of Figure 1–3? How rapidly are you moving from left to right? Where do your main business rivals' characteristics fall, and how quickly are they moving? How quickly are your customers' expectations changing?

Also consider these questions:

- ☐ What kinds of financial results will be experienced by companies that are mainly on the right side of the scale?
- ☐ What sort of employee morale level, job satisfaction, and long-term commitment to the company will be associated with the left and the right sides?
- ☐ Where will customer satisfaction be greater?
- ☐ Which business model is more likely to attract and retain long-term investors?

The net effect of these DBD benefits is *multiplicative,* not additive. Each shift from left to right produces a marked improvement in how you do business—one that customers, talent, and investors alike will recognize and reward. Together, the shifts produce a completely new way of doing business.

FIGURE 1–3   The DBD Benefits Scale

---

❶ Guessing — — — — — — — — — — **Knowing**

❷ Mismatch — — — — — — — — — — **Perfect Fit**

❸ Lag Time — — — — — — — — — — **Real Time**

**❹ Supplier
Service** — — — — — — — — — — **Customer
Self-Service**

**❺ Low Value
Work** — — — — — — — — — — **Maximum
Talent
Leverage**

**❻ Fixing
Errors** — — — — — — — — — — **Preventing
Errors**

**❼ 10%
Improvement** — — — — — — — — — — **10x
Productivity**

**❽ Separate
Silos** — — — — — — — — — — **Integrated
System**

As you think about your own business, use the tables and figures in this chapter to develop an agenda for change. If you've used check marks to indicate where your business is today, indicate with "T" (for target) where you want your business to move in the next twelve months (e.g., in the first line of Figure 1–2, *Selling* may have a check mark under 10 percent and a T under 50 percent).

Begin to consider these three issues:

1. Which moves are most important, given the specific business is-sues your company faces? (What's most important from a customer perspective? A talent perspective? An economic perspective?)
2. What's the right sequencing of improvements?
3. How many parallel initiatives can your organization sustain?

We'll refer to the DBD Benefits Scale throughout this book. One way to understand how the digital innovators profiled in these pages have transformed their ways of thinking and doing business is to recognize how far they've moved from the left side of the benefits scale to the right: from guessing to knowing, from customer mismatch to perfect fit, from operat-ing in lag time to operating in real time, and so on. You may be surprised to discover how fully these digital benefits can be realized even now, in these early years of the digital transition.

THE WELLSPRING OF DIGITAL INNOVATION

A final thought. Digital innovators share one quality in common: They are *energetic advocates*—for their customers, their employees, and their in-vestors. Their mindset is simple and obsessive, and they are frighteningly persistent in their pursuit of answers to a single set of questions:

☐ How can I exploit digital options to offer a better deal to my cus-tomers? To create a better system for my employees? To generate a better risk-adjusted return for my investors?

An unrelenting focus on these three concerns has produced some fas-cinating business designs. They are different in their details, but each started with the business issues and the problems of customers.

GETTING STARTED IN DIGITAL BUSINESS DESIGN

Digital Business Design (DBD) is an emerging discipline being pioneered by a handful of great companies. Each of these companies began moving to a Digital Business Design in its own way; your company will also find its own unique path. But one rule is clear: Moving to DBD should start not with technology, but with your business issues and the challenge of getting your business design right. Perhaps Michael Dell, president of Dell Computer, said it best:

> If you take a business that is a bad business and put it on-line, it's still a bad business. It's just become an on-line bad business.

Thus, plunging into new technologies before thinking through your larger business issues is a recipe for disaster. Instead, we suggest the following process as an entry point into digitization:

Moving to a Digital Business Design requires that you ask and answer (in the order given) these five key questions:

1. What are the most important business issues facing my organization today?
2. What are the smartest business design choices for responding to those issues?
3. Which of my key business activities involve managing atoms, and which involve managing bits?
4. How can I replace atoms with bits?
5. How can I develop bit engines that will manage the bits electronically?

These five questions provide the most effective entry point to thinking digitally about your business. Answering them in sequence gives you a better start than focusing on any specific technology.

THINK BUSINESS ISSUES FIRST

The first two questions on the list above may be deceptively familiar. On the surface, they have nothing to do with digital. Instead, they focus on issues every manager addresses. Let's start with the first question:

1. What are the most important business issues facing my organization today?

Among other things, this is a question concerning *strategic focus*. It challenges you to identify the crucial factors that will determine the success or failure of your company in, say, the next two years. The answers will vary from industry to industry and from company to company. They could include:

☐ Mismatch with customers' needs.
☐ Customer churn.
☐ Extreme competition.
☐ No growth.
☐ Excessive asset intensity.
☐ No profit.
☐ Talent leaving.
☐ Talent demoralized.
☐ Poor product/service quality.
☐ Lagging productivity.
☐ Lack of innovation.
☐ Industry consolidation.
☐ Rapid customer evolution.
☐ Unforecastable demand.

☐ Costs too high.
☐ Inability to recruit top talent.
☐ Problems with sales channels.
☐ Poor integration of acquisitions.

To answer Question 1, list below the *top five* business issues facing your company today. Use plain English, not industry or management jargon, and focus on the handful of truly critical issues you're wrestling with—the ones that will determine whether your company will be growing and profitable two years from now. When you have completed your list, share it with your colleagues. Is there consensus? General agreement about the key issues you face is a prerequisite to making smart decisions for leading the shift from a conventional to a Digital Business Design.

My Top Business Issues

_____

_____

_____

_____

_____

The CEO of a large technology-based company in a slowly growing but rapidly changing environment listed these top five issues:

"I don't know where our future growth will come from."
"My talent is demoralized."
"My customer churn rate is way too high."
"My selling prices are falling faster than my costs."
"I don't understand the new competitors we face."

The CEO of a highly successful young high-tech company in a fast-growing industry created a list of four issues:

"My customers are changing too fast."

"I can't hire and train enough good people to support my growth."

"My R&D isn't turning out new products fast enough to keep up with the market."

"My customers are killing me with technical service requests."

Notice that these issue statements are short and focused. That's the kind of list you need to figure out what DBD can do for your company. The point is that, unless you get the business issues right, digitization won't matter: You'll simply be spending time, energy, and money on the wrong problems.

THINK BUSINESS DESIGN

After you've identified the key business issues your organization faces, you're ready to consider Question 2:

2. What are the smartest business design choices for responding to those issues?

This *should* be—and may be—a topic you are already exploring.

> **Smart business design** involves deciding what your organization will and will not do to create unique value propositions for your customers and your talent, a robust profit model, and a way to protect the profitability you've created.

The hallmarks of a great business design include:

☐ High relevance to customers.

☐ An internally consistent set of decisions about scope (the products offered and the value-chain activities performed).

☐ A terrific profit model.

☐ A powerful source of differentiation and strategic control that gives investors greater confidence in future cash flows.

☐ An organizational system that supports the business design and leverages your talent effectively.

Given the recent explosion of digital technologies, the newest hallmark of a great business design is:

☐ A powerful digital system for managing and distributing information within and outside the company.

Every business embodies some business design, just as every structure, even a prefabricated tin shed, embodies some architectural design. The difference is that some businesses have been designed with a high degree of awareness as to what customers really want, where value can be found in the process of serving customers, and how an organization can consistently create and capture that value. Great businesses have created such designs and have continually updated and reinvented them as demanded by changes in the economy, technology, the competitive landscape, and customers' priorities.

Unfortunately, many businesses embody designs that evolve with little focus on customers, provide obvious vulnerabilities for exploitation by competitors, allow value to leak out in the process of serving customers, or have become outmoded due to environmental changes.

In this book, we'll show how digital technology expands the array of business design options from which organizations can choose. It also enables companies to execute smart business designs with a remarkably higher degree of speed, accuracy, and profitability. Smart business design *precedes* digitization and gives it value. Remember Michael Dell's warning: If you put a bad business on-line, it's still a bad business. An elegant digital solution that digitizes the wrong things is no solution at all. It's a big step backward. Digital multiplies the impact of smart choices, and bad choices as well. That's why, in the digital age, business fundamentals are more important than ever.

DIMENSIONS OF BUSINESS DESIGN

A structured approach to answering Question 2 ("What are the smartest business design choices for responding to my key business issues?") involves examining the eight key dimensions of business design listed in Table 2–1. The world's most successful businesses have smart, consistent, mutually reinforcing answers to each of these eight questions. A great business knows the customers it chooses to serve. It creates unique value propositions to retain those customers and to attract the best possible employee talent. It has effective ways to make money from its customer relationships and is capable of controlling and protecting those relationships and the profit streams they generate. It defines the scope of its activities so as to maximize its unique value propositions, profit model, and strategic control, and it develops an organizational system and culture that support the entire business design.

Take a moment to analyze your company by answering the eight business design questions. You can learn a great deal about your company, your industry, and your prospects for success by evaluating yourself within the dimensions listed in Table 2–1.

The truly great businesses of today, and those that will become great tomorrow, are also leaders along the eighth dimension of business design. They have powerful *bit engines*—digital systems for capturing, managing, analyzing, storing, multiplying, distributing, and leveraging information within and outside of the company.

The concept of the bit engine requires an understanding of the distinction between *atoms* and *bits.* As you'll see, the same distinction also underlies questions 3, 4, and 5.

MANAGING ATOMS, MANAGING BITS

The difference between *managing atoms* and *managing bits* was first formulated by Nicholas Negroponte of the MIT Media Lab. (His book, *Being Digital,* is one of a small handful of true must-reads in the flood of books that

TABLE 2–1   **What Is My Company's Business Design?**

Dimensions	Questions
Customer Selection	☐ What customers do I choose to serve?
Unique Value Proposition for Customers	☐ Why do they buy from me?
Unique Value Proposition for Talent	☐ Why do people work here?
Value Capture/ Profit Model	☐ How do I make money?
Strategic Control/ Differentiation	☐ How do I protect my profits and my customer relationships?
Scope	☐ What do I do to add value?
Organizational System	☐ What organizational architecture and culture do I create?
Bit Engines	☐ How do I manage and distribute the intelligence in the system?

have been published about the new technologies.) The distinction is important to understanding the value of Digital Business Design.

> *Managing atoms* **is manipulation of physical assets: stockpiling inventory, shipping products, buying equipment, installing machinery, building factories.** *Managing bits* **is manipulation of information: gathering, analyzing, modeling, sorting, sharing, and replicating data.**

Generally speaking, managing atoms is costly, slow, cumbersome, imprecise, and risky. Managing bits, when handled intelligently, can be cheaper, faster, more efficient, more accurate, and safer.

The shift from managing atoms to managing bits has been under way for millennia. The first great step in the process was the invention of language. Without language, a hunter would have had to roam the landscape personally in search of game; with language, he could sift the reports of other hunters and of travelers, and pinpoint the best hunting grounds in advance. The development of writing, mathematics, bookkeeping, and all the various forms of human communication were further advances in substituting the management of bits for the management of atoms.

The twentieth century produced a series of powerful breakthroughs in the management of bits, including the invention of the computer, the development of high-speed, high-capacity systems for storing and transmitting bits, and the emergence of the Internet. During the last decade, the accumulated power of these developments reached a point at which truly revolutionary changes in traditional business models were not only possible but inevitable. Electronic management of bits gives companies options that are otherwise impossible.

Here is an example. Roberts Express, an expedited freight carrier (i.e., a superfast delivery company), is an industry leader in digital business. Like its rivals, Roberts must pick up and deliver a wide range of packages—accurately, safely, and within hours—despite daunting and unpredictable obstacles: traffic jams, vehicle breakdowns, road repairs, wrong directions or addresses, and foul weather. Unlike its rivals, Roberts delivers 96 percent of its packages on time and boasts a customer-satisfaction rating of 1.9 on a scale of 2.

What makes Roberts uniquely effective? The differentiating factor has nothing to do with atoms. The trucks, phones, and computers Roberts owns are the same standard-issue equipment that is owned by thousands of companies. What distinguishes Roberts from other truckers is its speed, skill, accuracy, and flexibility in managing bits—the constant flow of information about deliveries, schedules, truck locations, road conditions, weather, traffic, and dozens of other factors. Using a powerful array of bit engines—including a satellite truck-location system, on-board computers, and a unique software package that tracks vehicles and forecasts demand—Roberts captures, manages, shares, and disseminates vital information more accurately and quickly than other delivery companies.

Without their system for analyzing and transmitting bits, the people at Roberts would be forced to manipulate atoms instead—as they used to, before the company went digital. The truckers would be forced to haul their rigs to side-of-the-road phone booths several times a day; the dispatchers would be forced to wrestle with cards, maps, pens, and papers in an effort to figure out which truck ought to go where. And because of the resulting loss of efficiency, Roberts would need to employ many more trucks and drivers (*more* expensive and unwieldy atoms to manage) to handle the same number of deliveries.

THINK ATOMS AND BITS

As Roberts illustrates, one key to DBD is a company's proactive, deliberate search for opportunities to manage bits:

- ☐ Bits *instead of* atoms.
- ☐ Bits *before* atoms.
- ☐ Bits *in addition to* atoms.

By carefully managing bits, Roberts has drastically reduced the need to manage atoms and has saved time, money, and energy in the process.

Consequently, Roberts is able to (1) provide its customers with faster, more reliable service, (2) reduce frustration among its own employees, and (3) boost sales and profits. This trifecta of business benefits is almost impossible to achieve without DBD.

Questions 3, 4, and 5 focus on the atoms/bits distinction as it relates to your business design:

3. Which of my key business activities involve managing atoms, and which involve managing bits?
4. How can I replace atoms with bits?
5. How can I develop bit engines that will manage the bits electronically?

Traditional businesses often manage atoms because the bits of information that could make the atoms unnecessary are (apparently) unavailable. The crucial vulnerabilities of many industries arise in just this way. Here is an example from among dozens that could be cited.

The automobile industry offers a classic case of atoms versus bits. Because neither car dealers nor auto manufacturers have a precise sense of what the public demand for a particular car model is likely to be, the manufacturers are forced to guesstimate the number of cars that will be purchased, physically produce and distribute them, and then see whether they will sell. The lack of reliable data about consumers' preferences (bits) forces everyone along the chain to produce and handle, at great expense, millions of profitless products (atoms). As a result, about seventy days' worth of inventory, representing a huge amount of unproductive capital, is on car dealers' lots at any given time. And dealers and manufacturers must spend an average of $1,500 per car ($22 billion annually) on rebates and special offers to get customers to accept otherwise unwanted vehicles.

By contrast, Dell Computer uses bit-management to eliminate guesswork and product mismatches from its business. Each customer designs his or her own computer on the Dell Web site, selecting the right processor, amount of memory, size and type of monitor, and so on. Only after the computer specs have been determined and the customer has authorized payment does the Dell production system go to work, assembling the computer for shipment. Thus, Dell manufactures only products that customers have already ordered and paid for. By managing bits first, Dell drastically reduces the need to manage atoms. Dell customers can select a product that perfectly matches their needs and wants.

Notice that DBD doesn't force Dell to make a trade-off between profitability and customer satisfaction; *both* are enhanced.

Automobile companies and Dell Computer face parallel business issues: Both manufacture costly and technologically sophisticated consumer products for which demand is difficult to forecast. The auto companies manage the resulting uncertainty mainly through the manipulation of atoms; Dell manages uncertainty through the manipulation of bits. Consequently, Dell has a far more reliable return on its investment, is growing faster, and enjoys much greater rates of customer satisfaction and loyalty.

> **Whenever your business can manage bits *in addition to* atoms— or, better still, *instead of* atoms—radical improvements in efficiency, profits, and customer satisfaction are possible.**

Look at your own business from an outsider's perspective. What is the relative importance of atoms and bits in your current operations? Which activities involve managing atoms and which ones involve managing bits?

Ask yourself: Where can I replace atoms with bits? Which of my processes are most ripe for transformation from atom managing to bit managing?

Where I am managing bits, how can I manage 100 percent of those bits electronically?

BUILDING YOUR BIT ENGINES

Digital Business Design is, in part, the art of developing bit engines that will manage information digitally for the maximum benefit of the business. The digital innovators profiled in this book are all distinguished by owning powerful bit engines that enable their unique (and remarkably successful) business designs.

A company's bit engines may include a wide array of technological tools and systems, from internal databases of product and service information to e-commerce switchboards and electronic marketplaces (auction sites, e-catalogs, and so on). (See Appendix A for a detailed list and description.) Which of these digital tools should be the bit engines that your company uses? The answer must be based on your entire business design. The key question is: *How can digital options help you provide a unique and better value proposition for your customers and your talent?*

DBD is never about technology for its own sake; it's always about using technology to create a unique and better business design—one that enhances what you can offer your customers and your employees while strengthening your profit model and your strategic control. Think: Business first, design second, digital third.

DIGITAL TECHNOLOGY EXPANDS YOUR BUSINESS DESIGN OPTIONS

Digital information systems can do a lot to enhance the productivity of your existing business. Their speed, accuracy, and efficiency can enable you to cut costs, reduce cycle times, decrease errors and improve services. All of this is good and important.

Far more important, however, is the potential impact of digital technology on your overall business design:

> **Digital technology greatly expands the range of business design options your company can use. Digital Business Design creates unprecedented opportunities for you to make your business *unique*.**

As this book will detail, DBD can enable you to consider many different strategic options, including:

- ☐ **New customer sets:** DBD can help you reach new customers who are geographically distant or different in size and type from those you have previously served, and connect you with customers at remote locations in the value chain.
- ☐ **New value propositions for customers:** DBD makes it possible to create new and more efficient marketplaces, to offer expanded arrays of products and services, and to improve the accuracy and timeliness with which you can solve customers' problems.
- ☐ **New value propositions for talent:** DBD lets you reduce the amount of low-value work your employees must do; it frees them to focus on creative problem solving, relationship building, and developing their own skills and knowledge.
- ☐ **New profit models:** DBD enables new sources of revenue and profitability; it allows you to maximize the value of the information in your system while reducing capital and operating costs.
- ☐ **New forms of strategic control:** DBD facilitates the creation of customer/supplier networks, broadens and deepens relationships, and generates new economies of scale, scope, and replication that will help you attract and retain customers.

These broader implications make DBD far more than a technology initiative. In a recent meeting with the CEO of a large insurance company, we outlined a number of on-line sales, marketing, and customer service programs we felt the firm should consider. The CEO demurred. "That all sounds good," he remarked, "but it sounds expensive. In our industry, we have a rule of thumb: Never spend more than three percent of revenues on your IT budget. I think what you're proposing would blow that rule out of the water."

In one sense, the CEO was right: Going digital might well require a higher level of spending on technology than his company was accustomed to. But the context in which he was considering the shift was the wrong one. "The issue isn't the three percent you're spending on IT," we told him. "It's the thirty percent you're spending on sales and marketing *that isn't working*."

Don't think about DBD as just another piece of your company's IT program. Instead, think about the ripple effect DBD can have, up and down all the dimensions of your business design.

DBD can help you redefine your scope, sharpen your customer selection, improve your value propositions, enhance your profit model, strengthen your strategic control, and empower your organizational systems. (See Appendix B for a list of ways DBD expands your strategic options.) In any given business design dimension, if you currently have, say, five options to choose from, the move to DBD may increase that number to ten or twelve. Expansion of your options is the true power of DBD.

> **If you take a good business and put it on-line, your job is half done. Now move your business to the *next* level. Use the new options enabled by Digital Business Design to create a unique business design that lets you provide new and different types of value for your customers.**

YOUR NEXT BUSINESS ISSUES

We started our discussion of business design by asking you to identify the five key business issues you currently face. A great business design—especially one that takes full advantage of digital options—can help you address those issues in a highly profitable manner.

But no business design can solve your company's toughest business issues once and for all. Solving *today's* business issues *always* leads to *tomorrow's* issues. Whether driven by internal forces, environmental shifts, new competition, technological innovations, or other changes, new business issues will inevitably rise to the top of your agenda tomorrow. Continual self-reinvention is required for long-term survival and success.

So what are *tomorrow's* top business issues for your company? How can you proactively use digital options to craft a unique solution to them?

The ideas and stories from today's digital innovators, presented in the pages that follow, can help you tackle this challenge.

We'll begin by examining one of the most powerful new bit engines, a digital tool for serving customers that has enabled innovative companies to dramatically improve their business designs and that is already transforming the competitive landscape of some of the world's biggest industries.

3

THE AGE OF
THE CHOICEBOARD

THE TRADITIONAL BUSINESS SYSTEM:
DESIGNED FOR FRUSTRATION

The last time I bought a car, I looked at a number of different models on dealers' lots. Not one of them met my needs precisely. Even the car I ultimately purchased represented a compromise, providing some features that I wanted (antilock brakes and a spacious trunk, for instance), some that I was neutral about (a sunroof and power mirrors), and a lot of others that I had no use for whatsoever (cruise control, fog lamps, heated seats). I bought the car, even with all its unwanted features, because I liked the way it looked and handled and because it was available at that moment. I didn't want to wait a month to get a car with a better mix of features.

What this car buyer experienced is what almost all customers go through today. Indeed, customer frustration is designed into most business systems. Companies create fixed product lines that represent their best guesses about what buyers will want, and buyers make do with the choices they're offered. There may be some minor alterations at the point of purchase—a few optional features or add-ons—but, by and large, the set of choices is fixed long before customers even begin to shop. Thus, whether they take home a car or clothes or a computer, it's probably not exactly what they had hoped to find.

> **Most buyers get too little of what they want and too much of what they don't.**

The fixed-product-line system frustrates suppliers, too. Predictions of future demand, no matter how well grounded, are inevitably inaccurate. That's why the pages of newspapers and catalogs teem with announcements of sales, factory rebates, and dealer incentives, and why off-price stores are always plentifully stocked. Retailers and manufacturers lose tens of billions of dollars every year because they must discount merchandise that isn't moving the way they thought it would.

They also have an incalculable hidden loss from sales they forgo on products they never produced or offered to consumers. They simply never knew someone might want them.

Until now, there has been no alternative to this inefficient and frustrating system. The slow, imprecise movement of information (bits) up the supply pipeline, and of goods (atoms) in the other direction, has meant that the manufacturing process had to begin long before accurate information about demand became available. Consequently, the traditional business system gets information in lagtime and operates largely on guesswork.

Going digital—shifting the focus of the supply chain from managing atoms (e.g., cars or stereo systems or wool suits or kitchen ranges) to managing bits (the information about what customers want)—has the potential to reverse this process, to largely replace *guessing* about customer demand with *knowing* what customers want before products are made. And that change is already happening.

ENTER THE CHOICEBOARD

Thanks to the Internet, an alternative to the traditional unhappy model of supplier–customer interaction is now possible. In all sorts of markets, customers will soon be able to describe *exactly* what they want, and suppliers will be able to deliver the desired product or service *without mismatch or delay*. The innovation that is catalyzing this shift is a powerful new type of bit engine known as the Choiceboard. Dell's on-line configurator, which allows customers to design their own computers to meet their exact needs and get a real-time price quote, is one of the most successful early examples.

> A *Choiceboard* is an interactive on-line system that allows individual customers to design their own products and services by choosing from a menu of attributes, components, prices, and delivery options. The customer's selections send signals to the supplier's manufacturing system that set in motion the wheels of procurement, assembly, and delivery.

Dell's Choiceboard expands consumers' options in the personal computer realm. Several competitors have created personal computer Choiceboards of their own. Here are some other examples of Choiceboards already at work in a variety of industries:

- ☐ **Mattel's My Design Barbie** lets fashion-doll fans custom-build a friend for Barbie. They can choose hair style and color, complexion, and eye color. The doll's image is displayed on a screen before it is ordered and manufactured.
- ☐ **De Beers's Design Your Own Engagement Ring** lets customers create a diamond ring with any of 189 unique combinations of cut, band, and sidestones, then connects them to a local jeweler who can help them buy it.
- ☐ **Cisco's Marketplace** is an on-line configurator that allows corporate customers to create the precise combination of data networking gear they need.
- ☐ **Charles Schwab's Mutual Fund Screener** allows customers to design their own investment portfolios by selecting from Schwab funds and from funds managed by other financial companies. (The Mutual Fund Screener is part of a broader system that Schwab provides to its customers. Typically, it is combined with other tools, such as an asset allocator, a performance monitor, and so on.)

☐ **Point.com's Service Plan Locator** permits wireless communications customers to research and buy wireless phones, service plans, and accessories. Hundreds of options from many manufacturers and suppliers are available.

☐ **Frictionless.com's** shopping site will allow partners to offer Choiceboards for a wide array of consumer products, making this the first Choiceboard "department store."

A Choiceboard model of doing business with individual customers becomes possible in any industry when a system of accessible, integrateable components is available from which customers can select and combine options based on their own priorities. Not every industry lends itself to the Choiceboard approach, but a surprising number do, and more will in the future.

Some industries that seem to cry out for Choiceboards currently lack them. For example, despite a host of on-line travel agents, no true Choiceboard exists for purchasing travel. Customers can buy airline tickets online, usually with a limited number of price and flight options; they can also scan a preselected list of vacation packages and perhaps choose one that more or less matches their tastes and requirements. But the wider array of options, the continual customization, and the freedom to select their own combination of features—all offered by the true Choiceboard—are not yet available on-line for would-be travelers.

(Perhaps by the time you read these words, that void will have been filled. Many opportunities for creating enormous new businesses are being opened up by the advent of the Choiceboard.)

CUSTOMER SELF-SEGMENTATION
VIA THE CHOICEBOARD

For consumers, the benefits of the Choiceboard are enormous. When a Choiceboard becomes available in a given industry, the level of customer frustration considered "normal" and "inevitable" in that industry drops dramatically. Some of the benefits of the Choiceboard for suppliers and manufacturers may be less obvious.

> **The Choiceboard enables customer self-segmentation, which is fast, cost-efficient, and far more precise than traditional manufacturer-imposed segmentation.**

Almost everyone agrees *in theory* with the concept of customer segmentation—marketing based on the specific interests, needs, and wants of particular types of customers. Translating theory into practice isn't easy, however. Hence the proliferation of systems for categorizing customers based on demographics, geography, gender, education, income, age, values, behavior, and so on.

The Choiceboard cuts through all such systems by placing product design choices in the hands of customers—in effect, allowing customers to segment themselves. The Choiceboard permits the ultimate in customization: accurate marketing to a target audience of one.

WHEN CUSTOMERS DON'T KNOW
WHAT THEY WANT

Choiceboards are great if customers know what they want. Suppose they don't? Choiceboard models are evolving to address this issue.

A great example is Sony's laptop Choiceboard. It asks a very simple set of questions about workstyle and usage; answering them takes just thirty seconds. Sony then suggests two or three laptop options that most closely meet the customer's needs.

Acumins does the same for vitamins customers. If the customer doesn't know what supplements are advisable, Acumins asks a two-minute series of lifestyle and health questions that help define the best usage. It then suggests a combination that matches the customer's specific situation.

These are just the first steps in the development of Choiceboard decision-making models. Over time, Choiceboards will embody increasingly sophisticated and accurate methodologies to help companies move their customer relationship from "mismatch" to "perfect fit."

CHOICEBOARDS AND PROFITABILITY

A well-designed Choiceboard not only improves customer satisfaction but can increase profitability as well.

> **The Choiceboard encourages upselling, cross-selling, and repeat business.**

By providing an easier, faster, and more satisfying buying experience, the Choiceboard increases the likelihood that customers will upgrade their choices to more attractive, sophisticated, powerful, and high-value products. Remember, the self-designed product contains *no* features that the individual customer hasn't selected. The money saved on unwanted features (which traditional buyer–seller relationships once forced customers to buy) is now available to spend on accessories, upgrades, or extra products.

Choiceboard customers who have been able to buy exactly what they wanted, instead of settling for a more-or-less unsuitable product, are more likely to repeat the experience sooner than with traditional selling. They may upgrade their computer system every two years rather than every three.

One customer described her experience:

When I went on-line to buy a PC from Dell, I was looking to spend $1,800 or so. By the time I was finished, I had designed a package that came in at $2,300. I got exactly what I wanted in the first place, and then I also bought additional capability that I knew would meet my changing (mostly growing) needs over the next few months. But I didn't have to settle for anything that I didn't want.

The process that I went through was painless. I had to hesitate at a couple of places, but the help button popped up a screen that explained my options in English (not techno-speak).

I have already started to tell my friends about this way of buying. Some found the system a little more difficult than I did; but, for most, it was a breeze. I don't know how Dell did it, but they made it really, really easy to use. I look forward to using it again in the future.

> The Choiceboard provides real-time market research. It offers more timely and more accurate insights into actual customer demands than were previously available.

Businesspeople have long bemoaned the imprecision of traditional market research—surveys, polls, and focus groups' or customers' feedback sent upstream via sales staff, dealers, and service reps. Many businesses have experimented with various ways of establishing direct links with customers in an effort to improve on the notoriously sketchy data produced by these sources. (For example, in 1993, unhappy with its reliance on subjective and partial reports from retail dealers, Apple Computer established a direct sales operation, not so much for the revenue it produced as for the data it provided on real demand and real trends in buying activity, and in customers' preferences, needs, and interests.)

The Choiceboard's real-time data about customers' preferences are based on actual customers' buying behavior, not on surveys or retailers' impressions. If you own a properly managed Choiceboard, it's possible to know how customers' tastes are changing day by day, not quarterly or monthly. You operate in real time, not lag time. Because you deal directly with the customer, it's possible to capture, record, and reuse the information in the future—for example, to customize the Choiceboard options the next time the same customer visits you.

The speed and detail of market information generated by a Choiceboard can't be duplicated in any other way. This enables pinpoint accuracy in your own operations. As Michael Dell explains:

You're sharing information in a real-time fashion. We tell our suppliers exactly what our daily production requirements are. So it's not, "Well, every two weeks, deliver 5,000 to this warehouse, and we'll put them on the shelf, and then we'll take them off the shelf." It's, "Tomorrow morning we need 8,562, and deliver them to door number seven by 7:00 A.M."

More subtly, the Choiceboard captures—one might even say *creates*—an entirely new *class* of information that has never existed before: information about what customers really want, as opposed to what they will settle for.

Here's what we mean. Say you're a traditional fixed-product-line supplier. Inevitably, there are specific combinations of features that *no* product offers. Think: Is it because the combination is illogical and unattractive, or because someone in your supply line (a knowledgeable retailer, for example) once told you, "Oh, no one wants a product like that," or only because it never occurred to anyone in manufacturing or marketing to create such a product?

Maybe this hypothetical product has almost no potential market. Then again, unbeknownst to you, there may be a potentially huge market. In the traditional model, there is no way for a customer to express a desire for a product that doesn't exist. With the Choiceboard, the product can be designed and ordered.

You may discover that your most popular and profitable product is one that has never existed before. The Choiceboard takes such discoveries out of the realm of creativity or serendipity and makes them *inevitable*.

> **The Choiceboard reduces costs for manufacturers and suppliers without sacrificing customer value—in fact, customer value is enhanced.**

The Choiceboard impacts the finances of manufacturers and suppliers in a host of ways—some obvious, some not so obvious. These companies no longer have to:

☐ Manufacture, warehouse, market, ship, and promote products without knowing whether they are salable.

☐ Invest in parts, equipment, factories, and workers to produce excess inventory so as to avoid being caught short in the face of unanticipated demand.

☐ Catalog, advertise, and promote a fixed array of products and then hope that customers' choices are in sync with their choices.

☐ Sponsor sales, discounts, factory rebates, and clearance deals to get rid of products for which demand was less than anticipated.

REVERSING THE VALUE CHAIN

The Choiceboard is more than an innovative way to sell products or services. It also holds out the promise of *reversing* the traditional value chain, a change that has larger implications for business strategy.

Here's how value flows in the typical nondigital business:

Assets > Inputs > Offering > Channels > Customer.

There's nothing "wrong" with this model. For centuries, it has been the only practical way of turning raw materials and talents into products and services, and then distributing them to the end users. But it's no longer the only way. At every link in the traditional value chain, information and value leak out.

The Choiceboard makes it possible for a digital business to reverse the value chain:

Customer > Channels > Offering > Inputs > Assets.

The process can now begin with the key source of information, the customer. The customer makes use of the Choiceboard to custom-design his or her own offering. In doing so, the customer generates the bits required to make the atoms productive, and guesswork disappears. Triggered by the customer's request, the production system orders the necessary inputs (computer components, for example). They are delivered to the factory or other center where the finished product is assembled and shipped.

The nondigital business system produces products and services, then sells (some of) them. The digital business sells first, *then* produces. As a result, in the digital value chain, far less information and value are lost. The customer's *precise* needs and wants are transmitted through the marketing, sales, and distribution channels, which define exactly the offering desired and the acceptable price. Only the inputs that are necessary are ordered. At every stage in this new value chain, guesswork is replaced by precise information, and every cent invested is based on real demand.

BIT ENGINES AND BUSINESS FUNDAMENTALS

The Choiceboard is one of the most powerful bit engines in the digital economy. As with all powerful tools, misapplications will occur: wrong customer groups, wrong part of the value chain, wrong sequence. Unless the business fundamentals are right, implementing a Choiceboard system is not a path to breakthrough performance.

A classic example of misapplication is occurring today in the automotive industry. Automakers are working mightily to create Choiceboards for consumers—even though a network to deliver cars quickly in response to customers' demands won't be built for several years. Meanwhile, auto dealerships lack the tools they need to serve their customers properly. For example, they often can't tell a customer whether a new car will arrive in five days or in fifty. A Choiceboard is desperately needed at the dealer level—*today*. When that step has been mastered, and after a responsive supply network is built, it will make economic sense to implement a Choiceboard system for the consumer.

If this sequence is short-circuited, huge effort will have been expended for meager, if any, strategic returns.

Implementing a Choiceboard before getting the fundamentals right will only create frustration. Think about your own business issues. Consider whether your highest returns on a Choiceboard investment will come from creating:

- ☐ An end-user Choiceboard.
- ☐ An intermediary Choiceboard.
- ☐ An internal Choiceboard.

Decide which of these should be your first priority:

- ☐ A product Choiceboard.
- ☐ A service Choiceboard.
- ☐ An information Choiceboard.

The most important question: Which types of customers is the Choiceboard intended to serve, and are those customers ready to be served in this way?

THE ISSUE OF DIGITAL READINESS

At this moment in the evolution of your business, your decision on introducing a Choiceboard may depend, in part, on your sense of the *digital readiness* of your customer base.

Digital readiness is a function of numerous factors, including how deeply a given market has been penetrated by personal computer ownership, the degree of computer literacy among members of that market, and the relative availability of broadband access to the Internet. Such factors help determine what fraction of those in the market are technically and psychologically ready to use Choiceboards. Digital readiness varies enormously from place to place and from market to market.

Evaluate your own industry. *Where* are its digital-ready customers? Dell has developed a highly successful Choiceboard for selling personal computer systems—in part because, almost by definition, the target customers are nearly all digital-ready.

In many other industries, the digital-ready customers may be purely internal customers or solely business-to-business customers.

A great example of Choiceboard application based on the right fundamentals is occurring in the brokerage industry. Charles Schwab's Mutual

Fund Screener is a powerful Choiceboard for individual investors. However, one of the old-line brokerages that competes with Schwab has recognized that its customer base is very different from Schwab's, and has acted accordingly. Its customers, mostly affluent older investors, are not digital-ready. They're not "keyboard jockeys"; they want to *talk* to their brokers. The key Choiceboard being created at this firm is at the broker level, to give brokers the support and leverage they need to serve their customers better.

But a note of caution: To establish a Choiceboard as a timely and profitable business option, it may not be necessary for a majority (or even a sizable percentage) of the customers in an industry to be digital-ready. Not all brokerage or mutual-fund customers are digital-ready even in the year 2000, and the proportion was significantly smaller when Schwab established its on-line mutual-funds Choiceboard. By moving when it did, Schwab was able to create a strategic presence and a mindshare position that still outstrips its competitors'.

> **If you wait for the majority to become digital-ready, it will be too late.**

CHOICEBOARD MINUS VALUE NET = 0

Like any great innovation in business design, Choiceboards can offer a decided *temporary* advantage to those who use them fastest and best. And, as we'll discuss below, to those who develop the most sophisticated strategies for *evolving* Choiceboards, a powerful *long-term* advantage will accrue.

The Choiceboard is a tremendously powerful strategic tool that can be used to capture a sizable portion of most industries' strategic landscape. Why haven't Choiceboards already swept the field in many businesses?

Three hurdles are currently holding Choiceboards back. The first hurdle is simply their newness. Many suppliers can't even imagine doing business through a Choiceboard model; they would have to restructure their entire manufacturing, logistical, and sales systems. Even more wrenching, however, is the fact that it requires restructuring the company's *thought process.* The sequence "Sell, customer-finance, and manufacture" simply goes against the habitual mindset of many traditional business managers.

The second hurdle is concern over customers' digital readiness. As discussed above, that is still a valid issue—but its impact is rapidly disappearing.

The third current hurdle for many industries is the lack of highly responsive, value-added supply networks that can deliver components and services as needed, including (1) fewer suppliers, (2) closer and deeper supplier–purchaser relationships, and (3) richer, fuller, and faster sharing of data all along the supply chain. This type of a supply system, which we refer to as a Value Net Design, has yet to be created in many industries. (For more information on Value Nets, visit http://www.valuenets.com.)

> **Without the necessary supply systems to support it, the Choiceboard model won't work.**

This is probably the single most serious obstacle to creation of a Choiceboard in many industries today. *But,* as more and more businesses wrap their minds around the importance of moving to a Digital Business Design, this obstacle will fall by the wayside, too.

CHOICEBOARD EVOLUTION AND THE WAR OF THE CHOICEBOARDS

Today, having a Choiceboard—*à la* Dell, Schwab, Point.com, and a handful of other businesses—can represent a strategic advantage over competitors in the same industry.

Before long, in many industries, having a Choiceboard will represent merely the price of entry—not a strategic advantage but a necessary starting point for doing business. When that happens, the companies that seize the lead now will be in the forefront of evolving their Choiceboards.

They will be able to provide greater customer value and to seize a portion of that value for themselves.

In the personal computer business, the on-line brokerage business, and a few other places, we can see early glimpses of the future evolution of the Choiceboard. Any firm that is the first in its industry to create a Choiceboard for its customers should *simultaneously* be looking toward the horizon and planning its second, third, and fourth versions. This is how to remain ahead of the inevitable competitors who will follow and imitate you.

Better Choiceboard Design

The best Choiceboards will continually evolve in the direction of greater transparency, improved ease of use, a more intuitive interface, more numerous choices, and more complete customization. Customers are already unimpressed by Web sites that greet them by name or merely direct them to the same category of merchandise they purchased on-line last time. They will quickly lean toward Choiceboards that remember their past preferences and can guide them effortlessly toward their next purchase decisions (or information retrieval) with a minimum of lost time and missteps.

Increased sophistication of design has already been demonstrated by some early Choiceboard leaders. Improvement should begin the day a Choiceboard opens for business, with the customer playing an active role in the improvement process. (A major insurance company created a business-to-business Choiceboard with only middling success. In analyzing the development process, the company noted, "The one thing we failed to do—and should have done—was to invest a lot of time just *watching* people use our Choiceboard. If we'd done that, we would have caught its design flaws, and its untapped opportunities, a lot faster.")

Providing Information

Choiceboards differ greatly in the amounts and kinds of information they provide to customers. The victors in the War of the Choiceboards will be those that are able (1) to figure out the details (about products, services, and other components) that customers need to make informed choices, and (2) to provide those details in the most effortless and intuitive fashion.

This will not be easy. No two car buyers, vacation planners, outdoor gear users, or DVD (digital video disk) aficionados are exactly the same. Information that a beginner finds enlightening and helpful may strike a veteran as condescending and insulting. Some shoppers enjoy having a salesperson at their elbow, offering information; others hate it. Extraordinary intelligence and sensitivity will be required to develop Choiceboards that adapt to the varying temperaments and needs of customers.

Fortunately, the medium itself provides an enormous advantage to designers: continual feedback from users as to what works and what doesn't. The smartest digital businesses will be those that make real use of that feedback in the most sophisticated ways. Which leads us to the next element in Choiceboard evolution.

Collecting Information

The ability of the Choiceboard to record and transmit data about current sales trends is a remarkable and genuine advance over the spotty information now available in most businesses. But it is only the beginning. Managed carefully (and with appropriate privacy safeguards), the Choiceboard can also develop a powerful file of information about individual customers. The Choiceboard itself can then be increasingly personalized.

Recommendation Engine

We are already beginning to see Choiceboards that operate as sophisticated recommendation engines. As these engines evolve, they'll proactively offer specific products and services based on individual customer profiles, company guidelines, ratings and reactions from similar customers, and predictive algorithms into which millions of pieces of data may feed. At first, the recommendations may be limited. (A computerized recommendation program developed by an on-line bookseller reportedly suggested the novels of Jane Austen to virtually every reader, no matter whether her previously recorded tastes ran to mysteries, romances, or sophisticated literary offerings.) In time, as they become based on a larger and more methodically sifted array of data, they may become more accurate and helpful than the advice of experienced human experts.

The skill and sensitivity with which Choiceboard designers create accurate personalization will help determine which Choiceboards emerge as winners in the coming contests for enduring customer allegiance.

Will these steps represent the end of Choiceboard evolution? Certainly not. Those who win in the next generation or two will need to be among the first to anticipate the *next* phase of the evolutionary process (even though that phase may be difficult to imagine today). Otherwise, they'll run the risk of forfeiting the strategic advantage they've gained through their early successes.

As in every aspect of business, the game never ends. There are always new opportunities to fail—or to succeed again.

CHOICEBOARDS AND YOUR BUSINESS

The Choiceboard, one of the most powerful new bit engines, is already beginning to transform the world of business. The following questions and activities will help you get started toward considering how a Choiceboard system may be able to help you to serve your customers better and to capture a greater and more secure stream of profits.

- ☐ If you're not familiar with using Choiceboards, visit one (or several) of those mentioned in this chapter. Better still, visit more than one Choiceboard within the same industry. Note any principles that can be applied toward creating the best possible Choiceboard for *your* customers.
- ☐ Read Appendix C, which introduces the Choiceboards Tour, an on-line guide to Choiceboards created for readers of this book.

- ☐ Is there an existing Choiceboard in your industry? If so, who owns it? What customers is it designed to serve? How does it add value to those customers? How is it helping the Choiceboard owner gain control over portions of the strategic playing field?
- ☐ In your industry, is there an existing value-added supply network to support a Choiceboard? If so, who owns it?
- ☐ If there is no existing value-added supply network, who owns the pieces from which such a network could be assembled? What would it take to create it?

4

DIGITAL INNOVATOR: DELL COMPUTER

MASTERS OF CHANGE

Founded in 1984 by Michael Dell, Dell Computer Corporation is the world's largest direct seller of computer systems and products that are designed and customized to end-users' requirements. Dell's customer selection focuses on large and small businesses; government agencies, schools, and other institutions; and the consumer market. Today, nearly half of all Dell products are purchased via the Internet.

The financial results Dell has achieved in this business arena have been phenomenal. In 1988, two years after going public, Dell was worth $1 billion. Three years later, it was worth $2 billion. Five years after that, in 1996, it was worth $4 billion (half the worth of its rival PC maker, Compaq). By 1999, it was worth over $100 billion (more than twice the worth of Compaq). How did this happen?

> Dell exploits patterns of strategic change better than just about anybody. It built a terrific business model (direct selling), reinvented it (build to order), and then, in 1996, crossed the threshold from conventional to Digital Business Design.

By digitizing virtually all of its processes—including sales and marketing, outsourcing, manufacturing, and service—Dell has (1) evolved a powerful value proposition for its customers and (2) developed a value-capture mechanism that works even in an industry that has become essentially a no-profit zone. This chapter explores how Dell has created and reinvented its unique business model, and considers the strategic options it faces in an always challenging future.

DELL BUSINESS ISSUES

The central business issue Dell faces is how to make money in a no-profit zone. Throughout Dell's history, the PC business has been crowded with competitors selling highly-comparable, near-commodity products based on technology that is constantly evolving. As a result, inventory that doesn't sell loses its value quickly, with a devastating impact on profit margins. In this environment, making money is extremely difficult.

A similar challenge confronts many manufacturing businesses today, from automobiles and consumer electronics to home furnishings, business equipment, and instrumentation. All share a series of potentially profit-killing characteristics, including too many steps in the value chain, too many markdowns, and too much guesswork about demand.

Dell's story is the story of how one company has managed to solve this dilemma through a series of reinventions, starting with a direct selling model and culminating—so far—in a highly successful shift to Digital Business Design.

THE FIRST DELL BUSINESS MODEL

From the beginning, Dell has been built on what it calls the Direct Model—selling PCs to customers without any intermediary. Like most other companies in the business of making IBM PC clones, Dell outsourced large portions of its manufacturing processes and handled only the final assembly of computer systems from components produced to Dell specifications by outside suppliers. However, in the late 1980s and early 1990s, as the North American PC marketplace grew and matured, Dell's Direct Model gave it several advantages over most of its competitors:

- Because of its direct connection to customers, Dell enjoyed real-time feedback about product offerings, service, and the competition. During the predigital period, this feedback came mainly via telephone calls (Dell received over 1,400 customer calls each day, as early as 1987). This feedback helped Dell avoid some of the more serious missteps of its competitors. The lesson here is: A large stream of value can be captured simply by controlling *one* crucial link in the process. In Dell's case, that link was the connection between customers and the supplier. Everything else could be outsourced. Dell made occasional miscalculations about customers' requirements and needs, but it never fell into the disastrous product mistakes that nearly destroyed Apple and other computer companies during this period.

- Dell's Direct Model eliminated the 25–40 percent price markup required by typical retail computer dealers. This enabled aggressive pricing for Dell products.

- Dell developed a specialist salesforce. Its representatives had a deep, focused knowledge of and commitment to Dell products. Other PC companies were forced to rely on dealers who carried six to ten lines of products from various companies and had no strong commitment to any of them.

- Perhaps most important, Dell enjoyed a streamlined asset base and consistently low inventory levels because it built products only to fill customers' orders. Rather than build computers and then hope it could sell them, Dell sold the computers first, then built them according to customers' specifications. The refinement and elaboration of this innovative business approach, and the full realization of the financial and other advantages it offers, would prove to be crucial aspects of Dell's success.

BUSINESS MODEL EVOLUTION:
LEARNING FROM MISSTEPS

In examining a successful business after the fact, it's easy to imagine that the great business model emerged full-blown and perfect from the mind of the CEO. That's never true, and it isn't true for Dell. Dell's history includes several major missteps that might have damaged the company. Instead, each misstep became an opportunity for Dell to learn, refine, and recommit to its core business model, and to become stronger with each step.

"Olympic"

In the late 1980s, "Olympic" was the internal code name for a proposed family of Dell products that spanned the desktop, workstation, and server markets and were laden with ambitious technology. Dell managers received a respectful but cool response from customers with whom they shared the Olympic plans. Nonetheless, Dell proceeded to develop prototypes and unveiled them proudly at the annual Comdex computer trade show in November 1989.

This time, the negative response from Dell's customers was unmistakable. Some of the elements of the Olympic product line were impressive, but the total package offered no compelling benefits. One customer summed it up: "We don't *need* that much technology." Chagrined, Dell bit the bullet and canceled the Olympic product line.

> **The Olympic Lessons: (1) Make customers part of the product development process—create products for *them*, not for yourselves. (2) Hear what your customers say, not what you want to hear. (3) Admit your mistakes early, fix them quickly, and move on.**

The Road to Latitude

In 1988, Dell entered the notebook computer market—at that time, the fastest growing and most profitable segment of the PC business. The first Dell notebooks were well designed, and they sold respectably. Later generations of Dell notebooks were increasingly complex—and late to market.

By 1993, a whole range of new Dell notebooks were behind schedule, largely due to *feature creep*—overdesign of the product, not to meet consumers' needs but simply because the features were possible and at-tractive. Dell then brought in John Medica, who had led the development of Apple's PowerBook. He soon concluded that only *one* of the notebook products currently under development had a chance to be competitive.

Again, Dell made the right decision, although it was costly and painful. Dell canceled all of the noncompetitive products and refocused the entire division on producing the sole survivor, known as Latitude XP, as quickly as possible.

Dell also made the risky decision to equip the Latitude with a new technology, the lithium ion battery. Customer feedback had told Dell that the single greatest gripe about notebook computers was the short period of time they could be used before their batteries gave out. The lithium ion battery—if it worked—could more than double the average working time, from two to five hours. The new battery worked, and the Latitude became a significant hit product for Dell.

> **The Latitude Lessons: (1) Don't overdesign. (2) Ask your customers what they most want—and act on the answers.**

The Retail Detour

Despite its history of success with the Direct Model, Dell experimented with selling its computers through conventional retail outlets. From 1990 to 1994, Dell products were sold through several retail chains, including CompUSA and Circuit City. Retail sales were growing relatively quickly (20 percent annually), and the business appeared healthy. Then a new corporate CFO entered the scene. He ran a separate P&L on the retail business, allocating costs and revenues accurately to that sales channel. He discovered that Dell was making *no* profits from retail sales—nor, apparently, were Dell's competitors. No identifiable profit core could be found in the retail PC marketplace.

For a third time, Dell made a difficult but appropriate decision: It left the retail business altogether. Because retail sales constituted a relatively modest portion of Dell's revenues, the financial hit was of relatively minor importance. Far more significant was the improved focus Dell enjoyed as a result. Dell personnel in sales, manufacturing, marketing, and service could now concentrate with much greater clarity on Dell's core customer set, undistracted by questions such as: "What kind of product will Circuit City want for next Christmas?"

Many media observers and Wall Street analysts considered it a serious mistake for Dell to drop retail sales from its business mix. They predicted that Dell's sales growth would soon slow or stop. Instead, it accelerated, leading to strong growth in shareholder value (albeit at a level that still trailed Compaq significantly, as shown in Figure 4–1).

FIGURE 4–1   In 1995, Compaq Was Worth Four Times as Much as Dell

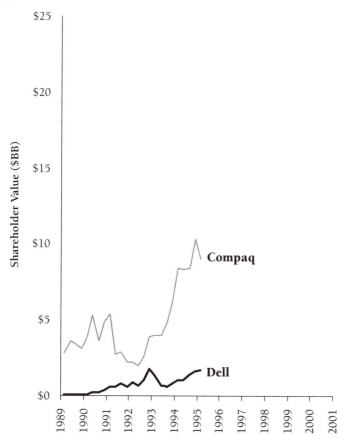

Source: Compustat, 7/00.

Lessons from the Retail Detour: (1) Focus on profitable growth, not growth for its own sake. (2) Stick to your unique business model as long as it works, no matter what others are doing. (3) Make sure that the scope of your business matches what you do best.

DELL GOES DIGITAL

Nineteen ninety-six was a watershed year for digital business. Cisco Systems started selling computer networking gear on-line. Charles Schwab created the eSchwab electronic brokerage business. And Dell started selling computers via Dell.com.

The business world didn't pay much attention to this confluence of events. (It's disquieting to reflect: "We missed the advent of digital business in 1996. What are we missing this year?") Ninety percent of all the businesses out there could have done what Dell, Cisco, and Schwab had begun to do—substituting bits for atoms. Ninety percent chose not to. Because of the choices they made that year, Dell, Cisco, and Schwab are still their industries' leaders today.

Dell had already made it possible to track order status via the Internet. In the late 1990s, customer readiness to use the Web for buying had increased to the point where selling via the Internet was the logical next step—especially for a PC company. By definition, everyone on the Web was part of the target audience for Dell's products.

Dell's transition to digital was not an overnight event. For a time, the vast majority of its business was still done by telephone. This transition to a hybrid business model is typical of smart organizations that are in the process of going digital: Schwab, Cisco, and Cemex have all employed similar mixes of on-line and nondigital business. Dell drove the mix to evolve toward digital very, very quickly.

The key step was the creation of Dell's on-line configurator, a digital system for designing a customer's own PC and one of the world's first Choiceboards. By permitting customers to design a PC that has only the options they really want, the configurator makes possible a *precise* fit between the customer's needs and the product's features, rather than the compromise for which customers have traditionally settled.

The Dell configurator still offers the easiest way to buy a PC anywhere. Among its benefits to the customer are:

- ☐ **Simplicity:** Dell offers two models of laptops and desktops, and three models of servers, so the differences are quick and easy to grasp. The models' simplicity is balanced by Dell's customization.
- ☐ **Customization:** Choosing from among a variety of options (memory size, hard drive capacity, modem type, and so on), customers can configure Dell's computers according to any of over *16 million* possible permutations.
- ☐ **Instant feedback:** For each choice a customer makes, the exact cost (or savings) is immediately available.
- ☐ **Digitized human touch:** Customers can easily request additional information to aid in their decision making.

Less obvious but equally important are the benefits to Dell:

- ☐ **Perfect accuracy and speed:** Because no salesperson or order-entry clerk is required to record customers' choices, there is no delay in processing an order, and no opportunity for costly errors or miscommunications.
- ☐ **Upselling:** The configurator makes it easy for customers to buy accessories or options that will upgrade the power and quality of their equipment. The fact that customers are no longer forced to spend money on features they don't want may encourage such upgrading.
- ☐ **Capture of customer information:** Because the configurator instantly records every customer's preferences, Dell can track buying patterns in real time instead of on a quarterly, monthly, or weekly basis.

Dell's configurator works only because of the information-intensive production system Dell has created. This system makes it possible for Dell to build computers to customers' specifications quickly, accurately, and without stockpiling inventory. The system's features include:

- □ **Radical reduction in parts:** In the PC industry, as in most others, 10 to 20 percent of stock-keeping units (SKUs) account for 90 percent of customer demand. Dell focuses on that vital subset.
- □ **Digitization of information:** Ordering details and specifications are transmitted down the line electronically—"following" the computer as it is assembled, and precluding errors and miscommunications.
- □ **Digital supply network management:** Dell has developed unusually close relationships with a small number of suppliers that are kept fully informed (electronically) of changing order patterns and component needs. They supply parts on a just-in-time basis, limiting the amount of money and space Dell must invest in stocking supplies.
- □ **Process simplification:** The original standard of 130 "touches" during assembly of a typical PC system has been reduced, over time, to just 60.

Dell engineers are continually working to improve and streamline these processes; collectively, they own over 200 process patents. As a result of these and other digitization steps, the total production time for a Dell PC—from the moment the customer places the order until the computer leaves the assembly line ready for shipping—is only six hours.

DELL VERSUS THE COMPETITION: THE CUSTOMER PERSPECTIVE

Dell is not the only company that sells computers on-line. Many of Dell's digital innovations, including its use of the Choiceboard, have been copied by rivals. However, no competitor has yet managed to match Dell in terms of ease of use, clarity, speed, cost, and personalization.

Jason is a small-business manager. When he recently needed to purchase a new PC, Jason's busy life and work schedule made on-line shopping the best alternative. His experience is instructive because it mirrors that of thousands of other customers. His shopping began not at Dell's Web site but at the Web site of a neutral information supplier:

> I started by visiting one of my favorite sites, CNET.com, which offers expert advice on tech-related items. They divide customers into several groups: Starving Student, Family, Multimedia Maven, and so on. For my category, which is Small Office/Home Office (SOHO), they recommended Dell, Toshiba, and Compaq.
>
> I then visited Dell on-line, looking for a flat screen and a CD–RW [rewriteable compact disk] drive, but trying to minimize my cost beyond that. Using the Dell configurator, I got to choose exactly what I wanted. The price was under $2,000—with shipping and tax, $2,175.
>
> My next stop was Compaq. I was amazed to find that their Web site looked almost exactly like Dell's—same list, same upsell prices, same menus, same help buttons. (When I last visited them, six months ago, the site looked totally different.) I configured my computer, and the process went pretty smoothly. But the total price ended up being about $200 more than Dell.
>
> I headed over to Toshiba's site, expecting a similar experience. That's not what I found. Navigating Toshiba's Web site was very confusing, and they didn't offer to configure a computer for me or even to sell direct. So I bailed out early.
>
> The fact that I could configure my own product, in addition to their brand name, sent me back to Dell in the end.

For another perspective, consider the experience of Terry, a recent college grad working at his first "real" job. He needed to buy a PC for the first time since he'd started college six years ago. Having decided that a laptop would better suit his peripatetic lifestyle, he also started shopping by visiting CNET.com for an unbiased opinion. CNET offered two recommendations: a Dell Inspiron 3800 and a Quantex W-1410, from a company Terry had never heard of. Here's what happened next:

> I traveled to my next on-line research destination—pcworld.com. I discovered that the Quantex W-1410 was number five in their "Midrange

Computer" category and that the Dell Inspiron was number one in the "Budget Notebooks" category. Both cost around $2,000, which I am comfortable paying. I saw, however, that one big downer on the Dell was its battery life—only two hours compared to Quantex's three hours. But Dell was rated "Good" on customer support, as opposed to Quantex's "Fair" rating.

I decided to click through to the Quantex Web site to see if it would tell me more. However, when I got there, I discovered that I couldn't find the W-1410. There was a W-1400, but no W-1410. I wondered: Are they the same? I spent a few minutes trying to find out, but I couldn't, and I gave up.

Should I continue to pursue the Quantex option, despite their somewhat frustrating Web site? And what about some of the other laptops in the pcworld rankings?

After thinking for a couple of minutes, I decided I simply couldn't go wrong with a Dell. I'm a risk-averse person when it comes to purchases over $1,000. For that reason, I chose Dell. Ordering it on-line was quick and easy, and I'm happy with the machine.

What are some of the lessons about digital business that we can learn from customer experiences like these?

> **Choiceboards compete on a dynamic playing field.**

As Jason's visit to the Compaq Web site illustrates, Choiceboards (like other on-line interfaces) are constantly evolving. Any innovation is likely to be imitated within a few months. Dell and other Choiceboard leaders cannot afford to be complacent. Instead, they must be constantly looking for ways to upgrade their services in order to stay two steps ahead of their rivals.

> **An on-line interface is relatively easy to imitate; behind-the-screen aspects of customer service are much harder to copy. Cosmetic parity ≠ customer parity.**

The visual appearance of the Dell configurator is easy to copy. It's much harder to duplicate the other business design assets that make Dell an industry leader. Among them are:

- ☐ The behind-the-screen accuracy, timeliness, and thoroughness of service that make Dell's configurator more reliable than its competitors' versions.
- ☐ The supply-network management expertise that allows Dell to offer high-quality products faster and cheaper than its competitors can.
- ☐ The brand name that makes customers feel more comfortable buying from Dell than from less-well-known rivals.

> **The speed of e-commerce is a double-edged sword. Abandoning one Web site for another can be done so quickly and easily that even momentary confusion is likely to drive away customers.**

A lesser-known brand like Quantex especially needs to do a superlative job of serving customers. All it took was a few moments of uncertainty ("Is the W-1400 the same as the W-1410?") without adequate customer help, and Terry decided that buying from Quantex wasn't worth the risk. Within seconds, he had traveled to the Dell site instead.

> **Risk reduction is a powerful value proposition that DBD can enhance.**

For decades, IBM thrived on the adage, "No one ever got fired for buying IBM." In much the same way, Terry decided, "I can't go wrong buying Dell." This sense of risk reduction—a feeling that, when faced with uncertainty and incomplete information, buying from Dell is a safe choice that the customer is unlikely to regret—is produced not only by Dell's word-of-mouth reputation and history but also by the ease, speed, efficiency, and accuracy of Dell's Choiceboard and other digital services.

Because the Dell Web site is clear and intuitive, it sends customers messages like these:

- ☐ "These people know what they're doing."
- ☐ "They seem to care about me."
- ☐ "They understand what I want."
- ☐ "They've been doing this a while—they've got all the kinks ironed out."
- ☐ "I can buy from them without worrying."

The implication?

> **Merely being on-line isn't enough. Providing digital service that responds to the totality of customers' needs, demands, worries, and wants makes the crucial difference.**

REVERSING THE VALUE CHAIN

One crucial feature of Dell's Digital Business Design is its *reversal* of the traditional value chain. By starting with the customer's placing an order electronically, and *only then* activating the production process (getting the bits about customer demand before committing the atoms of inventory), Dell is able to minimize inventory, virtually eliminate markdowns and unsold product, and collect revenues from its customers *before* it must pay suppliers.

In a market where inventory value plummets from week to week (one of the crucial reasons the PC business has proven to be a financial black hole for so many of Dell's competitors), this approach is the only way to protect your economics while delivering great value to the customer.

Compared to traditional business models, Dell's system almost appears a form of alchemy. But it's not magic; it is simply a highly sophisticated and thoroughly integrated collection of methods for getting the bits (information on what the customer really wants) before committing the atoms.

Designing such a system took breakthrough thinking of a high order. Making it work and maintaining it over time poses additional challenges.

Here is Michael Dell on one aspect of Dell's inventory management:

> Inventory velocity has become a passion for us. To achieve maximum velocity, you have to design your products in a way that covers the largest part of the market with the fewest number of parts. For example, you don't need nine different disk drives when you can serve 98 percent of the market with only four.

Notice what Dell does *not* say: You can reduce your disk drive offerings from nine to four only if you know for a fact which four drives your customers prefer *and* can anticipate when and in what direction those preferences will shift. Many manufacturers and retailers have only sketchy information about issues like these. Dell's digitization of the customer connection replaces guessing with knowing, lag-time with real-time data.

Michael Dell again:

> Once you reduce your inventory while maintaining your growth rate, a significant amount of risk comes from the transition from one generation of product to the next. Without traditional stockpiles of inventory, it is critical to precisely time the discontinuance of the older product line with the ramp-up in customer demands for the newer one.

Again, the challenge of digitization places a high value on the very flow of information that digitization itself makes possible. But note the enormous reward available to companies that can operate this way: In most businesses, a transition from one product line to a newer one inevitably involves unsold goods that now have almost no value and must be written off, usually at great expense. For Dell, this is impossible; there is never a warehouse full of PCs that might suddenly become obsolete.

Dell now maintains an average of less than six days' worth of inventory (its European plant has reduced inventory to four days' worth). This is possible because Dell's constant communication—through all channels, especially the Internet—enables suppliers to turn on a dime when demand for one particular chip, motherboard, or monitor suddenly morphs into another. Dell calls it "Trading inventory for information." This is another way of describing the atoms/bits trade-off.

EXPANDING THE CUSTOMER RELATIONSHIP

Michael Dell and Henry Ford are both economic revolutionaries, but mirror images in method. Ford's genius: Create one product—the black Model T, introduced in 1908—and make it affordable and available to millions. Dell's genius: Create one Choiceboard and supply network, and let millions design an infinite variety of products that will meet their individual needs.

Beyond the product customization offered by its PC configurator, Dell offers an additional layer of customization through its Premier Pages— customized Web pages that Dell has created for over 40,000 corporate clients. These pages, which are connected to the client's intranet, permit client-authorized personnel to configure their own PC systems, place orders for equipment, and check the status of those orders electronically. The pages also provide direct access to Dell technical support and, when necessary, help from a dedicated account executive.

Premier Pages offer a powerful combination of sales, service, and technical support in digitized form. They cut Dell's costs by freeing sales reps and technical support personnel from handling purely routine problems. They also constitute a powerful selling tool for prospective corporate customers.

Dell has also worked hard to add value to the customer beyond the "box" of the PC. One corporate IT manager comments:

> We've used Dell equipment for seven years, but we also had IBM and Compaq. Now we're buying only Dell, for four reasons. One, the products are built to order. Two, delivery is quick, on time, and consistent. Three, their services are great—we call the 800 number and get excellent response. Four, their prices are competitive.

> Right now, we use a purchasing software package that Dell doesn't support, so our ordering system isn't digital. But Dell is working with us, and within twelve months we expect a completely digital purchasing system to be in place, thanks to Dell's help.

Dell has recently taken another major step in this direction with its fast-growing equipment leasing, purchasing, and financing business, known as Dell Financial Services (DFS).

DFS is a wholly owned joint venture of Dell Computer in partnership with the CIT financial group. Launched in April 1997, it has grown in three years from zero to $1.3 billion in revenues and has a target of nearly $2 billion for 2000. Currently, about 80 percent of DFS's business is in Dell products. The other 20 percent consists of IBM, Compaq, Hewlett-Packard, Cisco, and other computer makers' gear.

Dell's objective is to make DFS a total IT equipment solutions provider that will make it easy for on-line customers to select, configure, lease, buy, trade in, maintain, and upgrade all kinds of computing equipment. Clients will order through a single source and pay a single monthly invoice. In combination with the customization of Premier Pages and Dell's intense focus on customer knowledge, DFS has the potential to make Dell the easiest, fastest, and most reliable supplier of IT products for thousands of businesses.

Another IT manager says:

> We recently put together a global team to choose our IT equipment leasing partner. We considered GE Capital, Compaq, and DFS. We chose DFS based on cost and service. Also, Dell has the best expertise and leverage. They make it easy to scale down to a standardized pizza-style menu of three equipment options for our individual customers, which streamlines the process and cuts our costs. We find that Dell provides quality products, and no one offers customers a more personal "feel."

In mid-1999, Dell moved to expand its customer relationships even more by creating a network of partnerships with other companies whose products and services can be sold through Dell. The first step was the launching of Gigabuys, an on-line store selling non-Dell products ranging from computer peripherals (printers, monitors, digital cameras, personal digital assistants) all the way to office furniture. More recently, Dell has added Web hosting, data storage, and other information services to its list of offerings. CFO Thomas Meredith describes the strategy as an *ecosystem model* in which Dell uses its customer expertise to sell goods and services from dozens of suppliers to millions of customers around the world.

Although Dell started off as a product-centric company, it is evolving toward a services/solutions model that is constantly looking to create the next new layer of value for the customer and the shareholder (see Figure 4–2).

FIGURE 4–2   By 1998, Dell's Value Had Reached Parity with that of Compaq

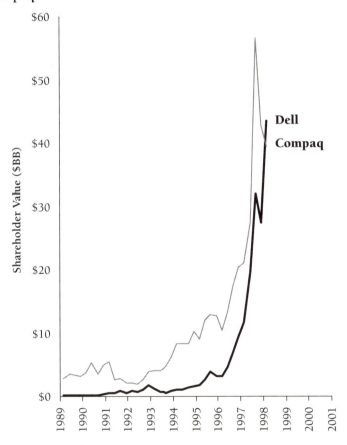

Source: Compustat, 7/00.

DELL'S BUSINESS DESIGN

Table 4–1 summarizes Dell's Digital Business Design. Its unique value proposition for customers includes fast response and high customization through its configurator system. It also includes ease of interaction, self-service (in numerous functions, from price checking to order-status checking to PC design), and the ability to provide corporate customers with extensive and accurate information about purchase patterns and usage. Through Dell Financial Services and Gigabuys.com, Dell's scope has evolved to include the availability of non-Dell and non-PC products.

Dell's unique value proposition for its talent includes:

- □ A digital infrastructure providing instant availability of data.
- □ Just-in-time, just-enough training that is closely matched to actual training needs.
- □ Opportunities for rapid advancement as the company continually segments and divisionalizes its operations.

Dell's configurator system has not only decommoditized the PC buying process but has made it easier for customers to "upsell" themselves. Dell's digital system has dramatically reduced the asset intensity of its business.

Dell's strategic control flows from multiple sources:

- □ Corporate-level customization through Premier Pages.
- □ Individual customization.
- □ The superior responsiveness of Dell's supplier network.
- □ The best-performing Choiceboard with the strongest brand behind it.
- □ Real-time demand knowledge.

BENEFITS OF DBD

Recall the Digital Benefits scale we introduced in Chapter 1 (page 20). Having examined in some detail the workings of a real, live digital business,

TABLE 4–1 Dell's Digital Business Design

Customer Selection	☐ Corporate
	☐ Government
	☐ Education
	☐ Consumer
Unique Value Proposition for Customers	☐ **Choiceboard/Customization**
	☐ **40,000 Premier pages/Information on usage**
	☐ **Speed and flexibility at a good price**
	☐ **Self-service (order tracking, design, etc.)**
Unique Value Proposition for Talent	☐ **Digital training ("Just in time, just enough")**
	☐ **Push-button information availability**
	☐ Rapid career development via divisionalization
Value Capture/Profit Model	☐ **Few markdowns**
	☐ **Cross-sell and upsell**
	☐ **Digital productivity**
Strategic Control/ Differentiation	☐ Relentless customer focus
	☐ **Choiceboard evolution trajectory**
	☐ **Supplier network cost and responsiveness advantage**
	☐ Customer relationships, brand recognition
	☐ **Real-time market knowledge**
Scope	☐ Desktops, notebooks, and servers via mail, telephone, or the Internet
	☐ **Peripherals and options at Gigabuys.com**
	☐ Dell Financial Services
	☐ Venture investments
Organizational System	☐ Customer-segment-driven divisionalization
Bit Engines	☐ **Choiceboard ordering system**
	☐ **Electronic links to customers and supply chain**

Boldface = digitally enabled.

we are now in a position to see how those benefits play out not just in theory but in practice.

Dell uses bits better than any other company today (except perhaps Cisco Systems). Dell's configurator Choiceboard ensures that Dell gets the bits (the information about what the customer really wants) before it commits the atoms. The configurator also ensures a near-perfect match between what customers want and what they get.

As Dell watches these transactions, it gathers real-time data on customers' behavior. It sees today what its competitors will see in a month, after the customer data wend their way through the networks of dealers and other channels that stand between most sellers and their customers.

Dell's system also enables customers to serve themselves—not just in designing and purchasing the product, but in other ways. For example, if a customer wants to track the location of a PC that was ordered a week ago, Dell's order-status checking system allows the customer to find out on-line, without talking to anyone.

Dell's talent has seen a huge shift from low-value-added work to leverage and growth. By eliminating most of the low-value administrative and processing work that steals too many workhours, digitization has freed up hundreds of hours to be spent with customers rather than on paperwork. Dell's just-in-time, just-enough training program enables workers to learn what they need when they need it, and to apply the learning within hours.

Finally, Dell has experienced the impact of nonincremental, 10X productivity improvements. Inventory turns have increased tenfold; order-status checking and supplier communication costs have plummeted. These order-of-magnitude improvements have radiated out to the customers. Using the Dell configurator, a customer can accomplish in five minutes what used to take two hours. More important, the customer satisfaction level is far higher than it could ever be under the old system (which still generally prevails at Dell's competitors).

THE FINANCIAL OUTCOMES

The reversal of the value chain, a key feature of Dell's Digital Business Design, leads to what we call *digital financing*. The customer pays Dell for the

FIGURE 4–3   By 2000, Dell Was Worth Three Times as Much
as Compaq

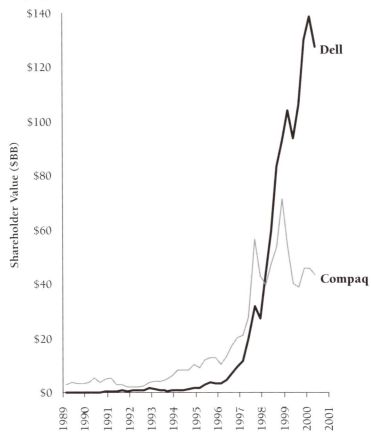

Source: Compustat, 7/00.

product; *then* Dell pays the supplier for components, thus upending the
usual relationship between accounts payable and accounts receivable.
This *negative cash-conversion cycle* creates negative working capital, allowing Dell to rapidly upgrade technologies and finance infrastructure
improvements.

Dell's shift to DBD has produced spectacular results (see Figure 4–3).
Between 1995 (just before Dell introduced its Digital Business Design)
and 1999, the following improvements occurred:

□ Return on sales: 7 percent → 11 percent
□ Profit growth: 15 percent → 33 percent
□ Market value/Sales ratio: 1:1 → 7:1

ESCAPING THE NO-PROFIT ZONE THROUGH DBD

Faced, like many manufacturing companies, with the challenge of making money in a no-profit industry, Dell managed to develop an extraordinary value-capture mechanism by reversing the value chain. Starting with the customer rather than the manufacturing side, Dell has virtually eliminated guesswork, obviated the need for price markdowns, and substituted a flexible, value-added supply network for the traditional rigid, slow-to-respond product pipeline with which most industries are saddled.

Perhaps Dell's reinvention of the PC business can point the way for other manufacturers to escape from the no-profit zones in which they're currently mired.

DELL'S NEXT BUSINESS ISSUES

Dell arrived at a digital business model two full years before any of its competitors, and the model is continuing to evolve at a pace that other firms cannot match. Thus, the gap between Dell and other PC companies continues to grow, at least for now.

But being the leader in the low-growth, low-profit PC business is not a formula for long-term success. Sales of PC desktops fell 3.5 percent in the United States in 1999, and Dell's annual sales growth has been cut in half from its early '90s pace of 60 percent.

In the Internet age, customers' priorities are changing. Value and profit growth opportunity are now migrating from PCs to other computing tools—servers, appliance servers, and storage devices—as well as an array of other products, services, and information that customers will need to digitize their businesses. Thus, the number-one business issue for Dell is how to make the transition from a PC company to an Internet infrastructure company, and how to exploit the "collapse of the middle" pattern one more time (as value shifts from PCs in the middle to access devices at one end of the spectrum and core products and services at the other end).

Dell sees the Internet stretching the company in two directions: (1) toward the "core," as companies demand infrastructure gear like servers and storage systems, and (2) toward the "edge," selling appliances like handheld computing devices and cell phones. Dell is also extending into the Internet service provider (ISP) market with DellNet, and into the services market with Dell Expert Services Group, a new consulting arm to help Dell's largest corporate customers launch digital businesses.

At the "core," Dell's opportunities appear great. Michael Dell believes server sales will grow twentyfold in the next five years. The challenges are just as great. Dell must compete, on the high end, against industry leaders like Sun Microsystems, which dominates the Web server market. The complexity of the products, the market, and the needs of customers poses a range of new challenges for Dell.

In storage systems, Dell's current presence is weak. It ranks sixth overall (with 4.2 percent market share) and twelfth in external storage systems (with just 1.6 percent share). What model will Dell design to compete against EMC Corporation, the leader in high-end storage?

Meanwhile, life on the "edge" offers other challenges. Dell plans to sell information appliances such as ultralight notebooks, handheld computing devices, and WAP phones. Although handheld computers and phones are new frontiers for Dell, it can leverage its Choiceboard expertise in this sector.

However, in the ISP realm, DellNet is a commodity provider arriving late to the game, with no apparent source of strategic control. And in the services and consulting arena, Dell will have to compete with a diverse range of players: specialized startups like Scient; Dell's traditional competitors, Hewlett-Packard (HP) and Compaq; and large end-to-end solutions providers like Andersen Consulting and EDS.

Dell's situation illustrates the inflexible realities of value migration. Being hugely successful in one cycle (even with an outstanding Digital Business Design) gives no assurance of winning in the next. But it *can* give you some advantages to work with. Dell's Digital Business Design has given it a tremendous four-year run. It has also created important residual values that could be exploited in the next shift:

- ☐ Excellent understanding of the customer.
- ☐ Enormous brand equity.
- ☐ Unmatched skill in the totality of Choiceboard design and management.
- ☐ Experience and talent in reducing administrative costs and hassle for customers.
- ☐ A fast, flexible, value-added supply network that has reduced inventory levels down to several days.
- ☐ Profound understanding of DBD, based on Dell's own experience as a digital pioneer.

These great assets from Dell's Digital Business Design 1.0 can help toward building a great DBD 2.0 to compete in the next cycle. But a simple carryover rarely works. Dell will remain effective only if it succeeds in answering the questions that will define tomorrow's winning design:

- ☐ What's my *next* unique value proposition for the customer?
- ☐ What's my *next* profit model?
- ☐ What's my *next* source of strategic control?

One thing seems likely: Michael Dell and the leadership team around him already have plans in place for the game's next two or three moves. Going digital doesn't exempt a company from the continuing surprises of change and competition. But it can create a very strong platform from which to launch your next reinvention.

5

DIGITAL INNOVATOR: CEMEX

THE TOUGHEST BUSINESS ON EARTH

Cemex is perhaps the most unlikely of today's digital innovators.

Its roots are in a single cement plant founded in Hidalgo, Mexico, in 1906. Today, Cemex manufactures and distributes cement in thirty countries, maintains commercial relations in about sixty more, and, with revenues of over $4.8 billion (1999), is the world's third largest cement manufacturer. It shares first place with Petrobras of Brazil and YPF of Argentina on the list of the most respected companies in Central and South America, and is the *only* Central American company to win a place in the world rankings.

Cemex's business performance has been extremely impressive. What makes the Cemex story extraordinary, however, is the highly *unpromising* nature of the industry in which Cemex operates.

A definition of the characteristics of the toughest business on earth might include: an asset-intensive commodity business with low profit margins, low rates of growth, and unpredictable demand whipsawed by changes in economic conditions, interest rates, and government policies. Throw in customers who are always changing their orders and are driven by uncontrollable factors such as weather, work stoppages, and traffic jams, and the result is a pretty good recipe for a business to avoid at all costs.

No wonder Amazon.com's famously ambitious president, Jeff Bezos, has been quoted as saying he'd like to position his company to sell *anything*—except cement.

Yet Cemex has produced some of the most remarkable financial results of any Central or South American company. *If the cement business can be transformed through Digital Business Design,* ANY *business can be.*

THE CUSTOMER'S STREAM OF CONSCIOUSNESS

Most businesspeople have a love/hate relationship with their customers.

Customers are the reason any company is in business; they provide the opportunity to compete and excel, as well as the resources needed to earn profits and grow. They are also demanding, irritable, fickle, unreasonable, and unforgiving, and they can drive company representatives crazy.

Nowhere is this truer than in the cement business. The customers are contractors and builders working on homes, offices, hotels, highways, bridges—the gamut of projects for a wide array of individuals, businesses, and government agencies. If you've ever been frustrated by the time it took a contractor to finish an addition to your home (or even just your kitchen) or been delayed on a highway by apparently permanent construction detours, you know that such projects rarely run smoothly and according to schedule.

Because the requirements of the projects are unpredictable and changeable, the demands builders place on their suppliers are unpredictable, too. They change, cancel, reinstate, and recancel orders for cement and concrete (the mixed construction material of which cement is the major ingredient). They postpone deliveries or call to say, "Can you get it to me three hours sooner?" They are totally unmindful of the complexities of running a cement operation—starting with the fact that a load of concrete is never more than ninety minutes away from spoiling in the rotating cylinder on the back of a delivery truck. All the customers care about is getting their concrete when and where they want it—even if they've changed the delivery day and time, on short notice, three times before.

If this description sounds like something *your* customers would do, whatever business you may be in—welcome to the real world.

It's natural (and easy) to impute malicious intent to customers. However, it's not helpful. Instead, try to mentally walk across the room and look at the world from your customers' point of view (or better, "*points* of view," because no two customers are the same).

If you were a local manager for Cemex and you were able to tap into a customer's stream of consciousness, this is what you might hear:

> I know it's the third time I've changed this order, Lorenzo, but the damned weather ruined our schedule. The forecaster promised "Sunny and mild," instead of which—a hailstorm, for God's sake! That's on top of our union troubles. Three months ago, the union people decided to organize an "unofficial work action" to soften us up for contract negotiations. We were shut down for half of each day for two weeks. Worse yet, they kept changing the half. Sometimes it was morning, sometimes it was afternoon. Sometimes it was both. They kept us guessing just to impress us with their power. It cost us millions. Then there was last week—our supplier of steel reinforcing rods left us the lurch again. We were all set Wednesday morning to lay the foundation for the new parking garage, but the rods promised for two days earlier never arrived. What am I supposed to do? Of course I have to change my order. You think I do this for fun? And just remember, Lorenzo—if you can't deliver on time, *I die.*

If you stayed tuned in to that stream of consciousness, you'd hear a lot more (and in much more colorful language).

These kinds of problems aren't unique to Mexico. We once presented the story of Cemex to a group of American manufacturing executives. During a break, one of them came up to us and said, "What you're saying about the concrete industry is really true. I used to work as a dispatcher for a construction company that built office buildings in the Southeast. I can tell you that when you have three hundred guys standing around a big hole in the ground and the concrete's *not there,* it gets real personal, real fast."

Problems like these are not limited to construction-related products or even to commodity businesses. The key to Cemex's customer challenges is *unforecastable demand,* a problem that plagues many other industries, from package delivery to pop music to financial printing to ready-to-wear fashions. The same sense of being at the mercy of an unpredictable environment permeates the customer stream of consciousness in each of these fields.

That stream of consciousness is an unacknowledged reality of business—a reflection of the dozens of things people would like to be able to say but usually don't. It's a truth most of us would prefer to go on avoiding—especially when we're in a business that, like the cement and concrete business, is plagued with seemingly intractable problems and we assume we must go on living with them. Anyone who wants to truly understand a company's most important business issues must take the crucial step of understanding the scene from the customers' perspective.

> **Don't avoid your customers' realities. Instead, by doing some hard-edged listening, try to understand them and help your customers articulate them. This is the first step toward responding to and ultimately *reshaping* the customer stream of consciousness in a positive way.**

Cemex became a digital innovator—and one of the world's most remarkable companies—because it had the courage to recognize its customers' realities and then remake its own business design to do something about them—even while operating in the toughest business on earth.

CEMEX BUSINESS ISSUES

Lorenzo Zambrano, a grandson of Cemex's founder and a Stanford MBA, became CEO of Cemex in 1985. An insightful man, he saw clearly the basic strategic and economic problems of the business. First among these was the endemic, seemingly intractable issue of unforecastable demand—a huge problem for Cemex's customers and, by extension, for Cemex. But there was also a series of challenges peculiar to the Mexican cement industry of the mid-1980s:

☐ Mexico had begun lowering its trade barriers, such as high tariffs, which had formerly blocked foreign competition and investment. This was good news for the Mexican economy in general, but not so good for specific Mexican producers that had enjoyed a near-monopoly of their home markets.

- □ Competing firms in the cement business, including the largest foreign multinationals, had begun to consolidate and to become more efficient. They were exerting significant price pressure on Cemex.
- □ The high volatility of the Mexican economic and financial systems was still increasing. Interest rates, the value of the peso, and the demand for building products were more unpredictable than ever.
- □ International cement makers, especially the low-cost Asian producers, had begun to look to Mexico for expansion opportunities.

(Cement, unlike concrete, can be profitably exported halfway around the world. Here's the calculation a producer in Indonesia would have faced in the mid-1980s: A ton of cement cost $12 to $15 to produce, $30 to ship to the Americas, and $5 to $10 for final processing. Thus, the prevailing price of $70 per ton yielded about $20/ton for profit.)

Cemex had complicated its own problems through a loss of strategic focus. The company Zambrano took over had become overly diversified. Besides its core cement manufacturing business, it owned hotels, petrochemical plants, mining companies, and other industrial holdings.

Under the circumstances, the text that would appear in the "excuses" section of the CEO letter in the annual report was predictable. But Zambrano didn't relish the idea of writing an excuses letter. He preferred to change the game. He started by selling, at opportune times, almost all of the various non-cement businesses Cemex had acquired. Then, in 1987, he hired Gelacio Iniguez, a Wharton MBA who today is often hailed as a "cyber-visionary," to serve as Chief Information Officer (CIO). A powerful partnership developed between Zambrano, a CEO attuned to the strategic possibilities of information, and Iniguez, a CIO with a genuine understanding of business. (This type of teamwork has become characteristic of many of today's most successful digital businesses.) Together, the two executives set out to solve Cemex's problems. Their starting point was a painfully clear statement of the company's business issues:

- □ How can we help solve the perennial problems of our customers—especially the constant, unpredictable changes in demand—without driving our own costs through the roof?

☐ How can we respond to the heightened threat of foreign competition created by deregulation?

☐ How can we differentiate ourselves from all the other suppliers of a commodity product so as to seize and hold the lion's share of the market?

☐ How can we grow the business while shielding ourselves from the economic volatility inherent in our industry?

As we've seen, Digital Business Design always starts by identifying the key issues the business is facing. Sometimes they are hard to identify. More often, they are easy to identify but hard to address. That was the case for Cemex.

WHO ELSE HAS SOLVED YOUR PROBLEM?

There's a natural human tendency we call *strategic sloth*—the reluctance to tackle big problems that were insurmountable in the past. Sometimes, the tendency can be your best ally, especially in a situation where an end run may be more effective than a frontal assault. Instead of addressing your business issues with a blank slate and relying solely on your own creative genius, ask who else has faced and solved analogous challenges. Survey the business landscape for practices and methods that are worth studying, learning from, and adapting.

> When you are looking for solutions to your business issues, don't survey only your competitors. The best answers may come from companies in other industries and other markets that don't appear on your competitive radar screen but *should* appear on your "best business models" radar screen.

If you find yourself responding to new ideas with a protest ("Oh, that'll never work in *our* industry"), stop yourself. By choosing *not* to learn from sources outside the familiar margins, you are condemning your organization to the trap of the hopelessly neurotic: repeating the same actions while hoping for different results.

Instead of getting locked into your industry's peculiarities, step back and generalize the largest business issues you face. What other companies have faced similar issues? How have they tackled them? Are pieces of a solution visible anywhere else on the business map?

Zambrano and Iniguez sensed that, if they could successfully solve their first and greatest business challenge—unforecastable demand—solutions to the other key business issues would begin to fall into place. This issue was at the heart of Cemex's difficulties.

The systemic problems were daunting. Fully half of all concrete orders were changed by the customers, often just hours before they were due for delivery, so managing a network of concrete plants and delivery trucks was exceedingly complicated and frustrating. Dispatchers had to take orders for any of 8,000 grades of concrete and then forward those orders to six regional mixing plants. Each plant had a large fleet of trucks for deliveries to customers.

Phone service in Mexico is often unreliable, and Cemex's phone systems frequently became jammed with calls from customers, truckers, and dispatchers. Lost orders and gaps in essential information were common events. As a result, the best Cemex could offer its customers was a three-hour delivery window—standard in the industry, but unacceptably costly for customers. If this cycle time could be significantly improved, the benefits for Cemex's customers would be huge.

A quest for answers led Cemex to Memphis, Tennessee, and Houston, Texas. In those cities, three organizations—Federal Express, Exxon, and Houston 911—had largely solved the same core problem. Cemex sent observers to each organization.

☐ Using Memphis as a shipping hub, Federal Express (whose customers never provide forecasts of demand) had built an international business. It achieved a previously unheard-of degree of speed and reliability for the delivery of packages to millions of destinations around the world, at a reasonable cost.

☐ Exxon had developed the world's most advanced systems for tracking, scheduling, and rerouting oil shipments. Its global fleet of tankers, which was at the mercy of ocean weather, political and military unrest, and changing market conditions, was efficiently managed and tracked to worldwide destinations.

☐ The Houston 911 emergency dispatch system had figured out how to coordinate hundreds of ambulances and fire and police vehicles in response to unpredictable, often life-threatening problems. City traffic, incomplete information, or inaccurate addresses were among the system's daily challenges.

All three organizations shared Cemex's problem: coping with unforecastable demand while using limited resources. If unlimited resources could somehow become magically available, all of these organizations' problems, along with Cemex's, would disappear. An infinite fleet of delivery trucks loaded with concrete could cruise the streets of Mexico City at all hours of the day or night, ready to deliver their payload anywhere at a moment's notice. It would be the ultimate in customer service—and in asset intensity. Cemex's challenge was to find a way to approach this level of responsiveness while driving down the need for capital assets as far as possible.

It was a conundrum that called for a different *mindset,* not just a different approach.

> All three model organizations had one thing in common: They had developed systems for quickly and accurately capturing, responding to, and sharing information about their customers' needs. As a result, they were able to substitute management of information for deployment of costly assets such as trucks, ships, and employees—bits in place of atoms.

Fortunately for Cemex, the company's top leadership was ready for change. Gelacio Iniguez recalls:

When I started to work for the company in 1987, we didn't have a workable IT platform or a strong company culture. Our management style was very traditional. Our competitive advantage was low-cost labor. But Zambrano said we didn't want to compete on that basis. Instead, we should develop and integrate a solution that would allow us to respond to market changes and move very quickly, with a lot of flexibility.

That's exactly what Cemex did. Over the next five years, it began to design and implement its own solution to the fundamental problem of un-forecastable demand. In the process, it became the only digital company in the cement industry—and one of the world's great digital innovators.

CEMEX GOES DIGITAL

The core issue Cemex faced was how to create a system for more reliable information flow and instantaneous transmission among customers, the cement plants, and the delivery vehicles. Using ideas borrowed from the three models and from other organizations, as well as its own research on the latest information technology, Cemex began to invest in bit engines that would connect the entire company in an efficient network.

The transition to digital wasn't painless. A small illustration: Gelacio Iniguez recalls how in the early 1990s, many Cemex executives were startled when they began receiving e-mails direct from CEO Lorenzo Zambrano. Some even phoned him to say, "Lorenzo, why are you wasting time typing on a computer keyboard? You have a secretary to send memos for you!" Zambrano knew what he was doing. Communicating on-line was a way of symbolizing his determination that Cemex would become a digital organization. This gesture by the CEO let everyone in the company know that it was time to rewire their habits, or be left behind.

One piece of the solution was put in place during the years 1987 to 1989: CEMEXNET, a satellite system for communications. This bit engine enabled electronic connections among all eleven of Cemex's Mexican cement production facilities. Rather than operating independently—and often in ignorance of the supply-and-demand situations at the other plants—the separate facilities would now be coordinated from a central clearinghouse.

An important benefit of the establishment of CEMEXNET was the gradual automation of the company's back-office functions. The dissemination of financial and other information was streamlined, and accurate decision making was facilitated. Generating and implementing a purchase order, for example, can be done in less than two hours using CEMEXNET. At most companies, it takes days.

During the early 1990s, Cemex developed a complete system for managing customer orders. The new technology was called Dynamic Synchronization of Operations (DSO). Cemex consolidated its several truck fleets into a single pool under central control. New computerized operations centers were built in Guadalajara, Mexico City, and Monterrey. Dispatchers had access to complete information and could choose optimal combinations of truck and mixing-plant locations. Filling orders for concrete took into account the traffic conditions en route, inventory, customer location, and other specifications.

A computer terminal was installed in every delivery truck. The terminal incorporated a Global Positioning Satellite (GPS) system like the one used by captains of ocean-going vessels. The dispatchers in Monterrey now knew the location, direction, and speed of every vehicle, at all times. With trucks now "independent agents within a network of plants, rather than appendages of a particular plant" (*Computerworld*), Cemex could quickly dispatch the right truck to pick up and deliver a particular grade of cement; reroute trucks when the chaotic traffic conditions of Mexico City or Guadalajara delayed delivery; and redirect deliveries from one customer to another if last-minute changes were made.

DSO was a complex solution to a seemingly intractable problem, and it took time to develop and implement. There were bugs in the early going, but the basic design of the solution was right and the execution was improved continually. That process is still going on today.

Cemex has reduced the three-hour delivery window to twenty minutes, and a goal of ten minutes is in sight. (If the delivery is late, the customer receives a price discount of about five percent.) This target is achieved with a reliability of over 98 percent. There are fewer lost orders because the phone systems aren't tied up, and Cemex enjoys large savings in fuel, equipment maintenance, and payroll costs. Cemex now uses 35 percent fewer trucks than were required under the old, nondigital system. Fewer trucks means less inventory in transit (and on the verge of spoiling) and fewer drivers to keep happy and productive.

> Managing bits rather than atoms—information rather than assets—improves speed, reduces errors, and saves money.

Most important, Cemex's customers are more fully satisfied. They know that when their plans change at the last moment, their concrete supplier can turn on a dime. The reliability of Cemex justifies a small price premium, which in effect funds the company's ongoing investments in technology.

MANAGING THE BUSINESS EQUATION

The basic system was in place by the mid-1990s, but continual refinement and upgrading go on. The World Wide Web is now a key part of the Cemex communications network. All of Cemex's operations are linked by wire, satellite, and the Internet. Over 90 percent of all communication within the company is handled by E-mail transmitted via CEMEXNET. As of June 1999, Cemex's customers, distributors, and suppliers became linked to Cemex on the Internet. They can quickly find out when shipments will arrive, check payment records, and gather other data without having to speak to a customer service representative.

All Cemex executives carry their laptops everywhere; they'll stay only in hotels that offer high-speed Internet access over their in-room phone lines. The statistics they gather, on every aspect of the business, are just twenty-four hours old. (Data available to competitors are thirty days old.) A Cemex executive traveling to Tokyo to discuss a possible acquisition can immediately access today's production data from a specific cement kiln in Venezuela. The entire company is moving toward operating in real time rather than in lag time, and from separate silos into one integrated system.

Like other cement companies, Cemex manages a very complex equation: kilns, trucks, ships, satellites, construction sites, traffic patterns, work interruptions, reroutings, down time, cost/ton, the strength of the peso, the changing value of company assets. Monitoring, understanding, and managing this complexity across the entire range of operations of a large and rapidly growing corporate organism can only be done digitally. Anything less would slow down the process, introduce errors, decrease responsiveness to customers, and cause expensive mistakes.

In his book *The Genius of the System,* an analysis of the business methods of Hollywood in the era of the great studios, author Thomas Schatz quotes an admiring description of Irving Thalberg, the boy genius who created the legendary MGM movie musicals, many of which were both artistic triumphs and financial bonanzas: "He had the whole equation of pictures in his head."

Even as far back as the 1930s, only a genius like Thalberg could hold the whole equation of an industry in his head. Today, it takes Digital Business Design to master and control the equation of an industry. The genius of Cemex lies in its development of a digital system that can contain the whole equation of the cement business and continually anticipate, plan, observe, react, and adjust—as needed and in real time.

Cemex's commitment to information technology requires significant investment, of course. However, it is less expensive than observers might assume. Total IT spending currently equals about one percent of Cemex's total revenues—an incremental cost easily justified by the company's remarkable growth and margin improvements, as we'll see.

In this summary sketch of Cemex's development of a Digital Business Design, two key elements should be noted.

First, Zambrano and Iniguez focused on business design first, electrons second. An intelligent plan for Cemex's IT systems couldn't be developed until it was clear what those systems needed to do in support of Cemex's operational mission.

Even more important, they started their reinvention of the company by focusing on Cemex's key business issues. As Gelacio Iniguez puts it: "Reducing costs internally is important, but we want to focus on external processes. Changes that remove competitive barriers and those that connect with the concerns of customers are the most important."

Business issues always begin with customers and their concerns. Ultimately, they also embrace a company's profit model and strengthen its ability to create and maintain strategic control.

The solution devised for Cemex customers' central issue—how to get needed deliveries of cement in a timely fashion, despite the chaotic vagaries of the construction business—opened up enormous opportunities for Cemex to improve its profit model and strengthen its strategic control.

THE VIRTUOUS SPIRAL

The Cemex system, which included such well-designed bit engines as CEMEXNET and DSO, gave the company a value proposition that was unique in the cement industry. In exchange for a modest price premium, Cemex was able to guarantee on-time delivery to its customers, no matter how many unpredictable order changes were forced by environmental conditions. This attention to customer value quickly differentiated Cemex from its competitors and elevated Cemex to the status of a brand name in a commoditized business.

(Note: Cemex's superior management of information, with no change in its product quality, made the difference. Again, bits, not atoms.)

As a result, Cemex gained an opportunity to take significant market share from its competitors in Mexico and elsewhere.

The concrete business is inherently local. (The physical nature of ready-to-use concrete places a practical limit of about 100 kilometers on the distance a delivery truck can travel.) Cemex was able to leverage its superior business design into leadership in its local market. It gradually earned more market share in Mexico as contractors and builders discovered the advantages of doing business with Cemex.

By generating a local upward spiral, Cemex created both efficiency and strategic control. After Cemex controlled a 45 or 50 percent share in its local market, no other company could replicate its economic position. The infrastructure needed to serve customers with efficiency comparable to Cemex's simply was not affordable with a smaller slice of the market. Cemex created profitability *and* a protected profit stream. The money generated could be used to expand Cemex into global markets, using CEMEXNET, DSO, and the other elements of the system that were already in place.

Cemex's formula for global expansion: Win in one local market, then use the profits produced and the efficiencies generated to move into the market next door. Succeed and repeat.

In the early 1990s, Cemex embarked on a series of global acquisitions that helped to catapult it to its current position among the world's cement suppliers. These acquisitions followed a deliberate plan. In terms of customer selection, Cemex opted to concentrate on developing economies, especially in Central and South America and in Asia. Growth prospects in these regions far exceed those of the developed world. Cemex also sought to diversify as widely as possible, to avoid the risks of relying too greatly on the growth of any one economy. A singular focus is highly risky in any cyclical commodity-based business.

> **By leveraging the advantages gained from its Digital Business Design, Cemex has largely overcome the disadvantages of its slow-growth commodity business.**

Cemex has bought minority positions in or outright control of cement companies throughout much of Central and South America, and in other countries. Its major acquisitions from 1987 to the present are:

1987	Cementos Anahuac (Mexico)
1989	Cementos Tolteca (Mexico)
1992	Valenciana and Sanson (Spain)
1994	Vencemos (Venezuela) and Cemento Bayano (Panama)
1995	Cementos Nacionales (Dominican Republic)
1996	Cementos Diamante y Cementos Samper (Colombia)
1997	Rizal (The Philippines)
1998/9	A minority stake in Gresik (Indonesia)
1998	APO (The Philippines)
1999	Cementos del Pacifico, S.A. (Costa Rica) and Assiut (Egypt)

Individual plants were also purchased in selected locations—for example, a facility in Texas was purchased from Lafarge in 1994.

Cemex has used its Digital Business Design to make these acquisitions exceptionally efficient and productive. In many cases, Cemex buys depressed, low-performing companies at bargain prices, planning to turn them around by the application of the unique Cemex business formula. Generally, Cemex has succeeded in improving productivity and doubling the profitability of the acquired operation.

The Cemex acquisition system calls for a post-merger integration team—internal consultants specifically trained for this job—to be sent to the new facility. The team begins by negotiating lower prices from energy suppliers, cutting labor costs, and improving the new subsidiary's marketing strategy. Technology experts link the new plant into CEMEXNET and set up E-mail, voicemail, and Internet access. The process is generally completed within two to three months. Here are a few examples of the turnarounds Cemex has orchestrated:

- ☐ After acquiring Valenciana and Sanson in Spain in 1992, Cemex reduced the combined workforce by 25 percent and trimmed the number of corporate offices from nineteen to one within a year. Operating margins improved from 7 percent to 21 percent within three years.
- ☐ After acquiring a plant in Texas from Lafarge in 1994, Cemex reduced downtime from over 20 percent to less than 5 percent within six months.
- ☐ After acquiring Vencemos, Venezuela's largest cement company, in 1994, Cemex reshaped the business into a low-cost exporter to Brazil and the Caribbean, and doubled its operating margin to 33 percent within eighteen months.

In 1994, 34 percent of Cemex's revenues came from business outside of Mexico; by 1999, the figure was around 53 percent. Cemex is building dominant, not marginal, positions in the markets where it competes. Cemex is the number one cement supplier in Mexico, Venezuela, Spain, Panama, and the Caribbean; it is number two in the Philippines and Colombia, and number seven in the United States (where it is active only in the Southwest).

Cemex's ability to use acquisitions as tools for rapid growth offers a parallel to another digital innovator, Cisco Systems. Between 1992 and 1999, Cisco made some forty acquisitions; between 1985 and 1999, Cemex made twenty. They share a common thread.

> When a company has crafted a Digital Business Design that captures value in a clear and systematic way, it's relatively easy to improve new acquisitions and integrate them rapidly into the overall business.

Cemex's expansion strategy was not in itself digital; however, it was made possible by the company's digital strengths. The execution of the strategy was influenced by Cemex's Digital Business Design (see Table 5–1). For example, the selection of companies to be acquired was driven, in part, by a consideration of where digitization would yield the greatest benefits.

> By greatly expanding the range of a company's strategic options, going digital can produce an enormous *nondigital* payoff.

CEMEX'S BUSINESS DESIGN

The Cemex operation illustrates in microcosm many of the features of a smart business model for today. Cemex has taken an asset-intensive, low-efficiency business and enhanced its profitability by adding a brilliantly integrated layer of information technology—a bits factory designed to complement and support the atoms factory.

The unique value proposition Cemex offers its customers consists of rapid response and reliability. The customer needs less advance planning, can worry less about late deliveries, and avoids the huge costs (idle workers, for example) that accumulate when deliveries are late. The formerly insoluble conundrum of unforecastable demand has been largely solved.

The unique value proposition to the talent includes an infrastructure with a digital design that provides leverage to workers and decision makers

TABLE 5–1   Cemex's Digital Business Design

Customer Selection	□ Construction projects
	□ Contractors
	□ Focus on emerging, high-growth markets
Unique Value Proposition for Customers	□ **Reliable, on-time delivery**
	□ **Requires shortest notice**
Unique Value Proposition for Talent	□ **Technology and business training**
	□ **Information is always only twenty-four hours old**
Value Capture/ Profit Model	□ **Lowest costs, lowest assets**
	□ Premium pricing
	□ Acquire and turn around traditional cement businesses
Strategic Control/ Differentiation	□ **Unique system**
	□ Local market leadership
	□ Emerging brand
	□ **Unique knowledge of local demand patterns**
Scope	□ Manufacturing and distribution of cement and concrete
	□ **Logistics to ensure reliability and efficiency**
	□ **"Bits factory"**
Organizational System	□ Ability to successfully integrate acquisitions
Bit Engines	□ **Optimized distribution system via trucks with GPS tied into a central network**

Boldface = digitally enabled.

at all levels. A Cemex executive can download data on the inventory levels in a specific plant in Colombia or Spain from an office in San Antonio or a hotel room in Malaysia—an illustration of the near-perfect information transparency that digital business demands and enables.

The Cemex communications network provides twenty-four-hour access to the organization's best thinking anywhere in the world. Any time a brand-new problem arises, there's a 60 percent chance that a colleague has already solved it. Thanks to CEMEXNET and Cemex's Internet-based communications culture, a manager in Panama can post a question on Monday afternoon and get answers by Tuesday morning from counterparts in Madrid and Manila.

The Cemex system provides tremendous information leverage to the talent working in the company. *In fact, Cemex—a cement company!—has developed a more sophisticated system for generating knowledge velocity than many professional services firms.*

The generation of knowledge is not occurring exclusively at the senior management level. A crucial element of the Cemex acquisition and turnaround program is the provision of high-level training to all employees at the new subsidiary—not just in technical skills but in the basics of business management, finance, and information science. An understanding of the entire Cemex system is being driven downward and outward to every corner of the organization.

In 1998, with certification by the Mexican government, Cemex launched a unique program designed to educate all its blue-collar workers to the high-school graduation level. Classes are offered at remote Cemex locations through the company's own satellite learning system. Upgrading of skills, for individuals and for the organization as a whole, is a standing commitment. The focus on training is a key part of the value proposition that Cemex offers to its employees.

With its Digital Business Design, the company is capable of renewing and replicating itself repeatedly because a high level of intelligence and knowledge is disseminated throughout the organization's talent base.

Cemex's profit model is dramatically enhanced through numerous sources of digital productivity, including an ability to acquire cement companies and double or triple their margins after the acquisition.

By focusing on local markets and using its digital systems to build a 2X–3X relative position, Cemex establishes a very powerful base of strategic control. Not only are its economics hard to beat, but it also knows more about actual patterns of demand than any competitor.

BENEFITS OF DBD

Cemex is enjoying a wide range of benefits from its digital transition. With its mix of atoms and bits shifted dramatically toward bits, Cemex has become a veritable "bits factory." There is much less guesswork in the system (information is made available in real time), and the proportion of information available in thirty hours rather than thirty days has increased sharply.

At one time, the Cemex system inevitably mismatched assets to needs because of the combination of three-hour response time and unforecastable demand. Today, there is a much more precise match of assets to needs, partly because response time has been cut to twenty minutes and partly because Cemex's industry leadership enables it to see and anticipate patterns and flow of demand better than any competitor.

Finally, the shift from low-value-added to high-value-added work has been extreme. Cemex's business design has not only reduced the earlier labor intensity but also has significantly upgraded what its talent, from truck drivers to senior managers, spend their time doing.

THE FINANCIAL OUTCOMES

The business payoff from Cemex's development of a Digital Business Design has been impressive. The company has grown rapidly, both through acquisitions and through internal growth. It is now the world's third-largest cement manufacturer, with an annual production capacity of over 65 million metric tons (versus 10.7 million in 1985).

More important, Cemex outstrips its major rivals in productivity and profitability and generates a cash flow fully 50 percent greater than that of its biggest rivals.

Earnings per share have grown rapidly along with sales, reaching $0.77 in 1998 (versus $0.35 in 1994).

Cemex's ability to lead markets and to generate powerful and stable cash flows has enabled it to expand globally. Among the unexpected benefits has been an ability to take advantage of changing economic conditions around the world. The 1997 financial crisis in Asian markets reduced growth in some of Cemex's export business (building in Japan and other Asian nations slowed), but it created acquisition opportunities when governments were forced to sell their stakes in local cement plants at bargain prices. For an asset-intensive business, investing at the bottom of the market is crucial. Cemex's geographic diversity shields its cash flow and provides the resources for transforming economic swings from crises into opportunities.

ANYONE CAN PLAY

Cemex stands out as an extraordinary anomaly. Of the hundreds of commodity-based, asset-intensive companies in the world—from such industries as steel, chemicals, aluminum, mining, rubber, timber, sugar, oil, and so on—it is one of the first to shift from conventional to Digital Business Design.

And it is not located near San Francisco, Seattle, Boston, or any other locale that radiates an intense sensitivity to smart business design or digital opportunity. It is located in the middle of nowhere, close to nothing but the U.S. border and the Gulf of Mexico. In 1988, when CEMEXNET was being built, Cemex's Huichapan plant outside Mexico City was in a town with only twenty phone lines. Cemex enjoyed no special advantages in terms of talent base or high-tech infrastructure. Yet Cemex won its industry's race to devise and implement a Digital Business Design.

> **In today's business world, anyone can play. Even if a company has a remote location, a small market, and/or an obscure economy, it has the capability to perform at a world-class level, so long as the quality of its thinking is world class.**

The shift from *scale* to *smart business design* as the dominant factor in business success opened the door to opportunity for companies in every area of the developed and developing worlds. The shift to Digital Business Design leaves that door open even for businesses that arrive late. Today, any permanent limits to a business's growth and profitability are not "out there." They are inside the business's collective mind.

Today's world-class businesses located "anywhere" include the following:

- **Nokia,** from Espoo, Finland, with a market of five million people (less than the population of Brooklyn and Queens) leads the world in digital telephone handsets and infrastructure equipment. Astute brand management, a deep understanding of customer needs, and smart business design are Nokia's recipe.

- **Zara,** a fashion apparel retailer from Spain (population: forty million, one-seventh that of the United States), has an unparalleled supply network that allows it to react to fashion trends within fifteen days.

- **Bang & Olufsen,** a manufacturer of high-end stereos, televisions, telephones, and other consumer electronics goods is based in Denmark (population: five million). During the 1990s, this supplier for European audiophiles brilliantly repositioned itself into a marketer of luxury goods for the same consumers who buy Gucci handbags, Rolex watches, and Moët & Chandon champagne. The impact on profitability was remarkable.

- **Swatch,** a watchmaker located in Switzerland (population: seven million), transformed a moribund craft-based industry into a fast-moving fashion business by creating an entirely new market for cool, colorful watches worn as clothing accessories and collected like caps or T-shirts.

Whether your business is headquartered in Frankfurt, Beijing, Fairbanks, or Little Rock is increasingly irrelevant. Bits know no borders.

CEMEX'S NEXT BUSINESS ISSUES

For the next five years, Cemex has significant growth opportunities. They beckon for expansion and acquisitions throughout the developing world—in Central America, South America, Asia, and Africa. World cement production in 1999 was an estimated 1.56 billion metric tons (an increase of less than 3 percent over 1998). Most of this production was in the developing regions Cemex has targeted; for example, fully one-third of the world cement market (over half a billion tons) is now in China.

Cemex's current share of the world cement market is only about 4.5 percent. There's a continuing opportunity for Cemex to increase its market share.

Cemex also faces significant challenges, however. Despite brilliant implementation of its Digital Business Design, its business model is still too asset-intensive. In addition, Cemex is carrying a heavy load debt, currently over $4.6 billion. (The company has announced plans to reduce its debt by half a billion dollars during 2000.)

A larger question is: Where can Cemex turn for new growth opportunities after 2004?

Every business faces challenges, but there are always significant opportunities for business design innovation. Opportunities available to Cemex might include:

- □ *Reduce the weight of its capital assets.* Cemex's strategic control grows out of information management, not the delivery trucks and cement plants the company owns. Others (GE, perhaps?) could finance and own the assets while Cemex retains control of the supply network.
- □ *Do more for customers.* Cemex is already working closely with customers, helping them to become more digital-ready and able to take advantage of the information flow Cemex generates. Gelacio Iniguez notes that construction practices are currently "very fragmented." He hopes that Cemex can develop ways to download data in handheld computers and other tools that can help construction

firms get a better grasp of the economics of their own businesses. "Our focus will shift from the internal network to the external network," he predicts.

□ *Expand the scope of the business.* One approach would be to expand into building materials and supplies, using the same smart technology to provide reliable, on-time delivery of bricks, steel beams and girders, roofing materials, copper and polyvinyl chloride (PVC) pipes—you name it. Or pick thirty of the best customers and develop ways to solve their biggest problems, perhaps by offering services such as scheduling and logistics management.

For the present, Cemex has such a large headstart over its major rivals that no one appears likely to dethrone it. But the central business lesson of the past two decades has been the danger of complacency. Cemex needs to be planning its next two moves now, while competitors are working to catch up. The company's track record over the past fifteen years suggests it is doing just that.

6

10X PRODUCTIVITY

Digital Business Design actually redefines the potential for productivity improvement and for business performance. It often enables order-of-magnitude (tenfold) improvement. We refer to the dramatic improvement DBD makes possible as *10X Productivity.*

> A *10X Productivity Improvement* is more than an incremental growth in efficiency. It is a fundamental change in the way companies do business. It liberates resources to serve customers, leverage talent, grow the business, and help toward achieving strategic leadership.

In industry after industry, as digitization takes hold, we are seeing productivity improvements at the 10X level, and sometimes *much greater,* along specific dimensions of businesses.

Productivity is measured as a ratio of *value created* to *resources used.* When an organization is able to create more value while using fewer resources, productivity grows. The Industrial Revolutions of 1780–1820 (driven by the harnessing of steam) and 1880–1920 (driven by electricity) produced phenomenal leaps in productivity because the creative power of existing resources was multiplied.

Digitization (the "substituting bits for atoms" revolution) is now beginning to yield productivity improvements on a similar scale—although, as was the case with the last two productivity revolutions, there has been a lag between the introduction of the new technology and the realization of its full benefits. Only now, a full twenty years after the onset of the PC revolution, is it possible to map the entire range of productivity benefits being driven by digitization. And so far, only a few companies—the digital innovators—have reinvented their business designs so as to take full advantage of these potential benefits.

WHAT MAKES 10X PRODUCTIVITY POSSIBLE?

Why are 10X Productivity improvements possible when DBD is employed? There are several reasons.

1. Most of the time, in most of the economy, atoms are used when bits would bring better results. Bits are cheaper. When bits are used instead of atoms, a lot of big costs go away.

2. Digital options make it possible to collect very valuable types of bits (such as information on what customers really want) *before* committing atoms. The result is that atoms (e.g., inventory or unused factory capacity) are not wasted. Huge costs vanish quickly when bits precede atoms.

3. Digital innovators have developed an entire array of bit engines (listed in Appendix A) to collect, process, and distribute bits with extraordinary efficiency. The goal is not just to focus on bits, but to have the tools to manipulate and distribute those bits in smart ways. When a collection of powerful bit engines is exquisitely tuned to the needs of customers, value can be generated at an extraordinary rate.

That's why it's important to be constantly asking: What bit engines have we put to work in our company? How can they be improved? What new bit engines will we need to address tomorrow's business issues?

The more a company selects the right bit engines and puts them to work, the more 10X Productivity improvements it will create.

THE KEYS: YOUR ECONOMICS
AND YOUR CUSTOMERS

Potential productivity benefits from DBD fall into three main areas: Capital, Cost, and Cycle Time. All three are valuable resources that are always in scarce supply. Digital Business Design can dramatically improve the efficiency with which all three are used. However, when mapping out a strategy for going digital, it's crucial to focus on the *right* functional areas in the *right* sequence. Not all 10X improvements are equal. In a particular business, reduction in Cost may be essential, while reductions in Capital and Cycle Time are relatively unimportant; in a different business, just the opposite may be true.

How do *you* decide which business functions to focus on, and in what sequence? The specific economics of your business and the needs of your customers should be the controlling factors. If you define productivity in terms of what matters to your customers, you can hardly go wrong; if you define it without considering the customer context, you can hardly go right, no matter how impressive your numbers may look.

CAPITAL

At one time, capital assets—land, machines, factories—were regarded as *the* key to productivity, so much so that the free enterprise system was named capitalism. Today, capital in the traditional sense is recognized as only one of the major factors of production.

The current focus is to reduce fixed assets, inventory, and accounts receivable—the labels for the three largest numbers on the assets side of most balance sheets. Digital Business Design can reduce all three—dramatically. Here are two examples.

☐ **Negative working capital at Dell Computer.** Dell's business model evolved, over a decade, from a very strong nondigital model to a very powerful digital model. As the new model matured, Dell's need for capital in all three asset categories fell dramatically. Today, Dell has *negative* working capital. Because it gets paid by its customers *before* it has to pay its suppliers, and because of the extreme efficiency of its production process, Dell always has more cash available in its coffers than it has tied up in capital assets.

The key component of working capital is inventory. Like most companies, Dell used to have a lot. Then less. Then very little. In

1992, Dell turned inventory six times; today, it turns inventory sixty times annually, a tenfold improvement. Any recent Dell balance sheet will show that the combined value of Dell's current liabilities exceeds the combined value of its accounts receivable and its inventories by more than a billion dollars.

In effect, Dell's customers are financing Dell's growth by paying for product before it is built. Unlike most other businesses, which must take on debt to grow, Dell's Digital Business Design enables it to *increase* its liquidity even as it grows.

☐ **Asset reduction at Amazon.com.** Another example of asset efficiency through digitization has been created at Amazon.com, the leading Internet retailer of books, CDs, and other products. Unlike traditional booksellers, Amazon does not need vast real estate holdings (usually in expensive downtown sites or upscale malls) for retail locations. Because Amazon maintains minimal stock in its own warehouses and buys books and CDs (from wholesalers and other suppliers) as they are ordered, inventory costs are minimized. And because customers pay for their books as soon as they are ordered—and *before* Amazon is required to pay its suppliers—accounts receivable are always lower than accounts payable.

COST

Digital Business Design can also produce order-of-magnitude improvements in cost by reducing the amount that must be spent on labor, raw materials, overhead, rent, and R&D. Delivering services electronically rather than in person (moving bits instead of atoms) is one of the obvious sources of cost reduction. But, as the following examples will show, smart business design can find potential 10X improvements in almost every traditional business cost category.

☐ **Sales and marketing at Dell.** For most manufacturers, marketing and sales support cost a small fortune to provide in person and a prohibitive amount to provide by phone. The same support costs very little on-line. Dell Computer creates an invaluable bit engine—its Premier Pages—for its best corporate customers. At these customized Web sites, customers can quickly and easily configure and order computers electronically. Premier Pages also facilitate requests for information and calls for technical troubleshooting.

The financial benefits to Dell are huge. Each week, about 50,000 customers use Dell's Web site to check their order status; another 90,000 download software files, and 200,000 access Dell's on-line troubleshooting tips. Each of these hits saves Dell between $3 and $15—the estimated cost range for handling such routine inquiries by phone. And because Dell needs to hire and pay fewer salespeople to handle orders and troubleshooting requests, resources are freed up to support experts who can provide superlative responses to complex problems. Thus, Dell's customers benefit by receiving quicker answers to basic questions and better access to top-notch talent when difficult questions arise.

> It's important to have hands-on, high-touch service available when needed. But, by digitizing services that *don't* require in-person assistance, the overall cost structure is improved, customers receive *better* service, and profitability is greater.

☐ **Travel services via the Internet.** A traditional travel agent equipped with a computerized airline reservation system must pay $8.00 to process a standard plane ticket. The same procedure costs less than a dollar when handled by an Internet-based travel business such as Expedia or Travelocity. Improvement: More than 8X.

☐ **Procurement at Corning, Inc.** A major player in the scientific products business, Corning traditionally spent an average of $140 on the process of procuring the parts and supplies needed to manufacture a single product. Corning recently switched over to a Web-based catalog system. Now the procurement costs associated with each product average just $6. Improvement: More than 20X.

□ **Consumer banking.** A typical bank transaction costs $1.25 when handled by a traditional teller, 54 cents via banking-by-phone, and 24 cents at an ATM—a fivefold saving over banking *à la* 1970. But the same transaction processed over the Internet by an on-line bank costs *two* cents. Improvement: More than 60X.

CYCLE TIME

The third dimension of productivity is cycle time. Moving from conventional to Digital Business Design can help many organizations generate 10X Productivity improvements in cycle times, which also yield financial improvements. People, equipment, and overhead all have to be paid for on a time basis. Fast response also increases customer satisfaction, thereby increasing sales. Responding to emerging customer needs in real time rather than in lag time improves the accuracy of the response and further enhances customer satisfaction. And quick turnarounds of inventory bring less loss of value and greater return on investment. Speed pays direct dividends in cash. Here are some examples:

□ **Delivery time at Cemex.** The greatest need of Cemex's customers is rapid *and flexible* delivery schedules. Using its Digital Business Design to manage information, customer service, and fleet deployment, Cemex has reduced its customer response cycle from three hours to twenty minutes, a ninefold improvement. Cemex has used this advantage to create its leadership position in the concrete market in country after country. Cemex's digital systems have also dramatically improved the cycle times in other crucial performance areas. Cemex executives can download within twenty-four hours financial and other operating data that used to take a month to access—a thirtyfold improvement. Partly as a result of such efficiencies, Cemex was able to reduce the number of offices maintained by its Spanish subsidiary from nineteen to one.

□ **The "virtual close" at Cisco.** Digital systems for managing financial data allow Cisco Systems to close its quarterly financial accounts within a day. (It took fifteen days only four years ago.) Specific subsets of information can be accessed even more quickly; for example, sales figures are updated three times a day. The availability of information in real time rather than lag time empowers talent at all levels and enables Cisco to grow more quickly than would otherwise be possible. CEO John Chambers comments:

> Now the decisions that once would have come to the CEO might be made by the first-line manager. For example, at the end of a quarter, I might have realized that one of our product lines didn't meet our margin expectations. Today, the first-line manager can see that our margins aren't in line with what we expected the second week into the quarter. And they can explode that information down—because of our use of Web-based architecture—to understand exactly what happened. . . . If those decisions are made by all 28,000 employees, that's how our company can scale and grow.

☐ **Delivery tracking at UPS.** United Parcel Service (UPS), the package delivery company, has made the transition from nondigital to digital tracking of customer account information, including the process of locating a parcel at any point during the delivery cycle. One UPS agent comments, "Five years ago, a customer who called would expect me to call back with information within, say, forty-eight hours. Now we respond in four hours." Improvement: 12X.

☐ **Spare parts at GE.** The cycle time to deliver spare parts used to be 100 days. For parts ordered via one of GE's Web sites, the cycle time has been reduced to three days. Improvement: More than 30X.

☐ **Order placement at Weyerhaeuser Door.** At the architectural door subsidiary of the giant Weyerhaeuser forestry concern, the typical process for ordering a custom-made door once took two weeks. Now, using a digital system for designing and ordering doors and transmitting the key information directly to the factory, most orders are processed in less than an hour. Improvement: More than 80X.

THE CUSTOMER CONTEXT

The need for improved productivity is no new concept for most businesses. It has driven a host of trends and fashions during the past two decades—from quality circles, Kaizen, reengineering, and Six Sigma, to downsizing, rightsizing, mergers, and divestitures. Some of these efforts have been worthwhile, and, for many companies, digitization is the next logical step. It promises even greater leaps forward than prior programs could achieve.

But remember the key point about Digital Business Design: It's about business first, design second, and only then about digital. When speaking about productivity, this moral is vital: *Productivity outside the customer context is self-defeating.*

A classic example of the traps that await businesspeople who forget this law comes from the brewing industry. Since 1957, the best-selling beer in the United States has been Budweiser, brewed by Anheuser-Busch in St. Louis. Before Budweiser, the beer that held the number-one ranking was Schlitz, produced by the Uihlein family of Milwaukee.

As recently as 1976, Schlitz trailed Budweiser in annual sales by just five million barrels: 29 million versus 24 million. In that year, company head Bob Uihlein made a crucial business decision. Determined to catch Budweiser, he decreed that Schlitz would increase the productive capacity of its Milwaukee brewery by reducing the brewing cycle time from forty days to fifteen. Not only would the brewery be able to produce and ship greater quantities of Schlitz, but enormous cost savings would result.

There was one significant problem, however. When lager beer (like Budweiser and Schlitz) isn't properly aged, the proteins it contains tend to bond at low temperatures with tannin, a naturally occurring acid, creating solid matter that settles to the bottom of each bottle. The resulting substance, called haze, isn't physically harmful, but it looks repulsive. Schlitz used a chemical additive in an attempt to stave off this problem, but it didn't work. Faced with a fateful dilemma, Schlitz shipped millions of bottles of beer with haze, gambling that customers wouldn't notice or care.

They did notice and they cared a lot. Today, Schlitz is nowhere to be found on the list of best-selling American beers.

> **True productivity is measured by the needs and desires of *customers* rather than a company's business objectives.**

If productivity gains, no matter how huge, lead to customer irritation or invite competition to come in and take away sales, they are never good ideas.

What does this mean for an organization that is considering going digital?

There are often trade-offs among various ways of doing business. When the choices are made, they need to incorporate the perspective of the customer.

Place yourself in the shoes of bookseller Barnes & Noble, a business in a rapidly digitizing environment. If your best customer wants a book this afternoon, she can go to one of your bookstores. There's a cost involved—in time, effort, energy, gas to run the car, perhaps a quarter to put into a parking meter. But she'll own the book today. She'll also have the opportunity to heft the book in her hands, see how the printing looks, and get a feel for the object itself. For some people, those things matter.

At another time, this customer—or another customer—can wait a day or two for the book. She may not always be able (or inclined) to run to the local Barnes & Noble. She has an alternative: she can order the book online and spend two minutes and fifty keystrokes placing the order rather than an hour or more traveling to the store. The book will arrive on her doorstep in one to three days, depending on where she lives and what delivery service she selects.

Barnes & Noble is moving to give customers that choice. Today, it still maintains over 800 superstores, complete with cappuccino bars and in-store events, but it also has B&N.com, providing customers with another alternative (and also reducing the overall asset intensity of its business).

Similarly, discount broker Charles Schwab offers on-line trading, telephone service, *and* branch offices for those who like to watch the ticker prices and chat with a real, live broker. Cisco Systems can provide service on-line, by phone, and in person. The option belongs to the customer.

SMART SEQUENCE

We've seen how Digital Business Design can be used to drive 10X Productivity improvements in three separate areas: Capital, Cost, and Cycle Time. Although 10X Productivity is very impressive, the goal is *big improvements,* not a literal reading of 10X. DBD has changed the definition of *big;* instead of 10 percent or 20 percent, DBD enables 10X or even 20X improvements. Many digital productivity gains will fall short of the 10X level; that's OK. In many other cases, DBD will put once-impossible targets within your reach at last.

Thus, it's important to redefine your standards for the magnitudes of productivity improvement that are possible. But don't base your digitization decisions on magnitude alone. Rather, ask which 10X improvements are most important, given the unique business issues facing your company, and invest to make those improvements happen first. For most businesses, improvements in all three areas—Capital, Cost, and Cycle Time—are *not* equally important or equally attainable. A smart sequence yields the best results.

Michael Dell provides a good perspective: "Understand your economics first, then build your strategy." Dell's economics are all about inventory. Capital has been Dell's main focus of 10X Productivity (although improvements in Cost and Cycle Time have also been achieved) because a key business issue in the computer hardware industry is the perishability of inventory. Chips constantly drop in price, thereby destroying the value of existing machines. By reducing the amount of capital tied up in inventory to six days' worth, Dell has eliminated a major drag on its balance sheet and its income statement.

For discount broker Charles Schwab, Cost has been the main driver (although improvements in Capital and Cycle Time have also occurred). A pure service provider, Schwab's dominant issue is the cost of providing high-quality, personalized, knowledgeable service to investors. By gradually increasing the mix of lower-cost services (especially on-line trading and on-line information access) and reducing the *relative* mix of high-cost services (especially flesh-and-blood brokers in branch offices), Schwab continually improves its bottom line while maintaining a high degree of customer satisfaction.

For Cemex, Cycle Time has been most crucial (although Capital and Costs have also been reduced). By meeting the demands of its customers for rapid delivery of concrete and by offering almost infinite flexibility in scheduling without having to increase costs—in fact, reducing them— Cemex has become the supplier of choice in virtually every market where it does business.

> **In mapping your digitization strategy, start by asking: Which of the three areas—Capital, Cost, or Cycle Time—is most crucial to the economics of my business and my customers' businesses?**

The answer to this question will help you determine where you should begin looking for opportunities to digitize your business and how you can develop your own smart sequence for going digital. If two or all three of the areas are equally crucial, ask how much *parallelism* your company is capable of pulling off. It can be risky to mount major change efforts in more than one area at a time. Issues of corporate culture, the flexibility of your systems, and the digital readiness of your people will all come to the fore. Most businesses will be better off picking one area and hitting it hard and fast, even while they are planning where the second beachhead should be.

These decisions will probably involve not merely an internal analysis of your company but a larger analysis of the economic system of which you're a part. Where are the greatest losses of value currently occurring? Where are the greatest payoffs possible?

These crucial nodes are often at the interfaces between two or more parts of the system. In some businesses, the value drain may be between you and the network of dealers (retailers, wholesalers) that connect you to (and separate you from) your customers. Or, the drain may be between you and your suppliers, or you and your customers. Examine the entire system carefully in order to identify the most vulnerable pressure point.

INVESTING IN THE FUTURE, IN SPITE OF WALL STREET

Remember the definition of 10X Productivity Improvement offered near the start of this chapter?

> A *10X Productivity Improvement* is more than an incremental growth in efficiency. It is a fundamental change in the way companies do business. It liberates resources to serve customers, leverage talent, grow the business, and help toward achieving strategic leadership.

We're now in a position to more fully appreciate its importance.

We all do business today in a Wall Street straitjacket. Companies that have forecast to market analysts a 20 percent increase in profits each year for the next five years often cannot afford to invest in growth (especially when the investment requires "expense" dollars rather than "capital" dollars). Every quarter is spent in searching for ways to trim costs still further. Most businesses have long since cut away the fat; they've been slicing into meat and bone for several years now. The investments in creative thinking that might generate the next big source of profit growth have suffered; managers are spending more time prodding slow-moving systems into compliance than brainstorming tomorrow's innovations.

> 10X Productivity is important not just because it can and will help toward meeting the next quarter's earnings forecast, but because it releases money and frees it for investment in growth.

The resources liberated through 10X Productivity gains can be invested in attracting, keeping, and equipping the best talent; expanding research and development; improving the quality of customer service; and keeping the costs of products and services unbeatably low. 10X Productivity can catapult your company into a position of market leadership that can be maintained for years.

THE NEXT FRONTIER: 10X PRODUCTIVITY FOR THE CUSTOMER

Besides taking advantage of 10X opportunities for their own operations, digital innovators have begun to focus on creating 10X improvements for their customers.

Cisco's product configurator (part of the company Web site known as Cisco Marketplace) has built-in software designed to prevent configuration errors—that is, the selection of particular pieces of networking equipment that won't operate correctly together or in the customer's environment. Cisco saves time and money, but what's the difference for the customer? Error-free on-line configuration of a typical customer order takes five to ten minutes. Off-line purchasing would take two hours or longer, and having to fix an error after the product arrives on site would add another two hours or more. Cisco's digital way of doing business delivers a greater-than-tenfold time saving for the customer.

Charles Schwab's performance comparator tool is a bit engine that allows Schwab's investment customers to assess relative performance (say, for a portfolio of fifteen stocks and ten mutual funds) in a few minutes. Without the comparator, gathering and juxtaposing the relevant equity benchmarks and Morningstar ratings (comparing investment performance for three months, six months, one year, and so on) would take the same customer a half-hour or longer.

GE's PartsEdge Web site is a bit engine that enables customers to compare and buy spare parts—either GE's or those of other manufacturers. GE customers who go on-line can accomplish in minutes what used to take hours (and multiple phone calls and searches) to do.

Dell's Premier Pages allow corporate customers to get price quotes on computer systems, software, and other accessories in minutes, compared to multiple phone calls and faxes that could easily consume the better part of an hour.

In each of these cases, the tenfold improvement is per transaction or occurrence. As the absolute savings accumulate, they reduce the total workhours for some functions by as much as 70 percent, which frees up time for activity of significantly higher value.

ORDERS OF MAGNITUDE

Scientists use the expression "orders of magnitude" to refer to large-scale differences, those involving tenfold increases or decreases. Order-of-magnitude changes are quantitative changes of such significance that they tend to produce qualitative changes as well.

For example, when the population of a city grows twofold—from half a million to one million (El Paso compared to Dallas, say)—this is noticeable growth that city planners, law enforcement agencies, highway departments, water companies, hospitals, and school systems will need to accommodate and manage. But when the same city grows into a megalopolis of ten million (Dallas compared to Osaka, Japan), it morphs into a different *kind* of city. It develops qualitatively different social, political, and economic problems and potential. No longer merely a regional power, such a city is capable of competing on a global scale for intellectual, financial, and political capital, and can be expected to dominate entire fields of human endeavor.

The same effect occurs within an organization that has experienced order-of-magnitude productivity improvements. The company morphs into a *different kind* of company. It's not just more productive, it's different. It creates new levels of performance for customers and a different environment for its employees. It is much more in control of its own destiny because it is constantly liberating resources and taking more command of its earnings. It is more capable of funding the extra strategic investments that will make it more competitive tomorrow.

The implication is simple. The more 10X Productivity improvements you make, the more strategic you can be. The resources freed up by 10X improvements can be used to enhance the value propositions you create for your customers and your talent, and to strengthen your strategic control. Your company will then be positioned for even greater profitability and success in the future.

10X PRODUCTIVITY AND YOUR BUSINESS

Consider the following questions. Take just a few minutes to answer each one in relation to your business.

- ☐ In the past two years, how many 10X Productivity improvements has my organization executed? How does that number compare to my competitors' efforts?
- ☐ What 10X Productivity improvements are on the horizon for the smartest companies in my industry during the next year?
- ☐ What type of 10X Productivity improvement would be most important to my business—an improvement in Capital? In Cost? Or in Cycle Time?
- ☐ What type of 10X Productivity improvement would be most important to my customers—an improvement in Capital? In Cost? Or in Cycle Time?
- ☐ What specific action steps do I have to develop *today* to make my most crucial 10X Productivity improvements possible?
- ☐ What is the full portfolio of 10X Productivity improvements that my organization should implement during the next two years?

7

DIGITAL INNOVATOR: CHARLES SCHWAB

CHANGE CREATES OPPORTUNITY

No other company in the financial services industry has moved toward a Digital Business Design as rapidly and powerfully as Charles Schwab. As recently as 1996, Schwab was a nondigital incumbent. Today, over half of the brokerage transactions Schwab handles take place on-line. The benefits are large cost savings for Schwab and improved speed, accuracy, and convenience for customers. Schwab's other processes, from customer service to employee training, have also been digitized, improving customer satisfaction and yielding more productivity gains. Most important, digital strategic options have enabled Schwab to keep and increase its leading position among discount brokers, even as new competitors flood the marketplace.

To some observers, it's no surprise that Schwab has been able to capture the high ground in the newly digital financial services arena. A tireless creator of differentiation, Schwab has reinvented itself repeatedly and has taken advantage of change to find new ways of serving customers and capturing value. Schwab's digital reinvention is only the latest one—so far. But the steps Schwab took to move from conventional to Digital Business Design were difficult and far from obvious. Powerful competitive challenges forced Schwab's hand, and new challenges continue to emerge from expected and unexpected quarters. In the next decade, Schwab will be hard-pressed to keep up with the evolution of its customers while maintaining the uniqueness of its value proposition.

One explanation for Schwab's historic success at anticipating and leading change has been its willingness to look for models and bellwethers everywhere, not just in the financial services industry. Here is how Schwab President and Co-CEO David Pottruck puts it:

> We don't study the brokerage industry. We study Home Depot, Wal-Mart, Hewlett-Packard—companies in incredibly competitive environments, and with no patents, that have somehow, year after year, over decades, regenerated their competitive advantage and grown.

Schwab built a culture that was unique in the financial-services industry: innovative, open-minded, unpretentious, empowering, and, above all, customer-centric. This culture positioned Schwab well to take advantage of the opportunities created first by a changing industry and then by the emergence of Digital Business Design.

SCHWAB'S BUSINESS ISSUES AND THE EVOLVING RESPONSE

Schwab's willingness and ability to repeatedly reinvent its business design have enabled it to respond to the three business issues that have been crucial for companies in the financial services industry during the past two decades:

1. **Customer evolution.** In few other businesses have the needs and wants of customers changed more rapidly than in personal financial services. Demographic, economic, regulatory, and competitive shifts have made personal finance consumers continuously moving targets.
2. **The challenge of differentiation.** For decades, brokerage, banking, and other financial services were virtually nondifferentiated commodities. That is changing, but service innovations in the field are still quickly imitated by competitors. Establishing and maintaining a unique value proposition is a huge challenge.
3. **The need to provide customer choice.** Customers have strong personal feelings and preferences about how their money is

managed. Few are satisfied by one-size-fits-all services. Customizing services while keeping them affordable is a major challenge for Schwab and its competitors.

As the customer base evolved, Schwab's responses to these issues also evolved. Its development of a series of business designs kept Schwab in the forefront of financial services innovation for over two decades. Schwab evolved from the world's leading value-added discount broker (1975) into a partner with independent financial planners (1984) and then into a mutual fund "supermarket" (1992) via its innovative OneSource system, which made it easy for investors to compare and buy mutual funds in dozens of categories from hundreds of fund management companies.

THE CONTINUING EVOLUTION
OF THE CUSTOMER

By the mid-1990s, Schwab was in an enviable position: It dominated the discount brokerage business. Schwab's customer and asset bases had grown steadily, and the ratio of its market value to sales had risen from 0.3 in 1987 to 1.1 in 1992 and 2.5 in 1996. The company was on a roll.

But success is funny. It always leads you back to the precipice. Every great achievement creates the next great opportunity to fail. To miss the shift. To fail to "get it." To change one step too slowly.

Schwab had enjoyed stellar growth by virtue of its being the most sure-footed innovator in the financial services industry. However, Schwab was *not* the first company to recognize the revolutionary impact of the Internet on individual investing. As often happens, Schwab's success was accompanied by the emergence of a brand-new threat—which was all too easy to overlook in the success of the moment. The lesson:

> **Whenever your business is experiencing a major high, look for the source of the next low. Chances are good that it is hiding in the underbrush nearby.**

In 1992, Schwab launched the phenomenally successful OneSource. In the same year, E*Trade was founded and began offering stock trading through such Internet portals as America Online and CompuServe. For several years, E*Trade operated just below the radar; like many Internet businesses, E*Trade didn't really begin to take off until 1996.

In that year, E*Trade launched the second dedicated on-line trading Web site. (K. Aufhauser, later bought out by Ameritrade, had executed the first on-line trade in 1994.) For investors who were comfortable with the Internet, this posed a direct challenge to discount brokers in terms of both convenience and price. E*Trade announced a flat $14.95 commission on stock trades. Schwab's average commission was around $60.00.

The cost savings were part—but only part—of what made E*Trade attractive. More significant were the ease, speed, and flexibility of investing that digital technology made possible.

The customer also wanted something else—control over the information, the processes, and the services needed to make and carry out smart investment decisions. The advent of the Internet now offered a powerful new tool for providing customers with that sense of control. Hence the power of the E*Trade challenge.

As that challenge grew, an intense internal debate erupted at Schwab: Should the firm go on-line—and if so, how? The specter of a 75 percent drop in commission income was daunting. The debate must have resembled those within traditional brokers over whether and how to respond to the challenge of the discount brokers. (The same debate is heard repeatedly whenever retailers are confronted with competition from a new, lower-cost sales and distribution channel.)

INSIGHT AND COURAGE: SCHWAB GOES DIGITAL

Incumbency is a double-edged sword. Schwab enjoyed clear advantages over its new on-line competitors: a great brand name, a history of innovation, an experienced and knowledgeable talent base, and financial resources. But the continuing evolution of the customer could render all of these assets irrelevant. If Schwab was to make the tough choices required to respond to the emerging set of customer needs that E*Trade had identified, two qualities would be essential:

1. *Insight* into how Schwab's customers were changing and how the new digital technologies could enable Schwab to stay one step ahead of those customers.
2. *Courage* to take on the risks involved in: entering an entirely new business arena; investing in a rapidly emerging technology; accepting a new, less-favorable price structure; and committing Schwab to meeting a new and more demanding set of customer requirements.

Two decades earlier, when brokerage commissions were opened to price competition by the Securities and Exchange Commission (SEC), the old-line brokers failed to respond effectively to the emergence of the discount brokerage, and Schwab made lasting inroads into their market share. Schwab wouldn't make the same mistake, especially since, as a discounter, Schwab is more vulnerable than Merrill Lynch or the other full-service brokerages to Internet-based incursions. By May 1996, Schwab had decided on a response. It founded eSchwab, an on-line Internet trading division completely separate from the core organization, with the mission of countering E*Trade.

eSchwab was the first reinvention in which Schwab played defense—responding to a challenge from a competitor rather than leading the field. Schwab was now in the position of an incumbent; it needed to protect its hard-won turf even as it moved to seize new ground. Tough decisions were required—the kind that only a highly successful incumbent faces.

Establishing eSchwab as a separate division offered both advantages and disadvantages to Schwab. On the one hand, it permitted eSchwab to be developed and managed as an entrepreneurial startup unfettered by the culture or systems of a large parent company.

On the other hand, customers no longer had the ease and simplicity of one account/one relationship, which had helped make Schwab's previous innovations, especially OneSource, so appealing. Customers of eSchwab had to open an on-line account separate from their traditional Schwab account, and they were permitted to transact business *only* on-line (except for a single toll-free phone call per month).

Schwab's decision to create a separate eSchwab division was understandable, especially since, in 1996, the future of the Internet was still considered speculative in many quarters. As Dan Leeman, Schwab's Head of Strategy, explained, "We created eSchwab because we wanted to learn. But we did not want to risk the whole company."

During the next two years, despite eSchwab's limitations, it exploded in popularity. By 1997, Schwab had become the market share leader. It serviced twice as many accounts as E*Trade even though eSchwab's standard commission of $29.95 was more than double that of E*Trade ($14.95).

That price differentiation had important strategic implications. Schwab's digital move was never primarily a low-cost play (although competitive pricing was always important). Rather, it was a response to customers' demands for the speed, convenience, and ubiquity of on-line investing.

Schwab's instinct, honed through years of competition in the off-line investment services marketplace, was never to compete solely on the basis of price. Schwab had invented the new category of *value-added discount brokerage* to differentiate itself from discounters whose only selling point was low cost. Applying the same mindset to the new on-line universe, Schwab became a *value-added on-line broker.* Rather than run the endless treadmill race of price competition, Schwab would (1) add value to its on-line offerings, thereby justifying a price premium, and (2) build a recognized brand name associated with customer service, integrity, and quality.

The cost efficiencies of being digital would help equip Schwab for the competitive battle but would not in themselves provide the winning edge. Service quality, great offerings of information and investment tools, and an unmatched brand would be the crucial differentiators that would set eSchwab apart from its on-line rivals, and help it compete more effectively against traditional industry leaders (Figure 7–1).

FIGURE 7–1   In 1998, Schwab Was Worth One-Fourth as Much as Merrill Lynch

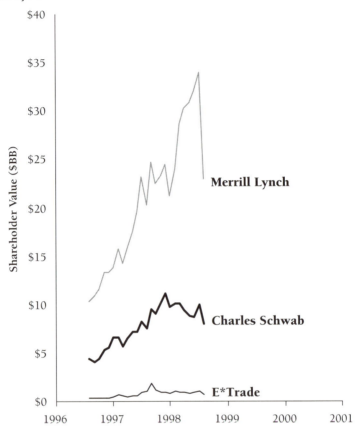

Source: Compustat, 7/00.

"CROSSING THE CHASM": REINTEGRATING eSCHWAB

The emergence of eSchwab as the leader in on-line investing was another major high for Schwab. And, true to form, the early signs of a potential low were already visible. In this case, the signs took the form of growing complaints from customers: "I don't want to have to deal with *two*

Schwabs." The dynamics of the separation between eSchwab and the rest of Charles Schwab were forcing customers to make a trade-off between low on-line prices and the richer array of services available through the parent company. And as the number of on-line brokers increased from twenty to more than 100, eSchwab appeared to offer less and less real differentiation from the pack.

Under the circumstances, it appeared eSchwab's success might be short-lived. Another crucial decision point confronted the company.

Customers were telling Schwab that reintegrating eSchwab into the traditional brokerage division was the right way to go. But the inevitable result would be commission compression: When customers were trading for the same account on-line and off, it would be difficult to justify radically different price structures for the two channels.

The logic behind the choice was both compelling and deeply painful. In a company less accustomed to reinvention and more wedded to tradition than Charles Schwab, action to implement the right decision might be delayed for several months or quarters. Schwab bit the bullet and went ahead. The reintegration move was announced, along with a new commission structure: $29.95 for *all* stock trades up to 1,000 shares, on-line or off.

In a symbolic rite that was designed to create an unambiguous focus on the importance of the transition, the entire Schwab senior management team, 120 strong, gathered on October 15, 1998, at the Golden Gate Bridge. Co-CEO David Pottruck handed out blue jackets emblazoned with the slogan, "CROSSING THE CHASM," and then led them on a walk across San Francisco Bay.

The need for a morale-building move was very real. In response to the huge, sudden hit to commission income, Schwab's stock price plummeted. By late summer of 1998, Schwab's market capitalization had fallen by more than $2 billion (from $11.1 billion to $8.7 billion).

Schwab's management refused to panic. Volume growth began to kick in. Schwab gained market share, and investors noticed. The stock price first stabilized, then floated up, then rocketed up. By Christmas, Schwab's market value had grown to $23 billion—more than double its late-summer low.

With 20/20 hindsight, the steps in Schwab's transition to DBD—responding to E*Trade by the creation of eSchwab, nurturing eSchwab as a highly competitive, independent line of business, then reintegrating eSchwab despite the company-wide impact on commissions—may seem obvious. In real time, they weren't obvious at all. Each step was crucial.

Suppose Schwab had waited two extra years before launching eSchwab. It might well have been too late to achieve a significant share of the on-line brokerage business.

Suppose Schwab had refused to reintegrate eSchwab into its core business. Schwab on-line might have remained a mere sideline, gradually cannibalizing an increasingly obsolete off-line company.

And suppose Schwab had mistakenly assumed that the crucial challenge of E*Trade was price rather than total customer value. A bare-bones eSchwab might have launched an on-line brokerage price war that could have shredded not only Schwab's profit margins but also the company's reputation as the high-value-added star of the discount brokerage business.

Deciding to launch eSchwab took insight and courage. So did avoiding each of the potential missteps on the subsequent journey.

THE POWER OF THE HYBRID MODEL

The newly unified combination of eSchwab and core Schwab created a hybrid business design—not a pure digital play, but a careful integration of products and services available through a variety of channels that were responsive to customers' preferences and convenience.

How many customers want to do business only on-line or only off-line? How many prefer to have a *choice* of channels, depending on time, place, transaction type, or other circumstances? A business that offers a choice is capable of serving the pure on-line *and* pure off-line markets, as well as the sizable market of customers who may prefer either channel on different occasions. The advantages of the hybrid model are clear.

Schwab customers currently have access to the widest range of financial service delivery systems in the industry. They can:

☐ Visit any of Schwab's 360+ branch offices and speak to an investment specialist face-to-face, gather printed information, or access price quotes and other data at a computer terminal.

☐ Do business by phone—speaking directly to a customer service representative in any of several languages, or using touch-tone or voice recognition software to obtain information or make transactions.

☐ Consult with one of the 5,800 independent, fee-based investment advisers who are served through the Schwab Institutional Division.

☐ Make trades over the Internet instantly at any hour of the day or night, as a growing percentage of Schwab customers do.

The mix of channels has important economic significance for Schwab. Currently, more than half (54 percent) of all the transactions handled by Schwab are generated on-line (the lowest cost alternative). Another 10 to 15 percent come in via telephone, and 5 percent are transacted live, at a branch office. The remaining 25 to 30 percent are submitted through financial planners.

The fact that only 5 percent of Schwab's transactions occur in a branch building might suggest that the branches are vestigial. Wrong. Over 70 percent of Schwab's new customer relationships are still launched in a physical branch. The permanence, stability, local presence, and personal attention symbolized by a branch office are crucial to a majority of new customers. Hence, they *prefer* to open their accounts in a branch office—even if they never set foot in there again.

Trust and its symbols are key variables in customers' decision-making process. This is especially true in the world of personal finance, where one's life savings may be staked on a business relationship.

> **Where a digital presence ("clicks") offers speed and convenience, the physical presence ("bricks") offers a basis for building trust. In many businesses, customers insist on both.**

This helps to explain (1) recent research suggesting that exclusively on-line banks will fail to attract and retain many customers, and (2) how Schwab has been able to hold its own against lower-priced on-line-only competitors. When asked why she chose Schwab rather than E*Trade, Ameritrade, or Datek, one investor said:

> I like the fact that Schwab has bricks-and-mortar buildings. I think it's the skepticism I have about the start-ups. I'm nervous because all their money is electronic. . . . It's worth the price to have the brand name and reliability of Good Ol' Schwab.

For Schwab, a company obsessed with understanding the customer, the branches are also crucial sources of information on the needs and attitudes of investors. Martha Deevy, Schwab's Senior Vice President for Electronic Brokerage Marketing, explains:

> Our branches are a tremendous advantage in that they let us really look at and understand customer behavior. Whenever we think about creating a relationship with a customer on-line, we step back and look at what the interaction looks like in the branch. One thing that happens in a branch is that when you walk in, you're met by a greeter, who can answer basic questions . . . before you need to meet with a rep or conduct business. We looked at the branch and said, "What do they [the branch officers] do? How do they create [customer] leads? How will we do that on-line? Recognizing that the investment process is a long one, how do we build a bridge to Schwab on-line?"

Insights gleaned from branch-based interactions and experiences help feed Schwab's on-line and telephone communication efforts. Technology enables every customer service rep to view a customer's entire portfolio while responding to questions or taking orders. Because every rep is trained on all products and services offered by Schwab, selling opportunities tailored to individual customers' needs and values can be fully exploited. All notes taken during a service call are automatically made available to the next rep who speaks to the same customer. This allows continuity and personalized follow-up.

The goal: To offer, at 20 percent of the cost, 80 percent of the service available from a full-service broker.

But offering the customer a choice isn't the only important dimension of Schwab's hybrid model. Schwab constantly struggles to enhance its answer to the toughest question of business design: "Why should I buy from Schwab?"

UNIQUE VALUE PROPOSITION
FOR THE CUSTOMER

For Schwab, the answer to that question lies not only in choice, convenience, and good price. It lies in providing unusually consistent support for the investor.

Schwab offers an array of information and tools that support investors at every stage of the investment process: developing strategy (Allocation Planner, Retirement Planner), getting information (Analyst Center and Insider Access), making investment choices (Mutual Fund OneSource and Stock Screener), comparing performance (Mutual Fund Report Card, Positions Monitor), and personalizing access to all information (MySchwab).

Schwab's unique value proposition for its customers hinges on this entire array of information and on analytical tools that help investors to make more informed investment decisions with greater confidence that their decisions are *right,* given their financial situation and investment goals.

The combination of digital services and available tools makes Schwab's Web site a uniquely attractive destination for hundreds of thousands of on-line investors. One Schwab customer commented, on behalf of many:

> I like the fact that I have all of Schwab's research tools at my disposal, even though I only use them when I'm about to make a trade, which is about twice a month. And I like the fact that I can personalize the MySchwab page. It makes me feel even more in control of my money. Being able to track a collection of stocks over a few days or weeks makes it easier for me to decide when I'm ready to buy or sell—and when the

time comes, the power to make the trade is always just a click or two away.

The Schwab system is both effective and cost-effective. It is a digital self-service system that offers personal backup when required. The hybrid approach catalyzes an upward spiral for the customer and for Schwab. Over time, as customers become more comfortable with the system, there are fewer demands for personal service on routine questions. Familiarity with the tools increases their use, reduces the in-person support required, and reduces the guesswork that customers feel they have to do in the investment process.

SCHWAB VERSUS THE ALTERNATIVES: THE CUSTOMER PERSPECTIVE

Has Schwab's drive to create a unique value proposition for its customers been effective? Its rapid customer growth would indicate that the answer is Yes. The set of benefits that each customer experiences is as important as the total number of customers.

For the past five years, Alan has maintained investment accounts with Schwab and with a major mutual fund company (we'll call it "Funds Family Inc."). Both companies have Web sites offering investment services and information, and many of the same investment options are accessible through both. But, from Alan's perspective, the experiences are very different:

> For three solid years, Funds Family never got a new investment dollar from me. Why? Convenience. To put money into Funds Family, I had to write a check and mail it in. With Schwab, I could transfer money from my bank account with two mouse clicks. Six months ago, Funds Family finally added the same feature—except you can only transfer funds electronically Monday to Friday between 9:00 A.M. and 3:30 P.M. With Schwab, I can do it 24/7. I don't get it: Why can't Family figure out how to hold my transaction until banking hours, the way Schwab does? It's a

real hassle having to remember to send money during the business day, which is when I'm most busy anyway.

Schwab's rivals are aware of the gap between their offerings and Schwab's, but closing that gap is easier said than done:

> For years, Schwab has made it possible for me to get daily and weekly news updates about a personal list of stocks I own or am interested in, plus a monthly investment newsletter. Family *just* added a similar daily news feature to their service—nothing weekly or monthly yet. Family recently improved their on-line trading service so it's about as good as Schwab's; for years it was painfully slow and cumbersome. But they still tend to push their own products on me when I'm trying to pick an investment. Schwab seems much more neutral in their advice.
>
> Every year, Schwab sends me an updated edition of Quicken—they know I use it to manage my personal finances. It's one of two or three freebies they provide. Family doesn't offer anything similar.

The Schwab system provides unique value not only for long-term customers, but also from the very outset of the relationship. One new customer described his initial experience:

> I'd heard so much about Schwab, I decided to try its system, even though I have a very good financial planner relationship.
>
> I got on-line, and after a couple of minutes on the site, I tried the asset allocation model. Within a few minutes, I got to the suggested asset allocation plan, which was dead accurate: a combination of 95 percent equities, 5 percent cash, which closely modeled what my planner had recommended. Within another couple of minutes, I got to a blended index fund, which matched my basic investment needs almost perfectly. It felt great.
>
> Then I tried to do the same thing through a mutual fund company. It took a few minutes longer; the Web site was a little less intuitive. It came up with the right asset allocation answer, but when it came to choosing a fund, it was a little more confusing. I finally sorted it out, but it was a bit cumbersome. Overall, I preferred Schwab.

Do your own comparison. Get on the Internet. Compare the experience of going through the asset allocation model on Schwab and other providers. Go beyond allocation to selecting the right investment. Are there any significant differences among the alternatives? What are they? Do they matter to you?

The Schwab value proposition is *not* ideal for every customer. For someone trading stocks or funds once a month, Schwab's $29.95 commission rate is probably a nonissue. By contrast, an active day-trader making many transactions every week is likely to prefer E*Trade, Ameritrade, or one of the other rock-bottom discount brokers. For a significantly lower price, these brokers will process a transaction with reasonable accuracy and speed, but without offering the array of information sources, digital tools, and other services Schwab provides.

Furthermore, customers who switch to a lower-priced on-line broker may sacrifice service quality as well. One customer commented:

> I moved to "Rock-Bottom Brokers" from a full-service on-line broker to save money on commissions. Now I stay with them because they give me one percent back on a free Visa card. It's not their smiling service, that's for sure. . . . By comparison with Schwab, their Web site is poorly organized and not user-friendly.

Notice how Schwab's unique value proposition for its customers plays into its customer selection strategy. Schwab charges more for most transactions but provides a much richer array of information, tools, and services. Investors who are more concerned with cost than with any other factor are likely to avoid Schwab. But such customers are likely to be chronic switchers, ready to jump to another broker whenever a little better deal is offered. Bypassing them means that Schwab reduces costly customer churn and focuses instead on a more loyal and profitable customer base.

Schwab is beginning to hear several important warning notes. Although Alan (the Schwab customer we quoted earlier) is very happy with Schwab, he sees a challenge for the company in the near future:

Schwab's been ahead for the last four years, but I see Family closing the gap. The question is: Will Schwab make the next leap up to reopen the distance between itself and the competition?

In fact, for me, the question is how soon will Schwab provide me with the kind of powerful tools that nontransaction sites (like Smart-Money.com) provide. That is the kind of functionality that I'm looking for.

CUSTOMER-CENTRIC CULTURE AS A UNIQUE VALUE PROPOSITION FOR THE TALENT

Schwab's Digital Business Design creates a genuinely unique value proposition for its customers. Schwab works just as hard to create a unique value proposition so that its talent will give a decisive answer to the question: *Why should I work at Schwab?* (This is becoming the toughest question many companies face.)

At Schwab, the answer to this question goes beyond "great stock options." Schwab has built a genuinely customer-centric culture and a sense of mission. In the words of Co-CEO David Pottruck: "We are the keepers of our investors' dreams." For many employees, this is a uniquely attractive job description.

Recently, a new customer (we'll call her Karen) walked into a Schwab branch office to open an investment account. A broker named Alex helped Karen with the paperwork and accepted her check for an initial investment. Then Karen said, "I've heard a lot about what a good company Schwab is, and I'm considering investing some of my money in Schwab stock. Can you please print out for me the research reports from Credit Suisse First Boston and Hambrecht and Quist about Schwab?"

Alex typed Karen's request into his computer terminal. In just a moment, the answer he expected came back: "No."

Karen was puzzled. "Why not?"

Alex explained, "Here at Schwab, we have a very strong conflict-of-interest policy. We don't believe in using our position as your broker to promote our own stock."

"But I asked for *third-party* reports, not your own recommendation."

"It doesn't matter. Our rule is never to behave in any way that runs even slightly counter to the customer's interest. In fact, even when the customer is *wrong,* Schwab bends over backward to act on her behalf."

Now Karen was intrigued. "How do you like working at Schwab?" she asked.

"Well, I worked at three other brokerages before coming here. My compensation there was commission-based, which is not the case at Schwab. So the focus was always on the transaction, not the customer. There was constant pressure to generate trades. Some were good for the customer, but many weren't. I hated it.

"Schwab is like a different world. The philosophy is: We want you and your friends and your children to be customers of Schwab, and we'll treat you so as to make that happen. It's an amazingly long-term view.

"You know what? If I hadn't discovered Schwab, I wouldn't be working in the brokerage industry any longer."

Schwab's unique value proposition for the talent goes beyond its genuinely customer-centric philosophy. Schwab is also beginning to apply digital options to providing leverage for its people through programs like customized training. The Learning Intranet, launched in August 1999, delivers continuing education to almost 20,000 Schwab employees. Each staffer can have a Web page with a personalized curriculum based on job requirements and his or her individual history of both on-line and classroom training.

The Learning Intranet is one of a series of moves designed to bring digital leverage to the employee much as Schwab's array of digital tools provides support for its customers.

SCHWAB'S DIGITAL BUSINESS DESIGN

Schwab has worked very carefully to achieve uniqueness, and it has succeeded—for now.

Schwab's unique value proposition to customers and to its talent lies at the heart of its Digital Business Design (Table 7–1). Schwab's profit

TABLE 7–1 Schwab's Digital Business Design

Customer Selection	☐ $5k to $1.5MM+ investors ☐ Mutual funds ☐ Financial planners
Unique Value Proposition for Customers	☐ **Choice** ☐ Reliability ☐ **Information and tools** ☐ Value ☐ Single source of financial services ☐ Multiple tiers of service
Unique Value Proposition for Talent	☐ Customer-centric culture ☐ **Talent leverage (e.g., Learning Intranet)**
Value Capture/ Profit Model	☐ Fees ☐ Commissions ☐ **Rapid productivity improvements**
Strategic Control/ Differentiation	☐ **Strong, trusted brand, both off-line and on-line** ☐ **Strong branch presence, strong on-line presence** ☐ Dominant share of wallet ☐ Customer and financial planner relationships
Scope	☐ **Hybrid model (branches, phone, mail, on-line)** ☐ Wide range of investment and financial services ☐ Personalized services (U.S. Trust)
Organizational System	☐ Customer-centric culture ☐ Integrated system ("One Schwab for the customer")
Bit Engines	☐ **Integrated, real-time account information at all points of service** ☐ **Choiceboard** ☐ **On-line trading** ☐ **Tools for comparison and analysis**

Boldface = digitally enabled.

model is based on multiple revenue streams—brokerage commissions, financial planner fees, mutual fund fees—and rapidly declining costs per transaction (and per service interaction) as a consequence of external and internal digitization. Its strategic control derives from its brand, its branch network, and its deep relationship with customers and with financial planners.

A critical component of Schwab's Digital Business Design is the array of bit engines powering the system. A linked database makes it possible for service reps to access—instantly—all the relevant data on a customer. Schwab's intranet is the key source of knowledge-sharing and leverage for the talent. Schwab's portfolio of analytical and comparison tools enables

FIGURE 7–2   By 2000, Schwab (with Less Than One-Seventh of ML's Revenue) Was Worth as Much as Merrill Lynch

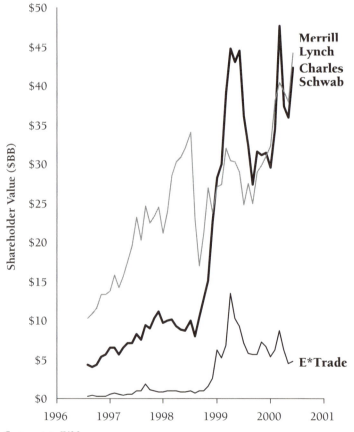

Source: Compustat, 7/00.

both customers and employees to convert the data they receive into decisions and profitable actions.

The creative use of digital options throughout the design has created outstanding financial results. Schwab's market value–sales ratio, which rose from 0.3 in 1987 to 1.1 in 1992 and then to 2.5 in 1996, has continued to improve. It reached 5.5 in 1998 and 7.0 in 2000.

As of the end of 1999, Schwab managed 6.6 million active accounts and over $725 billion in customer assets. The latter figure is still significantly lower than the $1.5 trillion managed by the industry leader, Merrill Lynch. But Schwab's asset base rose 39 percent in 1998 (versus 17 percent for Merrill) and grew by an additional $74 billion during the first three quarters of 1999 (three times as fast as Merrill). By 2000, Schwab's shareholder value was equal to that of Merrill Lynch (Figure 7–2).

BENEFITS OF DBD

Schwab has moved very far along the spectrum from atoms to bits. More than half of its customers' trades now take place on-line. More important, on-line customers can access a whole world of investment information electronically and conveniently.

Schwab gives its customers tools (mutual fund evaluator, mutual fund report card) to design what they will need to create the right match, and to enable easier and more accurate decision making. The system facilitates self-service and immediate response. It also leverages Schwab's talent, removing low-value work. Training is structured to be convenient, accessible, and a major ingredient in personal and professional growth.

Schwab's systems enable employees to detect and fix trading errors before they go through. The results are huge cost savings and, more important, a huge reduction in problems for customers.

SCHWAB'S NEXT BUSINESS ISSUES

Given Schwab's outstanding business design, is the company's current position of strength secure?

Not at all, for two reasons: (1) the continued evolution of Schwab's customers, and (2) the threats posed by competitors eager to capture parts of Schwab's business space.

Today, the average Schwab customer's account has assets of $94,000. It's still a small amount compared with the average Merrill Lynch customer's $400,000, but the gap is narrowing: Today, over 40 percent of new Schwab customers bring assets of $100,000 or more, as compared with only 10 percent in 1998.

Keeping up with a customer base that is growing more sophisticated, more affluent, and older is an ongoing challenge. Currently, the category of individual investors with assets between $1 million and $5 million is the fastest growing (by percentage) in the marketplace. Many of these investors are looking for quality, breadth, and depth of service—not price. Schwab has launched an ad campaign to help rebrand itself as a company with an emphasis on service. To keep these households in the Schwab fold, advertising expenditures were doubled from over $100 million in 1998 to $200 million in 1999.

As their asset base grows past the million-dollar mark, investors are likely to move elsewhere, especially to have their money privately managed. Schwab's recent acquisition of US Trust, an old-line, upscale private banking firm, is a key move to address this concern. It's a strategic move, not a digital one. With its range of financial services—from private banking and trust products to sophisticated techniques of wealth management—US Trust will enable Schwab to meet the needs of high-net-worth individuals.

As it makes these changes, does Schwab run the risk of losing focus? That's always a danger, but Schwab is better positioned than most companies to avoid that pitfall. One reason, of course, is Schwab's remarkable track record as a reinventor of itself and of its industry. Another is the fact that the migration Schwab is now making follows an organic logic. Rather than simply moving to grab a new market segment, Schwab is largely *following* its traditional customers—the increasingly affluent baby boom investors—as they shift into another region of the personal finance marketplace. Schwab is methodically building a service pyramid, with carefully tiered offerings designed to respond to the different needs of customers with $100,000 or $500,000 or over $1 million in assets.

As Schwab works to modify its business model in response to a broader spectrum of customer needs, it faces new threats on several fronts:

☐ In November 1999, **Merrill Lynch** launched Merrill Lynch Direct, which matches Schwab's flat commission rate of $29.95 per trade and offers, for a sliding annual fee, a customized on-line trading-plus-advice program. In the broadest terms, Merrill's strategy is clear: Facing commission pressure from on-line rivals, Merrill views the future as based mainly on the selling of advice and research. Schwab is seeking to enter that space from below; Merrill is pushing into it from above. Who will get to control the center first?

☐ On the international front, **E*Trade** has been moving aggressively. With 37 percent of Western Europeans (over 110 million people) expected to be on-line by 2003, and with Japan currently in the process of deregulating stock-trading commissions, U.S.-based on-line brokers are pushing for growth in burgeoning overseas markets. E*Trade, the current leader, is pursuing a plan to build a global on-line investing network embracing the world's top twenty financial markets. The plan began with an international blitz. Operations were opened in the United Kingdom, Sweden, France, Canada, and New Zealand, and a joint venture with Softbank has been launched in Asia. Schwab is slightly behind, but is pursuing its hybrid strategy with a branch expansion plan for the UK, Hong Kong, Canada, and Japan, and has partnered with Sharelink in the UK and with Tokyo Marine and Fire Insurance in Japan. Schwab hopes to be active in fifteen countries within three years. Is that pace fast enough to leapfrog past E*Trade?

☐ **On-line financial information sources** like SmartMoney.com, Equitytrader.com, and Yahoo!'s financial Web site are increasingly attractive. By providing fast, intuitive, and comprehensive access to investment data, research, and digital decision-making tools, these sites are undermining the uniqueness of Schwab's value-added discount brokerage model. They don't compete with Schwab's brokerage services—yet. But they raise a question: Can Schwab continue to enhance its information offerings quickly enough to justify the cost of doing business with it?

☐ **Renewed price pressures.** With its $14.95 trades, E*Trade continues to undercut Schwab on the price front, and upstart Datek pushes the line still lower ($9.95). Some on-line companies have begun offering five-dollar trades, and *commission-free* trades are on the horizon—a development comparable to the "free" PCs being offered by some manufacturers in exchange for Internet service contracts. How is Schwab preparing for this eventuality? Has the firm conceptualized the next profit model for a world in which commission income continues to shrink?

Although several important business issues are confronting Schwab in 2000, the single overarching issue is the same one the company confronted four years ago, eight years ago, and twenty years ago:

What's the next major layer of differentiation that will set us apart from all the customers' other alternatives?

In 2001, how will Schwab stay different? How will Schwab be unique? What choices will Schwab make in creating its Digital Business Design 2.0 so as to remain its customers' first choice?

8

HYBRID POWER: THE INCUMBENT'S ADVANTAGE

THE BENEFITS OF INCUMBENCY

There are few purely digital plays in business today—appropriately so. Not all customers are ready to transact all, or even most, of their business on-line. Nor is the technology in place to provide, in digital form, every kind of service customers demand. The smartest digital businesses today are organized along hybrid lines: They offer customers a *choice* of various ways to do business.

The hybrid model takes various forms and can be approached from different directions. A traditional off-line business can establish a profitable beachhead on the Internet; a dot-com startup can gain a bricks-and-mortar presence by building or buying it, or by forging an alliance with an off-line company. Either way, the hybrid model offers companies some unique strategic advantages, because the Internet itself can perform only a subset of the activities required to run a business that responds effectively to customer priorities. Success with customers will involve the ability to manufacture high-quality products, distribute the products, educate customers, answer questions, handle returns and repairs, and perform maintenance and service. Most of these capabilities (and the required assets) exist in the physical rather than the digital world, and they lie with traditional incumbents. For example, the bricks-and-mortar contribution to a digital business design can include the ability to:

- ☐ Leverage a trusted brand.
- ☐ Reach a large, established customer base.
- ☐ Allow customers to touch and test a product.
- ☐ Capture urgent and impulse buys.
- ☐ Provide aftermarket services.
- ☐ Provide places for returns and pickups.

Even the much-maligned "storefronts" of traditional commerce will continue to create value for incumbents. Most forecasters believe that e-commerce will account for only about 9 to 10 percent of total U.S. retail sales by the year 2003. And at least for some purchase occasions (filling an emergency prescription, or buying a sweater on impulse) or for a particular class of products (those requiring a high degree of "touch" in the purchase process, such as autos), physical distribution channels will continue to play a critical role in the buying process.

Despite the initial advantage of the dot-coms, bricks-and-mortar incumbents are well positioned to win in a hybrid world. Internet businesses are easy to start and expand rapidly because of their virtual nature and low capital requirements, but they are also easy to replicate and commoditize. E-commerce copycats who flooded markets with the same basic, low-price value propositions, are already going bankrupt or failing to find new financing. By contrast, most industries have a handful of traditional manufacturers, distributors, and retailers that have painstakingly built competitive barriers through investments in physical assets and infrastructure, brand building, organizational expertise, and patent and distribution rights. These barriers, if harnessed to the right hybrid business design, can provide some initial protection against dot-com upstarts.

If done well, integration of the Internet into a seamless hybrid can also create significant advantages relative to slower-moving traditional competitors in a number of areas:

- ☐ **Channel multiplication:** A hybrid model can extend a company's reach to new sets of customers. Milacron, a maker of machine tools, has discovered this with its on-line Milpro unit, which reaches previously underserved small machine shops through the Internet.

□ **Wider, deeper access to customer data:** A pure Internet company can track customer behavior on-line only; a pure bricks-and-mortar company can interact only with customers who visit the store. A hybrid business has access to both.

□ **High tech plus high touch:** A hybrid can combine the advantages of on-line business (speed, convenience, accuracy, flexibility) with those of off-line business (personal contact; the ability to see and touch the product; the sense that the company is trustworthy, solid, and real).

□ **Customization:** A hybrid model allows for more precise customization of products, as Mattel has emphasized with "My Design" Barbie.

□ **Assets:** A hybrid model can also enhance asset efficiency (e.g., Dell on-line) and leverage an off-line brand quickly. (For example, CVS, the drugstore chain, moved on-line through the purchase of pharmaceutical e-tailer Soma.com.)

BUILDING A HYBRID:
THE GATEWAY EXPERIENCE

Incumbents and dot-com businesses alike face a challenge: Having decided that they need a hybrid model that blends the digital and physical worlds, how do they develop it? The answer can be found by breaking down a successful clicks-and-mortar business design into its essential elements and working through a set of critical questions.

A handful of incumbents, including Charles Schwab and The Gap, have done just that. But the process can perhaps best be illustrated by looking at one of the most experienced hybrid players to date: computer retailer Gateway. From a 1–800-phone and direct-to-customer Internet model, Gateway moved to a business design that capitalizes on a powerful combination of direct sales and retail storefronts. Gateway's creation of a winning hybrid business model, built around the following four questions, holds lessons for managers planning their own move to e-commerce.

1. **Who are the target customers, and how can digital and physical assets be combined in a way that better addresses the customers' needs?**

In the mid-1990s, Gateway moved away from competing against Dell in the large corporate market and chose to sell PCs primarily to home users, small businesses, and first-time buyers—a rapidly growing market dominated by local value-added resellers and retailers. Company research suggested that the majority of first-time buyers wanted to see and touch the computer prior to purchase, and one-third of these buyers were unlikely to use the phone or the Internet to make a purchase.

Gateway also recognized that low-price computers with small and declining gross margins would increasingly dominate this market. Taken together, these market dynamics raised a significant issue: Could the company reach a large, underserved group of PC customers while also building profits in a rapidly commoditizing industry?

To reach this attractive market, Gateway deftly blended physical and digital capabilities by moving beyond the Internet to open 130 Gateway Country stores. These are not traditional stores; Gateway carries no inventory. Instead, the small stores allow consumers to test-drive Gateway computers, seek sales advice, and take classes.

Gateway has also leveraged its on-line capabilities. When a customer decides to buy, the PC is custom-built (typically, within forty-eight hours) at a centralized assembly-and-distribution facility, and shipped directly to the customer. This arrangement uses assets more efficiently while giving the customer the convenience of custom ordering and delivery.

2. **How can a hybrid approach enhance rather than reduce profitability?**

E-commerce has created low-cost, low-asset business models that can rapidly increase the scale of a firm's digital infrastructure. At the same time, many e-commerce companies have struggled to achieve sustained profits. Hybrid models, if built right, can combine the economic advantages of both Internet and physical businesses in a profitable way.

Gateway understood that the economics of simply selling low-margin computers were increasingly unattractive, whatever the sales medium. It moved aggressively to capture profit from the services associated with owning the computer: leasing and financing, training classes, software and accessories, Internet access, and a trade-in program designed to keep customers coming back. The product sale, which earns the customer's allegiance, opens the door to these more lucrative services. Gateway's robust profit model can withstand the low barriers to entry and price competition in the Internet space.

The merging of physical and digital assets underpins this profit model. The store plays a critical role in gaining the initial product sale, and salespeople in the store can effectively sell many of the add-ons (40 percent of buyers sign up for Gateway's Internet access). The stores also provide training and handle trade-ins. Rather than abandon bricks and mortar in the Internet age, Gateway plans to build a total of 300 to 400 stores by the year 2002. The Internet, in turn, provides a more effective medium for on-line support, order taking (through a 30,000-item electronic catalog), and an ISP through Gateway.net.

During the past five years, the company has achieved a 25 percent growth in earnings per share, and its market value has grown tenfold, despite a volatile and increasingly low-margin PC market. It became the largest shipper of consumer PCs in the first quarter of 1999, and, within this market, it ranks first in terms of brand strength and repeat business. While other computer retailers, such as CompUSA, are reeling, Gateway is achieving: 20 percent annual growth within its stores; operating margins twice those of traditional computer stores; and, because of its low inventory, a 45 percent return on capital.

3. **How can the unique aspects of a hybrid model keep profits from being diverted to competitors or to customers?**

Taking a hybrid approach creates more options for building competitive barriers that protect the profit stream. One such mechanism involves owning the hard-to-replicate assets associated with delivering after-sales support services to the customer. Gateway uses storefronts to serve the customer at the front end of the buying process and to provide consultation and training. The Internet helps to build customer loyalty by providing ongoing technical support. Gateway thus can maintain a relationship with its customers in the PC market, which is usually characterized by one-time transactions.

4. **How can an organization become quickly aligned with a hybrid business design?**

Creating a hybrid approach requires a mindset that is unfamiliar to most bricks-and-mortar companies. Whereas careful planning and deployment of resources in a stable market are typical characteristics of a mature business, a company moving on-line must emphasize speed and experimentation. The magnitude of the resources being directed at the Internet, the ability to grow rapidly, and the value of a first-move advantage require companies to move fast and lock up not only valuable customers and brand awareness, but also key talent, strategic alliances, content, and technology. (When Gateway decided to move away from the large corporate market and concentrate on the consumer and small-business segments, it changed its entire senior management team and moved its headquarters from North Sioux City, South Dakota, to San Diego, California, in order to recruit the right talent.)

Incumbents must be willing to cannibalize their existing products, revenues, and ways of doing business. One of the thorniest issues incumbents face is an Internet move that conflicts with traditional distribution channels. Gateway didn't face this challenge because it already was a direct seller. But other companies have had to address this issue in several ways: creating links to dealers' Web sites (Ford); giving traditional sales channels a commission on Internet sales (John Deere); and creating stand-alone competing entities (American Airlines' Sabre) and brands (Procter & Gamble). Given an opportunity to enhance their business through the use of the Internet, incumbents *must* cannibalize themselves or be devoured by competitors.

ORGANIZING A HYBRID

For a company branching into e-commerce, a key decision is how to position the new on-line operation relative to the existing organization. Managers can choose from four basic structures, each of which offers a series of tradeoffs (see Figure 8–1).

The choice of structure is generally based on how the company plans to fund the on-line initiative, how fully integrated the digital and physical

FIGURE 8–1   Tradeoffs for Different On-Line Structures

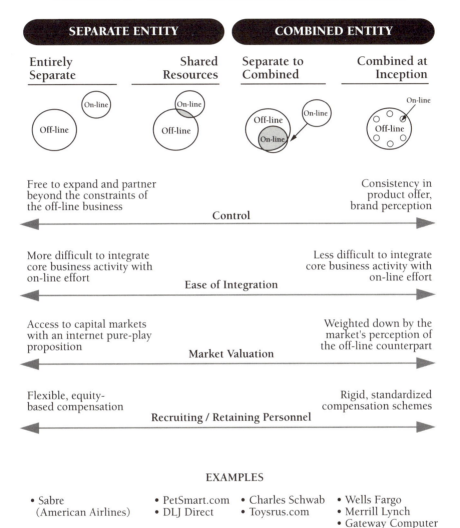

EXAMPLES

- Sabre
  (American Airlines)
- PetSmart.com
- DLJ Direct
- Charles Schwab
- Toysrus.com
- Wells Fargo
- Merrill Lynch
- Gateway Computer
- AA.com

operations will be, and how quickly the broader industry is incorporating digital technologies into daily business activities.

When an *entirely separate* structure is chosen, the on-line and off-line businesses operate as independent companies. Many investors and industry experts support this approach because it allows capital markets to value the on-line business as a pure play. For example, the spinoff of Barnes & Noble's Web site, barnesandnoble.com, unleashed an additional

$2.1 billion in market value. Initial public offering (IPO) funding options also make it easier to attract key management and technical talent, and they create a currency with which to make acquisitions and develop new products.

However, one drawback of the entirely separate structure is that it may make it difficult to take full advantage of the traditional business's strengths.

When a *shared resources* structure is chosen, the on-line company leverages the capital, infrastructure, brand, or content of its off-line parent. PetSmart, for example, merged its on-line business with PetJungle.com to launch PetSmart.com. The partnership gave PetSmart the necessary e-commerce technology, and the on-line business leveraged PetSmart's catalog distribution center and pre-existing awareness of its brand.

In the *separate to combined* structure, the off-line company incubates an on-line entity separately and later folds it in. Charles Schwab chose this route, launching eSchwab as a separate division that was later reintegrated into Schwab.

Finally, in the *combined at inception* structure, the off-line company incorporates on-line activities from the start. Merrill Lynch came late to the Internet, roughly two years after Schwab. Merrill considered launching a separate Internet unit, but decided it needed to maintain a close link to existing customers, because many of them had already opened accounts with on-line competitors. So Merrill created an Internet business internally.

The experiences of Gateway, Schwab, and other pioneers illustrate that incumbents can adapt a hybrid design and still win in the digital economy. But not all transitions to a hybrid business design are trauma-free. A transition may require significant lead time for promotion, and different patterns of customer buying behavior must be learned.

Williams-Sonoma, the upscale housewares retailer, found this out the hard way. Its Web site was launched on November 1, 1999, and plenty of inventory was brought in, to meet an expected high volume of customer demands. But the site was underpromoted. Expected demand levels didn't materialize, and inventory writedowns were severe (postholiday inventory was up 40 percent over the prior year's level).

In spite of these missteps, the business made significant progress. The company won new customers (half of its on-line sales were to people not already in the retailer's 19-million-name database), and 10,000 catalog requests per week started coming through the company's Web site.

BEYOND CLICKS AND MORTAR

Most discussion of the hybrid model has focused on integrating the advantages of bricks and mortar with the advantages of digitization. A second level of hybrid management involves integrating the mix of electronic and personal communication. Few, if any, good business designs seek to eliminate *all* personal communication. Companies such as Dell, Schwab, or Cisco try to optimize the right blend of the on-line and the personal. The overriding objective is to *enrich* the value and the impact of personal communication by enabling customers to perform for themselves any activities that don't require the expertise of a specialist.

When Cisco enables 85 percent of customers' inquiries to be answered on-line by the customers themselves, the conversations that do occur between customers and Cisco specialists involve higher order, more challenging problems—great leverage of Cisco talent.

Some situations require confidence, not expertise. Schwab enables its customers to solve most of their issues on-line, but if they feel they need help from a knowledgeable and sympathetic representative, it's only a phone call away.

Clothing retailer Lands' End goes a step further. It encourages a blend of on-line and telephone interaction because a telephone representative can often assist customers in making decisions and judgments that lead to incremental sales. Bill Bass, Lands' End's head of e-commerce, comments on the company's hybrid approach by noting that "Our new shopping tools bring an unprecedented level of human interaction to the Web and clearly strengthen our position as an on-line customer service leader."

For example, Lands' End Live offers two options for on-line customers to receive real-time, interactive customer service:

Option 1: Customers are linked to an on-line chat area where they can ask questions of personal shoppers.

Option 2: Customers can request a call back from a personal shopper. The call back automatically connects the two by phone and Internet browser, so they can talk while viewing the same Web sites. The live feature also helps Lands' End by providing immediate feedback about problems on a site.

Bass notes: "People thought the Internet was self-service, like a gas station. But there are some things you cannot program a computer to provide. People will still have questions, and what you get are much higher-level questions."

In the Lands' End business design, the personal *and* the digital play critical roles for customers. One digital tool, "Your Personal Model," allows women to create a three-dimensional virtual model of themselves, based on personal measurements, hair color, and skin color. The Web site can then suggest outfits and styles that flatter the customer's body type, indicate sizes based on the entered measurements, and show what the outfit would look like on the virtual model. A second tool, "Oxford Express," helps customers move quickly through a graphic database of colors, patterns, and styles. They can then choose from among more than 10,000 tailored shirts.

Lands' End also carefully integrates actual stores and on-line shopping. Its outlet stores, catalogs, and Web site are mutually reinforcing and supportive. Catalog mailings drive lots of traffic to the Web site and are the best way for customers to browse. Bass acknowledges: "You can flip through the pages, and it's a pleasant experience . . . you can't curl up in front of your fireplace and page through Internet images." The Internet site provides *flexibility*—by offering products that are not available in physical stores—and *ubiquity*—customers can access it at any time. Actual stores satisfy customers' need to test-drive products.

The company's hybrid approach has produced excellent results. Landsend.com, launched in July 1995, is now the number-one site for selling apparel on the Internet (and the sixteenth most popular retail site online). The e-commerce division's sales increased from $18 million in 1998 to $61 million in 1999; it now accounts for more than 10 percent of the company's $1.4 billion in revenue.

THE NEXT LEVEL OF
INTERACTIVE TECHNOLOGY

Experimentation in new ways of interacting with customers is accelerating. Emerging technologies will help create even more finely tuned hybrid models. For example, Liveperson.com offers the ability to respond to customer queries on-line, in real time, with a live person typing in responses to customers' questions. Because of the technology supporting multiple responses, one person can actually interact with several customers (like a chess master playing games against several opponents simultaneously). Responders have quick access to answers to frequently-asked questions (and sequences of questions), so they can respond to inquiries from several customers, achieving high satisfaction levels and significantly lower cost than a purely telephone operation could.

THE CHALLENGES OF HYBRIDIZATION
AND THE INCUMBENT'S EDGE

Incumbents can win by shifting to a hybrid model, but the transition can't be made without paying close attention to the very real challenges involved. The challenges will differ from one business to another. For Gateway, the crucial challenge was low-inventory locations. For Schwab, the challenge was commission compression, and for Williams-Sonoma, it was inventory management. For your business, the challenge may be different from all of these.

Every successful hybrid represents a unique business model, one designed to *integrate* the management of bits with the management of atoms in a way that is most advantageous to a particular set of customers. As always, the right design decisions will emerge from a deep understanding of what your customers want.

Invariably, some form of pain (financial, organizational, or both) is involved in making the shift to a hybrid model, and the same approach won't work in the same way for every business or every customer group. But the whole point of the hybrid model is to use a combination of modalities (on-line, "Liveperson" on-line, mail, telephone, salesforce, and physical location) that gives customers a choice, creates an optimal match between cost and customer needs, leads to higher customer satisfaction, and enables a more profitable business design.

A handful of players in the Internet space will successfully morph into a customer-relevant, hybrid Digital Business Design.

But the story of hybrids is the story of the incumbents' (largely unutilized) advantage. An incumbent's hand contains products, a customer base, physical plants, bricks-and-mortar storefronts, the company history, and the brand, all of which are difficult, if not impossible, to rapidly duplicate. What some incumbents lack are the characteristics of the best Internet firms: speed, flexibility, a customer-centric culture, upside potential, and so on. Emulating these characteristics requires a mindset shift more than a capital outlay. Strong internal marketing and careful design and organization of the new venture can create this mindset shift.

Despite the dot-com hype, incumbents have the edge in the hybrid world. The only question is: Will they use it in time?

QUESTIONS FOR INCUMBENTS

If you're a leader at an incumbent firm that is considering the move to a hybrid business model, begin your analysis with the following questions:

☐ In my increasingly competitive landscape, how will the shift to a hybrid Digital Business Design create new strategic control and differentiation from both traditional and Internet competition?

☐ How will a hybrid Digital Business Design allow me to enhance my service to existing customers while also providing access to previously unreachable or unprofitable customers?

☐ Which elements of my business design could be more efficient with a digital system, and which elements are best served by a traditional approach?

☐ What will be required, in terms of physical investments *and* mindset shifts, to make my company a true hybrid?

9

DIGITAL INNOVATOR: CISCO SYSTEMS

GROWTH AS AN EXTREME SPORT

In many ways, no two companies could seem further apart than Cemex and Cisco Systems. Cemex makes and delivers cement and concrete (an industry that is at least 250 years old); Cisco develops and sells equipment and software for computer networking (an industry created within the past fifteen years). The companies are also worlds apart in terms of customers, scope, and strategy. Yet both have become business leaders by moving from a conventional to a Digital Business Design. And although Cemex launched its digital transition earlier than Cisco, speed and focus have now made Cisco into one of the world's most digital businesses—and one of the most successful.

Cisco was founded in 1985 by Sandra Lerner and Leonard Bosack, who had met as graduate students at Stanford University. The new company filled an immediate need. Cisco was one of the few companies producing *routers*—electronic devices for connecting otherwise incompatible computers, thereby allowing them to share data. With the computer revolution in full swing, thousands of organizations, including universities, government agencies, and businesses, were in desperate need of some way to let their machines talk to one another. Cisco's routers helped make that possible. Within a year, the fledgling company was earning profits of $250,000 to $350,000 per month.

Early on, the basic DNA of Cisco's business had been established: It was a high-tech manufacturing company, producing and selling equipment that embodied leading-edge technologies capable of performing mission-critical data-processing tasks for all kinds of organizations. Thus, it was ideally positioned to take advantage of the major trends in business and technology of the late 1980s and 1990s.

By 1990—the year the firm went public—Cisco had grown significantly, fueled in part by venture capital from Sequoia Capital, a well-known force in Silicon Valley. Under pressure from the venture capitalists, the founders had been replaced by a new CEO, John P. Morgridge. Under its new management team, the company achieved even higher rates of growth. Revenues mushroomed from $70 million in 1990 to $340 million in 1992 and $1.24 billion in 1994. Cisco's compound annual growth rate for this period was a startling 105 percent. The employee head count ballooned, the company built and quickly outgrew a 120,000-square-foot facility in Menlo Park, and a Japanese subsidiary was opened.

All this turned out to be only the beginning. The explosion of interest in the Internet—and Cisco's courage in moving to where the customers were going—set the stage for an even more spectacular period of growth.

During the subsequent six years, Cisco's revenues increased fifteen-fold, to almost $18 billion. Now led by John T. Chambers, one of the most highly respected CEOs in the world, the organization continues to expand (an average of 1,000 employees are hired each month), and the wealth created by Cisco has gone through the roof. At its current valuation—far in excess of one hundred times earnings—Cisco's stock price makes it one of the most valuable companies in the world, rivaling such older and larger powerhouses as Microsoft and GE.

The leaders of a company that has experienced such unprecedented growth are in an enviable—and dangerous—situation. Hypergrowth demands an acute sense of balance, incredibly fast reflexes, and impeccable timing, like skiing the Himalayas or surfing a *tsunami*. Cisco could easily have been destroyed by its own almost uncontrollable momentum.

Instead, Cisco has thrived. It continues to grow and to move into new markets while maintaining profit margins significantly higher than those of its competitors. Today, Cisco is the leading company in sixteen of its twenty distinct businesses (it is number two in the other four) and is rapidly moving to seize its next opportunity, possibly the greatest ever: a major share of a converging telecom/Internet business.

> Cisco's adroit management of explosive growth would have been impossible without the company's mastery of the art of Digital Business Design. Being digital has permitted Cisco to understand, communicate with, sell to, serve, and adapt to its customers in real time. It has also liberated resources for expansion, research, and talent development so as to maintain and widen Cisco's edge over the competition.

The degree to which Cisco has been an innovator in Digital Business Design is widely recognized (although the significance of its innovations is not always understood). It's equally important to recognize Cisco's adroit management of its business fundamentals. Remember: It's always business first, design second, digital third . . . even with so brilliant a digital innovator as Cisco Systems.

CISCO'S BUSINESS ISSUES

As we'll see, the use of Digital Business Design has enabled Cisco to deal effectively with several major business issues. We'll focus first on the two most important issues of all:

- ☐ **Rapid customer evolution.** In the past fifteen years, few technological fields have seen more thorough and rapid change than that of computer networks. And as the uses for computer networks have changed, so have Cisco's customer base and the demands made on the company's products and services. Satisfying customers' needs and making it easy for customers to rely on those products—*risk reduction*—is especially difficult in such a quickly changing environment.
- ☐ **Corporate hypergrowth.** Because it operates in an industry that is growing at a frenetic pace, Cisco has had to grow even faster—to

serve customers and to stay ahead of competition. Managing such hypergrowth is a huge challenge for Cisco's business systems as well as for the skills of its leaders.

FOLLOWING THE CUSTOMERS

From its earliest days, Cisco has had to cope with a continually changing landscape of technologies and customers. The fundamental business design principle of *customer closeness* has played a crucial role in making this possible.

During the late 1980s and early 1990s, Cisco's engineers and its sales force were practically one and the same; the techies who connected with the customers were the same people who installed the networking equipment, trained customers in using it, fixed it when it broke, and upgraded it as necessary. Furthermore, the customers and the engineers considered one another "peers," as John Morgridge put it. Networking was so new that Cisco's clients and staff often collaborated to design, implement, and improve Cisco's products. This readiness to listen to and understand the customers, and to work with them to make solutions happen, is one of Cisco's greatest business assets.

By 1995, Cisco had become the leader in a highly competitive industry (see Figure 9–1). But it was not at all obvious which networking company was destined to leapfrog to the very top of the NASDAQ listings. The race was fast and very, very close. However, within the next five years, Cisco moved far ahead of its competitors. It gained first place by obsessing about the changing needs of customers and responding to them more accurately and more quickly than anyone else.

Customer Shift

In the early 1990s, Cisco's core market was the so-called *enterprise customers*—the international companies and other large organizations that were the first to develop major internal computer networks called local

FIGURE 9–1 In 1994, Cisco Was Worth Three Times As Much As Its Chief Rivals

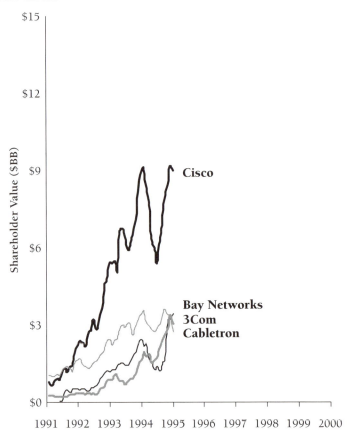

Source: Compustat, 7/00.

area networks (LANs). They required the various kinds of equipment that Cisco made, including *routers, hubs,* and *switches.* (A *router* is an information network's "traffic cop"; it reads every packet of data and chooses the right path to send it down. A *hub,* also called a *concentrator,* is a data re-broadcasting device; generally, it is used to tie together the systems in a single LAN. A *switch* makes a collection of hubs work together more efficiently by reducing needless traffic. A complex network needs all three devices.)

By the mid 1990s, Cisco's customer set had begun to change. Cisco was now serving both a wider array of enterprise clients and an emerging market of Internet service providers (ISPs)—companies that linked their own customers with the burgeoning World Wide Web. This new customer base required Cisco's high-capacity, high-reliability switches and routers plus an array of new products—asynchronous transfer mode (ATM) technology, wide area network (WAN) switches, and remote access, for example.

Cisco was able to respond to this shift more effectively than its competitors because it recognized and exploited two patterns of strategic change: Product-to-Solution and De Facto Standard. (For more information on these and other patterns, visit http://www. profitpatterns.com.)

> **The Product-to-Solution pattern involves moving from a product-centric view of the business to a customer-centric one. It requires learning customers' systems and economics, and creating unique solutions to improve both.**

Rather than viewing itself as a company that makes routers and switches, Cisco had to learn to see itself as a provider of computer networking solutions—a very different type of mental "job description." (Think of your own company for a moment. Is it a product-maker or a problem-solver?) The force driving this change was the growing complexity and riskiness of computer networks. As these networks became more complicated and more in demand for business operations, customers were eager to purchase all their networking products and services from a single source if this could be done economically and, most important, reliably. (When a company's financial network goes down, the CFO doesn't care whether the problem is with Company A's routers, Company B's switches, Company C's modems, or Company D's software. The CFO just wants it fixed, *now!*)

In response to its customers' demands, Cisco kept expanding its product line beyond its traditional routers and switches. From a strategic perspective, it had no other choice. Company acquisitions were a major tool. Cisco bought whatever technology its customers required, in an effort to transform Cisco into a complete and reliable source for the customer's full range of networking needs. By 1997, acquired companies and technologies were contributing fully half of Cisco's annual revenues.

> **The De Facto Standard pattern involves creating, controlling, or aligning with a standard (usually technological) that rationalizes activity within an industry.**

Cisco had always owned a loose collection of software programs that served to manage its networking equipment. During the mid-1990s, Cisco moved to integrate this software and brand it under the name of Internetwork Operating System (IOS). By 1997, as Cisco's sales continued to grow, and as Cisco actively promoted itself as *the* comprehensive solutions source, IOS had become the industry-wide standard for moving data among connected computer systems.

A network manager for a large professional services firm has described the advantage that the customer and Cisco derive from IOS: "To manage a complex system, I want more of the same, less of the different. The more standardized the equipment and the protocols, the better." Furthermore, a de facto standard has cumulative power: "I've now built up an enormous skill set on Cisco products. The more I use them, the more experience my support staff have in touching, installing, upgrading, and programming them. If I were to start changing suppliers, I'd lose all that."

Cisco didn't shut off other companies from access to its proprietary technology; on the contrary, it licensed IOS to companies ranging from Compaq, Intel, and Microsoft to direct competitors such as Bay Networks and 3Com. These licenses became a revenue source for Cisco. They also helped make IOS virtually ubiquitous in the world of networking. Cisco became positioned as the "keeper of the standard" and therefore the supplier of choice. The decision to license IOS proved to be crucial; if Cisco had adopted the wrong mindset and opted for secrecy and control, it would not have achieved the leadership position it currently maintains.

Today, Cisco routers and IOS software handle 70 percent of all network traffic, both across the Internet as a whole and within corporate

LANs and WANs. The IOS standard is a major asset for Cisco. The sense of risk reduction it creates for Cisco customers—"I'm buying from the people who created the standard"—is a key link in the Cisco value proposition. Like Microsoft in the PC operating systems arena, Cisco owns 80 percent of customer mindshare in the networking business. Its powerful sales pipeline needs only to be continually replenished with the best new products.

Nonetheless, Cisco faces intense competitive pressures. Continual change in the networking field fuels a steady stream of start-ups offering new tools to complement or replace existing technologies. If Cisco had allowed success to make it complacent, it would have quickly been displaced by one of its many eager rivals. Instead, Cisco has constantly pushed itself forward.

CUSTOMER-DRIVEN ACQUISITIONS

Cisco's ability to keep up with marketplace demands has been driven by an unusual willingness to listen to customers' stream of consciousness and respond appropriately. The Cisco response has often involved strategic company acquisitions. Here's an example.

Prior to 1995, Cisco's customers had made one specific form of networking technology, referred to as Fast Ethernet, the dominant product. In fact, Fast Ethernet was outselling the main alternative, asynchronous transfer mode (ATM), by five to one. But during 1995, a shift occurred. More of Cisco's enterprise customers sought to equip their wide area networks (WANs) with an ability to link up to multiple local-area networks (LANs) so that data could be distributed among various business partners. For this purpose, ATM technology was better than Fast Ethernet.

However, Cisco wasn't the leader in ATM technology; two competing firms, Cascade and StrataCom, owned that technological advantage. (A recent Cisco acquisition, LightStream, was developing a new ATM platform, but the project was far from completion.) Fearing that the products might become obsolete within a year or two, customers shied away from buying ATM technology from Cisco.

It would have been easy for Cisco to hunker down defensively in response. One option might have been to invest time in adapting Fast Ethernet to LAN-to-LAN requirements. (Cisco had in fact managed to increase the transmission speed of Fast Ethernet to a level competitive with ATM, and could have used this fact as a justification for ignoring ATM altogether.) Or, Cisco, as the market leader, could have asked its customers to be patient while its LightStream division worked to perfect its own ATM product.

Instead, Cisco moved boldly. Unable to quickly meet an undeniable customer need, Cisco decided to buy the technology it lacked. In April 1996, Cisco bought StrataCom for $4.5 billion. It was Cisco's largest acquisition to date (exceeded only in 1999 by the $7 billion purchase of Cerent Corporation). Cisco instantly became a leader in ATM, the fastest-growing networking market.

The StrataCom acquisition was an unusually large one; in fact, Cisco was widely criticized for overpaying (not for the first or last time). But it was typical of Cisco's strategic use of acquisitions as a way of serving customers' needs. Cisco has made technology acquisition a mainstay of its growth strategy. In fact, since 1994, Cisco has completed over 50 acquisitions and continues to acquire companies at the rate of about ten per year.

Taking on technology from other companies doesn't come naturally in Silicon Valley. Like Cisco Systems, most high-tech companies are founded by very smart engineering minds that are justifiably proud of their own creative prowess. The Not-Invented-Here syndrome is an easy trap for them to fall into.

> **A company built on great technology can all too easily fall in love with that technology and end up defending it when the world has turned the page. Judge your company and its product offerings through your customers' eyes, not those of a proud parent.**

When Cisco recognizes the need for a new product (usually because customers have begun to ask for a new type of solution to their networking needs), it first analyzes how and when it can bring the product to market through internal development. If that process would take longer than six months (just one-third the average time for launching a new product), Cisco will buy its way into the market by acquiring a company with a technological head start. *And* it will make the acquisition only if a Cisco-branded version of the product can be delivered by the time the deal closes—usually, in three to six months.

Cisco's acquisition values, often considered shockingly high by traditional Wall Street standards, are dependent on the target company's ability to meet these aggressive deadlines. The company pays so that it can reduce the two most common risks of internal R&D—*uncertainty of outcome* and the *likelihood of delays*—and replace them with *near certainty of outcome* and *high speed.*

> **For Cisco, company acquisitions aren't primarily a way to increase revenues and market share (though they do both). Instead, they are a way of accelerating the product development cycle in order to meet customers' needs more efficiently.**

Because serving customers (rather than growth for its own sake) is the driving force behind every Cisco acquisition, the company has not been riven by the culture clashes, incompatible visions, turf wars, and jealousy that destroy many cobbled-together enterprises.

Cisco's acquisitions offer one additional benefit to the company: Each provides an infusion of great engineering talent, which is in short supply in the technology business.

Cisco's astute exploitation of the Product-to-Solution and De Facto Standard patterns, its accurate tracking of the evolution of its customer base, and its skilled use of acquisitions as a way of seizing control of new ideas for serving customers, produced, in combination, a business design that masterfully addressed the company's key business issues. Without getting these fundamentals right, being brilliant at digital would not have mattered.

CISCO VERSUS THE COMPETITION: THE CUSTOMER PERSPECTIVE

Cisco's customers are among the most technologically knowledgeable in the world. They are also highly demanding, especially when it comes to the *reliability* of their network systems. Their attitude is understandable: When a company's network goes down, even for a short time, customer service, internal communication, data availability, and work process flows are all disrupted. For any IT manager, this is the worst nightmare. The office quickly fills up with angry colleagues demanding not an explanation (they couldn't care less *why* the network is down) but either a quick fix . . . or the manager's head.

One IT manager at a midsize company responded this way when asked to rank his priorities as a networking customer, and to rate Cisco in comparison to the competition:

> Uptime and reliability rank first on my list of priorities. And with Cisco products and services, our network is almost never down. A couple of years ago, when we were using mainly equipment from another supplier, we had to shut down the network whenever we had to upgrade a router. Not with Cisco. Now that Cisco products dominate our system, no one served by the network even knows when an upgrade is happening.
>
> My next priority is the technology and product features available. We're always looking for the latest network capabilities. I like the fact that Cisco generally seems to be ready just about the same time we are. There's a new technology called Layer 3 switching that offers greater bandwidth capacity, higher data security, and other benefits. We don't need it right now, but a year from today we will. Our Cisco rep says they'll be offering it to us in about six months. I've found they're very good about meeting the schedules they set.
>
> Next, I'm concerned about global presence and brand name. I'm very comfortable buying Cisco because the reputation of the company is excellent and widely known. I'd hesitate to buy even a very good product from a lesser-known company that people in our branch offices

in Frankfurt and London might not have heard of. If we experienced problems, I'd have to talk fast to justify having bought something other than Cisco.

The availability and quality of the sales and service people would be my next priority. I rate Cisco high in this area, although I rarely have to call for on-site service. Almost all of my questions and problems can be handled with a visit to the Web site or a phone call. I don't have the same sense of confidence when it comes to other providers. When I've had occasion to call other companies to find out about some of their products, they often seem confused as to who handles my account. And even when I have questions about products I actually own, they seem to want to make it hard for me to get answers. I've had to fax one company copies of my proofs of purchase before I could get the information I needed.

Next on my list of priorities would be on-line presence. Cisco's Web site is tremendously useful—much better than the competition—though it's not perfect. You have to be pretty sophisticated to work your way through some of the choices, and I actually ran across a logic error in the product configurator recently. Still, the Cisco Connection does make it easy for me to download software upgrades, and product data is readily available on-line.

Please understand: On-line presence is important to me, but only if the first four priorities are met.

Actually, in all five areas—uptime, technology, brand name, sales and service, and on-line presence—Cisco is clearly head-and-shoulders ahead of the other networking companies. So it's not hard for me to choose Cisco when I'm upgrading or expanding my network—in fact, it would be hard to make any other choice.

CISCO GOES DIGITAL

In 1995, when John Chambers became CEO of Cisco, he faced a classic opportunity/dilemma. It's easy to imagine him asking: "How can we keep growing our sales and customer base by 40 percent a year without having to grow our service staff—those highly trained and expensive engineers—

at the same rate?" The answer lay in the new options created by Digital Business Design.

Cisco had been one of the first companies to experiment with the business potential of the Internet. As early as 1993, an Internet-based self-service capability for Cisco's enterprise customers was launched by Doug Allred, Cisco's Vice President for Customer Advocacy. (Note the job title. It isn't merely cosmetic. A title like that changes the way people think about themselves and their work.)

In an unusual gesture of transparency, every known bug in Cisco's software and equipment was openly posted on the Cisco Web site. In addition, customers began to post messages about *their* technical problems on the Cisco site, hoping that the company's staff could resolve them. In time, the Web site became a popular gathering place for Cisco's customers and they began offering suggestions and solutions to one another: "Our network was out for two hours with the same problem, and here's how our engineers fixed it. . . ."

To multiply this unexpected benefit, Cisco installed on its Web site a function that triggered an automatic E-mail to alert a customer that a potential answer to its query had been posted. By capturing the sheaves of ideas and insights thus generated, Cisco produced its own digital library of information about how to use Cisco products more effectively. In time, Cisco.com grew into one of the first on-line corporate communities, a virtual gathering place where IT professionals could exchange ideas and solutions that would improve their networks and their businesses.

As a result, countless customer problems were solved or sidestepped through customer self-service. According to Doug Allred, if not for Cisco's Web site, Cisco would have had to hire an extra 10,000 engineers just to keep up with the company's growth.

John Chambers and Peter Solvik (Cisco's Chief Information Officer) subsequently digitized virtually every area of activity within Cisco: customer sales and service, manufacturing, administrative processes, and talent recruitment and training. Cisco became one of the first examples of how DBD transforms *all* aspects of a business.

CREATING A SCALABLE INFORMATION SYSTEM

In 1994, Cisco had taken another major step toward going digital. Peter Solvik made the critical decision to stop fixing Cisco's increasingly over-burdened IT system with duct tape. It was time to replace it with a comprehensive enterprise resource planning (ERP) system that could keep up with Cisco's rapidly expanding needs. Rather than a collection of silos or islands, an integrated system was needed to manage cash flow, manufacturing, human resources, purchasing, and other major functions from within a unified framework.

Oracle, a company with little experience in the ERP field but with a culture highly compatible with Cisco's (smart, fast, and aggressive), was chosen to create the software—a massive undertaking. The new program was initially installed in January 1995. For four months, it crashed frequently, but by May was running effectively. It remains at the heart of Cisco's Digital Business Design and is frequently studied as a model of information technology by business school students and executives of other Fortune 500 companies.

The Oracle initiative required a major investment of money, time, energy, and talent. It was also absolutely essential, given the incredible growth surge on which Cisco had embarked.

> Only inherently scalable, digital business systems can serve as the sustaining basis for a rapidly expanding organization. Lacking such a basis, the growing enterprise will inevitably collapse under its own weight. Does your business have a scalable business system capable of supporting your future growth cost-effectively?

Scalability has proven to be one of Cisco's crucial capabilities. Chambers observes:

> We don't do something that, if it works well, we couldn't replicate. So we try to set it up in a way that, if it's really successful, it's replicable across

the whole company. Without that attention to discipline, you can't scale with the speed that is needed.

Thanks to the Internet, the information captured, generated, organized, communicated, and retained by Cisco's information system can be shared with customers, suppliers, and other outsiders. Cisco's leveraging of this fact (through one of the first and best corporate extranets) is a major source of the productivity gains Cisco has enjoyed since going digital.

ON-LINE SERVICE AND SALES

Cisco has one of the most effective and fully developed digital sales chains in the world. It has been a front-runner in Choiceboard development. The customer Web site, Cisco Connection Online, allows customers to compare products, configure the complex assemblages of networking equipment needed for today's businesses, and then purchase the best package, all on-line. Cisco has moved far down the path from fixing to preventing errors. Ordering errors, which formerly delayed as many as one-third of faxed orders, have been virtually eliminated. So have configuration errors, an even more common problem with today's complex networks.

One typical Cisco customer—a corporate IT manager we'll call Ken—notes that other companies have Web sites that permit on-line purchases. Only with Cisco, however, does Ken feel comfortable "configuring a system and making a purchase without ever talking to someone. Cisco's site provides all the information I need and makes it easy to drill down through several layers of data. Furthermore, unlike other manufacturers' sites, it alerts me to configurations that won't work."

The resulting benefits are significant. For example, when the Cisco configuration tool warns Ken that a particular combination of products isn't appropriate for his needs, he may spend five minutes on-line fixing the error. By contrast, if the problem weren't discovered until Ken opened the carton containing his new system (and uttered a colorful expletive or two), he would have to invest at least two hours in calling a service rep, changing the order, and repacking and reshipping the product.

Is the Cisco Choiceboard perfect? Ken wishes that the Cisco configurator would warn him *immediately* about combinations of products that won't work together, rather than waiting until he's almost ready to confirm the order. Furthermore, the Choiceboard doesn't track all the equipment purchased by a particular customer. "I bought twenty routers for our West Coast office last year. The Web site should know what I have and be able to tell me what I need without asking."

Ken's behavior as a customer is not atypical.

> **As soon as customers learn to use your latest digital capabilities, they take them for granted—and expect more. Thus, when you upgrade your customer offerings, you need to begin work on the next generation of improvements immediately, if you hope to stay one step ahead of your customers' expectations and your competition.**

Because many of Cisco's product offerings consist of software, huge savings and improved efficiency have resulted from on-line software distribution. Before going digital, Cisco delivered software by shipping CDs via Federal Express. Now, 90 percent of Cisco's software upgrades (over 20,000 per week) are downloaded by customers from the Internet, saving money for customers and Cisco alike.

More important, the quality and accuracy of service are greatly enhanced by customer self-help and digital delivery. One Cisco customer says:

> Cisco has hundreds of software versions, and it's important for me to order the right one for my needs. The way Cisco's Web site walks me through the process—looking at the equipment I'm using, the features I want, and so on—I *can't* download the wrong software.

Downloads using the proprietary CiscoWorks software generally take only five minutes or so, and customers' use of a network is disrupted minimally, if at all. By comparison, software upgrades from other net-working companies often require system shutdowns, which cost time and money.

Cisco currently receives more than 90 percent of its revenues through on-line sales, up from 57 percent in 1998, 13 percent in 1997, and just 1° percent in 1996; by contrast, Dell, another digital innovator, gets about 50 percent of its revenues on-line.

As with Charles Schwab, going digital at Cisco has not meant elimi-nating human contact.

> **The power of Cisco's digital sales and service processes lies in the artful integration of on-line components with traditional off-line resources. The digitized services leverage the value of human contact and multiply its impact on customers.**

Every customer relationship begins with a face-to-face meeting, and Cisco maintains a network of 2,000 direct sellers, another 2,000 value-added resellers, a team of on-site system engineers, and call-in centers staffed by 150 technical experts who are able to respond to questions in thirty languages. All of these human resources are available to customers before, during, and after a sale. As with Schwab, the key is: Give the choice to the customer.

Most customers are eager to take advantage of the convenience of on-line ordering and customer service. Currently, 85 percent of Cisco's cus-tomer support requests are handled on-line (up from 10 percent in 1994). Consequently, since 1995, sales have increased by 600 percent but the support staff required has only doubled. Cisco account managers are able to devote their time to problem solving and customer dialogue, not to pa-perwork or routine transactions. Thus, without digital service, Cisco's hy-pergrowth would have been impossible to manage.

A library of nearly ten million pages of product information is avail-able to customers electronically through the Cisco Connection Online, which has over 150,000 registered users. Customers can access support information and on-line training sessions at their convenience. When problems arise, they can be communicated via E-mail, where they are tracked electronically. If a problem is not solved within a specific time frame, it moves up rapidly through a hierarchy of human contacts. Within forty-eight hours, an unfixed problem lands on John Chambers's desk, where, as Chambers notes, "the fact that we focus on it so heavily helps us to resolve it quicker but also helps us to prevent it."

In a typical month, customers access the Cisco Connection over 1.5 million times, including 300,000 times to check the status of orders and 380,000 times to download software. They can access human help immediately, though it's needed less than one-quarter of the time. The customers who declared themselves satisfied with Cisco's service rose from 65 percent in the mid-1990s to 85 percent as of 1998.

Cisco estimates that over $380 million is saved annually because of the digitization of its sales and service operations.

> **Virtuous cycle: A smart business digitizes its processes, creating productivity gains that liberate resources for investment in technology, talent, and research. The company becomes still smarter, creating even further productivity gains.**

Customer service is not a necessary evil for Cisco; it is a major source of revenues and profits. One customer estimates that, for every $6,000 router he buys, he spends about $1,100 annually on a Cisco service contract. It's relatively pricey, he admits, but he adds, "Considering how crucial this equipment is to my business, I'd be crazy not to spend the money." And how many times a year does he actually need on-site service? "On average, zero. Before we switched to Cisco, our network was up about 95 percent of the time. With Cisco, it's more like 99.9 percent. And when we do have a problem, a simple reboot usually fixes it."

Note the cascading benefits of DBD. The product quality enhancements, customer self-service, and accuracy and timeliness of information enabled by digitization all help to reduce customer downtime and increase the profit margins on Cisco's service revenues.

LEVERAGING THE TALENT

The value growth of Cisco since 1994 (Figure 9–2) has needed to be supported by employee growth, both in numbers and in the mix and depth of talents available. Meeting this need is difficult in an economic climate characterized by low unemployment and an acute shortage of high-tech talent. But even if talent were abundant, the task would be different but still difficult: the challenge would change to finding and keeping the *best* employees available.

FIGURE 9–2   By 1997, Cisco's Value Was More Than Six Times Greater Than That of Its Chief Rivals

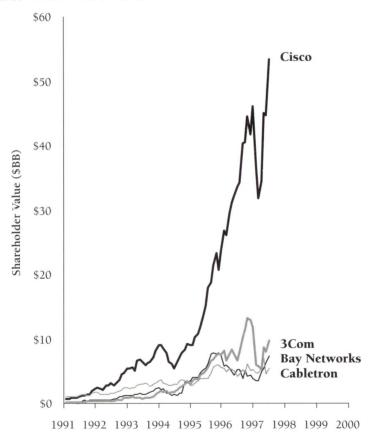

Source: Compustat, 7/00.

Cisco has been very public about its ambitious plans in the human resources area. It has announced its intention to employ the top 15 percent of the best talent in the industry. The only way to find, train, and retain enough people to meet this goal is to recruit digitally.

Recruitment

Eighty percent of Cisco's incoming resumes are now managed electronically. (The recruitment Profiler on Cisco's Web site draws thousands of job-search hits every month, and over 100,000 electronic profiles are received every year.) As a result, Cisco's cost per hire is $6,000 versus an industry average of over $10,000. More important, the cycle time for attracting candidates is greatly shortened; and, most important of all, the *quality* of the people hired is unexcelled.

The Profiler is also a source of competitive information. For example, Cisco tracks the E-mail addresses and current employers of job applicants; a sudden influx of queries from a particular rival firm may suggest internal turmoil there.

The "Make Friends @ Cisco" program links Cisco employees (who volunteer to participate) with potential hires of similar backgrounds. Discussion topics include common interests, life at Cisco, and potential jobs. As with all aspects of its business design, Cisco's recruiting integrates smart design choices with smart digital implementation. Employees receive a $1,000 bonus for every successful recruitment referral; such referrals now account for over half of all new hires.

Training

Mike Cousens, Cisco's Director of Communications and Training, describes the challenge: "Everyone, across the board, finds it hard to justify hours on a plane and in a classroom to receive training. The net result is: Training takes a low priority, which in today's skill-starved IT industry is a bad thing. By contrast, the Internet offers a way of training people in a cheap, convenient, effective way."

The three adjectives Cousens uses are given in *ascending* order of importance. Cost is important, of course. The convenience of being able to access training anywhere, at any time, is even more significant. But most important is the *effectiveness* of digital training, thanks to the *level matching* it enables. That is, Cisco employees can study *precisely* the topics they need to know about, when they need to know them, at the appropriate level of detail and complexity—a dramatic shift from mismatch to perfect fit.

To digitize the training process, Cisco set up video servers in twenty-five global sites. It was estimated that moving 10 percent of the training on-line would repay the investment; instead, within one year, twenty-five percent of training had been moved on-line. Cisco expects on-line training to reach 50 percent by the end of 2000. (The long-term goal is 80 percent.)

Internal staff members are now taking twice as many courses as before. They realize that they can access training modules two or three times a day for twenty minutes at a time, rather than take a day or more out to learn, so they have started fitting courses in around their jobs. Participation, relevance, and timeliness of learning have all increased sharply.

The Impact on Talent

Cisco benefits financially from its digitization of employee recruitment, training, and other functions. A recent estimate of the total savings is $58 million, including $25 million in reduced travel costs for training alone. Far more important, however, are the nonfinancial benefits derived from Cisco's unique value proposition for its talent.

Cisco's digital culture, including its efforts to digitize repetitive, costly, and uninteresting tasks, offers an enormous attraction to the industry's best minds. The typical Cisco employee taps the company's internal Web sites an average of thirty times a day. Digitization means less low-value work: fewer administrative hoops to jump through, less searching for data, fewer dead-end ideas to explore. Everything from purchasing and invoicing to time and expense reports is handled electronically. Time and money are saved, and countless sources of employee frustration are eliminated.

When the tools for the work are readily available, the work improves, the workers thrive, and the workers stay. Cisco's attrition rate is about 8 percent annually, compared to an industry average of 16 percent.

Cisco's success at maintaining ultrahigh rates of morale and employee satisfaction disproves the common assumption (often unconscious) that going digital is an "antihuman" process that turns workers into machine-tenders. Just the opposite is true.

> **Digital Business Design can liberate your company from the either/or trap of "Serve the customers"** *or* **"Satisfy the talent" and enable you to move into a both/and space.**

DIGITAL MANUFACTURING AND DESIGN

Cisco's products are manufactured in thirty-four plants located in various places around the world. Cisco owns just two of the plants, but, by using the Internet, Cisco is able to maintain quality control and production schedules across operations in a manner that is transparent to suppliers, customers, and employees alike. The community this represents in one of the most powerful Value Nets in operation. (For more information on Value Nets, visit http://www.valuenets.com.) Every week, suppliers can tap into Cisco's own enterprise resource planning (ERP) software to receive an updated twelve-month sales forecast. They can then adjust their own production plans accordingly. The result has been a 45 percent reduction in inventory with no negative impact on on-time shipping.

By outsourcing production of 70 percent of its products, Cisco has quadrupled output without building new plants. Outsourced products built and shipped directly to customers, never touching Cisco's hands, account for almost 40 percent of total revenues.

The process of designing new products has also been streamlined. Formerly, each of the four or five prototype versions of a new product would take about a week to complete, and much of the time was spent in gathering, disseminating, and comparing information and ideas among engineers. Cisco developed a New Product Information database that reduces this entire process to about thirty minutes and has saved almost *half* of its engineers' days and an estimated $100 million per year.

> By digitizing the design and manufacturing process, Cisco has freed its talent to concentrate on aggressively managing the flow of bits among customers and suppliers, rather than on manipulating atoms. The company's enormous value lies in being the knowledge manager in the center of the value system.

CISCO'S BUSINESS DESIGN

As shown in Table 9–1, Cisco today has one of the most highly evolved Digital Business Designs in the world.

Cisco's customer selection includes enterprises, Internet service providers, and small businesses, plus an expanding reach into the consumer marketplace. Its unique value proposition for customers includes a breadth of product line that matches the full spectrum of rapidly evolving customer needs, end-to-end solutions, and risk reduction. Buying Cisco is a career-protecting move.

Cisco's unique value proposition for its talent is compelling. It includes:

- ☐ A high probability that good engineering work will get to market quickly.
- ☐ Enormous leverage; routine tasks, from customer inquiries to daily internal processes, are handled on-line, which leaves time available for higher-value interactions with customers.
- ☐ The push-button availability of real-time data supports better decision making.

Cisco's profit model relies not only on hardware and software margins but on a powerful base of recurring service revenues. Profitability is enhanced by large-scale cost savings gained from digital productivity. The

TABLE 9–1 Cisco's Digital Business Design

Customer Selection	☐ Enterprise customers ☐ Internet service providers (ISPs) ☐ Small business market ☐ Moving into consumer
Unique Value Proposition for Customers	☐ Risk reduction (superior product, service, brand) ☐ Positioned as the end-to-end solutions provider ☐ **Configurator-enabled system**
Unique Value Proposition for Talent	☐ Creative work has the highest probability of getting to market ☐ **On-line customer service (frees time for value-added work)** ☐ **Digital recruiting** ☐ **Digital training** ☐ **Real-time information availability (internal and external)**
Value Capture/Profit Model	☐ Hardware/Software margins ☐ Recurring service contract revenue ☐ Installed base upgrades and product extensions ☐ **Productivity advantage over competitors**
Strategic Control/ Differentiation	☐ Dominant share, with embedded *de facto* standard ☐ Low-risk option compared to competitors ☐ Executive level customer relationships ☐ Partnerships with leading technology suppliers
Scope	☐ Outsourced R&D (via acquisitions) ☐ Outsourced manufacturing and software design ☐ **Internal knowledge management**
Organizational System	☐ Product-based divisions ☐ Ability to rapidly and successfully integrate acquisitions ☐ Customer- and talent-centric culture
Bit Engines	☐ **Choiceboards** ☐ **Internal ERP** ☐ **Electronic links to customers and supply chain** ☐ **Digital software distribution** ☐ **Remote diagnostics** ☐ **Database of frequently asked questions**

Boldface = digitally enabled.

company protects these profits by owning and managing the de facto industry standard, by nurturing very powerful customer relationships, and by earning a high level of commitment from its talent.

BENEFITS OF DBD

The impact of DBD on Cisco's operating style is pervasive. The business model centers on managing bits. Manufacturing has been outsourced, and most functions are deeply digitized. Thanks to the Cisco Marketplace, Cisco doesn't have to guess what customers want. It knows, and it can match those wants with near-100-percent accuracy.

Cisco's digital model has also moved information flow from lag time to real time for customers' orders, suppliers' communications, and internal functions like finance (the "virtual close").

Tools like the Cisco Connection Online, the Cisco Profiler, and others, have moved the company from a supplier-serve mode to a customer-self-serve mode. Customers perform more of the functions in their relationship with Cisco, and their satisfaction scores are higher because they're enabled to do so.

Digitization has also driven Cisco far along the spectrum from low-value-added activities to maximum leverage and growth for its talent. Routine repetitive work and "administrivia" have been largely eliminated. The probability that an employee's creative work will get to market quickly has been greatly enhanced—one major reason why many very good engineers are deeply committed to Cisco.

THE FINANCIAL IMPLICATIONS

Cisco's high profitability and unparalleled track record of growth have produced an enormous reservoir of company value. As of mid-2000, Cisco has the *largest* market cap of any company in the world. Its market value has far outdistanced that of its original rivals (Figure 9–3).

FIGURE 9–3   By 2000, Cisco's Value Was Over Twenty Times
Greater Than That of Its Chief Rivals

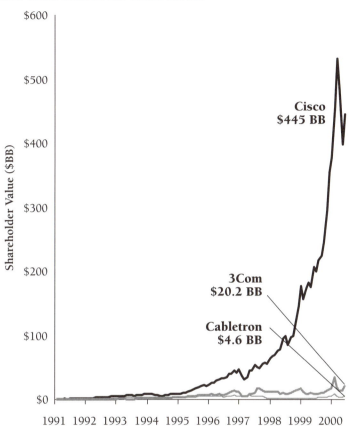

Source: Compustat, 7/00.

* Bay Networks was acquired by Northern Telecom for $9.1BB in 6/98.

THINK BUSINESS DESIGN

Cisco is perhaps the most fully evolved digital business in the world today.
But all of Cisco's digital functions—the on-line sales and service, the Cisco
Connection, the virtual close, and so on—would be meaningless if Cisco's
business design had not been built around responding effectively to customers' priorities.

If Cisco hadn't developed its model for outsourcing R&D through company acquisitions (an essentially nondigital strategy), it probably couldn't have kept pace with the speed of customer evolution.

If Cisco hadn't been able to keep pace with its customers' needs, it wouldn't have experienced the past half-decade of hypergrowth.

Is Cisco a digital business? Yes—but, more important, it's a business that understands the needs of its customers and does whatever it takes to respond to their priorities. That's the solid foundation on which Cisco's DBD is built. Business first, design second, digital third.

CISCO'S NEXT BUSINESS ISSUES

No company that has enjoyed 40 percent-plus growth can normally expect to maintain such a pace for long, especially when it has achieved the significant size Cisco has attained. Remarkably, however, trends in today's technological developments open up the potential that Cisco may continue to grow at a stellar pace for years to come. Over 75 percent of all Internet traffic today is handled by Cisco products. With the world's wired population expected to nearly quadruple in the next five years (from 275 million to one billion), there's clearly room for enormous growth for Cisco. Yet there are serious strategic challenges as well. Cisco could fail—spectacularly. Anything from sheer hubris to a single fatal misperception of the next customer shift could threaten its leadership.

Accelerated Customer Evolution

Cisco's customer mix and the needs of those customers continue to evolve rapidly. Cisco's product and service offerings must continue to evolve at the same rate as well. Enterprises now constitute 50 percent of Cisco's market; service providers are another 35 percent. The emerging market is small businesses, which are now about 15 percent of Cisco's market base but are growing. This new customer base primarily demands networking services that are cost-effective and easy to install and maintain. To meet both the new needs of existing customers and the demands of new customers, Cisco is focusing on vertical and horizontal solutions, and simplified entry-level versions of its services.

In time, Cisco's customer base may extend all the way down to the home user. Intel, 3Com, and others are already developing home network solutions to get a foothold in that market. How will Cisco respond?

Convergence

A triple convergence pattern is emerging. Three formerly separate data pipelines (wireline, cable, and wireless), three separate forms of content (voice, data, and video), and three separate forms of switching (circuit, packet, and optical switching) are all beginning to overlap and merge. New competitors are clashing in each of these businesses, and life is becoming more complicated for customers.

Internet telephony (transmission of voice by computer networks) is spreading rapidly and offers significant cost advantages. Telecom convergence may open up both a gigantic new market for Cisco (estimated currently at over $500 billion worldwide) and a whole new set of competitors.

Early maneuvers in this area appear promising for Cisco. In March 2000, Merrill Lynch announced that it plans to use a 5,000-phone system from Cisco at a new campus in New Jersey; Texas Instruments is also experimenting with a Cisco phone system.

It's unclear what form this new industry will take. John Chambers has been ruffling feathers among the old-line telecom firms by predicting that, soon, all long-distance telephone calls will be free. Maybe. In any case, it seems clear that telephone equipment makers like Nortel and Lucent will increasingly play in the spaces occupied by Cisco, Cabletron, and 3Com, and vice versa. Thanks largely to its de facto standard, Cisco has been able to dominate the smaller Internet data players. Will Cisco have equal success competing on an unfamiliar playing field against such giants as Nortel, already a powerhouse in the voice/data arena?

New Technologies

Cisco's switches rule the digital-based Internet, but what will happen as new data transport methods increase in popularity? Optical switching promises faster and cheaper data transfer with virtually limitless bandwidth. However, even optical switching requires a physical connection. As the demand for wireless solutions inevitably increases, what will happen to Cisco's dominant land-based network?

Furthermore, even within the seemingly secure Internet haven, Cisco will not go unchallenged. Cisco's products tend to be considerably more expensive than those available from competitors. It's important for Cisco to maintain its mind-share dominance to prevent erosion of its pricing premium.

Startup companies may threaten Cisco's hegemony. For example, Juniper Networks, founded in 1996, has developed new-generation routing devices that are currently four times faster than Cisco's. As a result, this tiny company (only $100 million in sales in 1999) already has a market capitalization of $43 billion. Can Cisco stave off such small, nimble competitors in its own backyard even as it takes on some of the world's corporate giants on their turf? What next-generation Digital Business Design will it have to build to do so?

10

THE ACTIVE CUSTOMER

THE FRUSTRATION FACTOR

Think about the last time you called an airline to make a travel reservation. We have no idea which airline you chose, or the time of day you placed the call, or what destination you had in mind. Nonetheless, we feel safe in describing your experience as follows:

1. You had to sort through at least five different telephone menu options, and one option was sufficiently ambiguous to make you say, "Hmm—maybe *that's* the one I want."
2. You had to spend a minute or two—or ten—listening to music that you didn't want to hear.
3. You had to spell out your name, address, telephone number, credit card information, and other relevant data at least once, even if you've done business with the same airline several times before.
4. You had to correct at least one error or misunderstanding on the part of the (well-meaning and hard-working) service rep.
5. You ended up buying a ticket that wasn't exactly what you'd hoped for in terms of the time of the flight, the location of the seat, or the price you paid.
6. When you hung up the phone, you were left with the nagging question, "I wonder if I could have done better with a different airline . . . or a travel agent . . . or an online service . . . or my company's travel department?"

This is a microcosm of how most service happens. The frustration and impatience are enormous. When you call a service person for help—whether it's a broker, an appliance repair person, or a utility-company rep—you typically have to wait a few hours, or a day or two, for a response. Sometimes the person you reach can answer your question, sometimes not. If the person has to search for an answer and get back to you—in another hour, or another day—your life may be on hold.

This process—the current standard—causes deep frustration for customers and service people alike. You've probably found yourself saying, in exasperation, "There's got to be a better way!"

Actually, there is. Here's another (true) service story, with a twist.

In preparation for an upcoming meeting in Stowe, Vermont, I phoned my auto club to request a current map. I used the 800 number listed on my membership card for "24-HOUR MAPS AND TRAVEL GUIDES." After several menu choices and an eight-minute wait, I was greeted by a service rep with the words, "Hello; Emergency Road Service!" When I explained what I wanted, the rep asked me to call back during business hours.

Later that day, having flown to Toronto on business, I tried the same number. A different rep said he couldn't help me with a U.S. map because my call had been automatically forwarded to the Canadian branch of the auto club.

The next day—back in New York—I tried again. This time, during yet another on-hold wait, I heard several recorded messages, including this one: "The easy way to get maps is to visit our Web site!" I hung up, and sixty seconds after logging on I'd solved my roadmap problem.

Digital Business Designs that build a system to allow customers to meet their own needs erase the traditional frustrating process. Instead, a few minutes on-line and a few dozen keystrokes gets customers to where they need to be, with much less pain and aggravation. Digital services let customers be *proactive* in solving their own problems.

Most customers respond to this option the same way: "Why would I want to do business any other way? I have better things to do with my energy than play call-and-wait."

THE CHANGING ROLE OF THE CUSTOMER

We all love sharing stories about the frustrations of traditional customer service. But a larger point is at stake: *The role of the customer in our economic system has changed dramatically in the past three decades.*

This change has occurred across three dimensions: *power, specificity,* and *activity.* Each change is important; the cumulative effect is enormous.

The first and most obvious dimension of change is *power.* Three decades ago, when many products were unique and when demand was growing more rapidly than supply (thanks, in part, to the burgeoning baby boom generation), suppliers—manufacturers, wholesalers, and retailers—generally held the upper hand.

In the past two decades, rapid imitation and widespread overcapacity have shifted the balance of power. Customers have more choices and more power, and they know it. They're using that power freely, with a clear impact on prices and profitability. As a result, life for commodity suppliers has never been more miserable.

The dimension of *specificity* is more subtle. Customers used to pull from the shelf standard products that more or less met their needs. Gradually, as choices began to multiply, customers started choosing segmented products that more closely matched their preferences. Today, customers are increasingly unwilling to compromise. The proliferation of Choiceboards is increasing the number of customers who have enjoyed a perfect-fit, no-compromise shopping experience. For more and more customers, access to the specific array of features and benefits they want is quickly working its way up their hierarchy of priorities.

The third dimension of change deals with *the role customers want to play.* For the past three decades, customers have been extraordinarily passive. They evaluated and selected, but did little else. That is changing quickly. Today, we are seeing the passive customer giving way to a customer who is not only more informed but much more active than customers in the previous generation.

> **In the 1980s, power shifted from the supplier to the customer. In the late 1990s, the customer shifted from passive mode to active.**

THE DIGITAL RESPONSE

Helping to produce and encourage this trend are digital technologies—not only Choiceboards but all forms of e-commerce. Today, as digital tools continue to proliferate, companies can take advantage of customers' growing activism to benefit both parties. They can create additional value by making it easy for customers to help themselves without reliance on company talent.

Schwab's Active Customer

Charles Schwab has assembled a great collection of systems to empower active customers. Schwab offers an array of on-line tools for every phase of the investment process, from asset allocation to ongoing monitoring of a portfolio. These tools include:

- □ **Asset Allocation Plans** created by an on-line modeling program in response to specific customer investment profiles (age, objectives, asset base, risk tolerance, and so on).
- □ A **Retirement Planner** that stores and updates information about any current investment plan, and offers specific advice about how to reach the desired retirement goals.
- □ The **Analyst Center,** an investment data source that rivals the information many stockbrokers receive: company and industry reports from Standard & Poor's; earnings forecasts from First Call Corporation; insider trading data from Vickers Inc.; price and volume data from BigCharts; interviews with executives and industry experts from Briefing.com; and news stories from Dow Jones.
- □ **Insider Access** to initial public offerings, and Web cast interviews with CEOs (Andy Grove, Michael Dell), stock analysts, and mutual fund managers.
- □ **Mutual Fund Screener,** a Choiceboard that allows users to screen thousands of funds based on their own criteria. Schwab funds and those managed by other companies are included.

□ **Stock Screener,** a sorting tool that finds stocks according to personalized criteria such as price performance, earnings expectations, market capitalization, sector, and industry.

□ **Mutual Fund Report Card,** which provides detailed information on the past performance, risk profile, Morningstar ratings, and expense ratios of over 7,000 funds.

□ **Positions Monitor,** which allows continual measurement of personal investments' performance against appropriate benchmarks—the S&P 500, the Dow Jones Industrials, the Russell 2000, and the NASDAQ market index.

□ **MySchwab,** a personal Web page that offers quick access to all Schwab services, as well as a customized array of news, from the latest price quotes for stocks to how favorite sports teams fared in last night's games.

Schwab's unique value proposition for its customers hinges on this entire array of information and analysis tools. In combination, they enable investors to make more informed investment decisions, and to do so with confidence. A customer can call for help at any step along the way. But a rapidly growing number of customers don't need or want help and are quite happy running their own show.

Cisco's Active Customer

Cisco has also developed an extraordinarily extensive system to enable customers to meet their own needs directly, quickly, and efficiently. The Cisco Tour (see Appendix D) illustrates how Cisco lets customers study product information, design their own networking gear, download software, participate in seminars, and perform a host of other activities—all digitally. This suite of self-activated capabilities has grown rapidly in the past three years, and will accelerate its growth in the next few years.

The Schwab and Cisco self-service systems provide customers with three new benefits: *immediacy, control,* and *efficiency.* Customers of both firms are given tools and information that enable them to say:

I'm in charge. I can do what I want exactly when I want to do it. Best of all, I know the results will be right, because I'm running the show, and because there's a great company at the other end of the computer line helping to make it all happen.

YOUR ACTIVE CUSTOMER CHECKLIST

What's going on here? It's more than just an improvement in the way customers are served (important though that is). The change amounts to *a significant redistribution of activities in the system.* As we saw in our analysis of Choiceboards, Digital Business Design allows companies to reverse the value chain and start the process with the customer. Now we can see that DBD also enables companies to make completely new decisions as to who does what—to redefine the roles that different actors in the system will play.

The economic logic of this rearrangement is compelling. As the universal frustration with traditional service demonstrates, many aspects of customer service are handled poorly most of the time. *Why should a company continue to do a bad job at high cost when a well-crafted digital system can let its customers do a perfect job, at low cost to the company and to them?*

Here is an important new criterion for evaluating a business design: *To what extent does my business design enable customers to perform for themselves the tasks for which they are best suited?*

Think about your own business design for a moment. How many of the following activities can your customers do for themselves? [Check all that apply.]

    _____ Find general information.
    _____ Find detailed product information.
    _____ Configure an order.
    _____ Place an order.
    _____ Check the status of an order.
    _____ Answer their own technical questions.
    _____ Connect with another customer to answer their own technical questions.

_____ Make comparisons.
_____ Self-schedule for repairs.
_____ Configure a service contract.
_____ Create content.
_____ Test configurations.
_____ Download software.
_____ Read reviews posted by other people.
_____ Post a review or commentary for others to read.
_____ Perform other activities relevant to your business.

The _fewer_ the items you've checked, the greater the inefficiency, waste, and frustration your customers and your talent are probably experiencing. Look at the checklist again. Which three to five items that you did _not_ check are most important to your customers? Can you develop a bit engine (or adapt an existing one) that will enable customers to serve themselves in those areas?

Remember, the self-service system you create needn't be perfect or all-inclusive. There will always be processes for which help from your in-house talent will be required; there will always be complicated or specialized problems that only an in-house expert can solve. That doesn't make digitizing the other 90 percent of your customer support less important. If anything, just the opposite is true. Enabling customers to solve most problems themselves will free up your talent to devote time and energy to the really knotty questions. The results: More satisfied customers, and company talent that's excited about the opportunity to use some high-level skills rather than fix routine problems for the thousandth time.

THE BLENDING OF ACTIVITY CHAINS

Schwab and Cisco represent excellent examples of companies that are absorbing customers into the supplier's activity chain. In a conventional brokerage house, it is a company function to find and send out research reports about a stock that a customer is considering buying. At Schwab, the customers help themselves—and get the information faster, easier, and more accurately. Similarly, at most technology companies, an in-house technician would answer questions about how to configure company products to tackle a new task. Cisco customers can answer such questions themselves by referring to the appropriate page on the Cisco Connection Online. In both companies, the customer becomes part of the supplier's activity chain—to the benefit of both.

GE AND THE CUSTOMER'S ACTIVITY CHAIN

DBD also makes it possible for the supplier to provide tools that enhance activities within the customer's activity chain.

As we describe in Chapter 12, GE is a major nondigital incumbent that is rapidly moving to digitize many of its processes and customer relationships. As it digitizes, GE is enabling its customers to reach into the supplier's activity chain and perform some of the tasks that the supplier used to do. But GE is also crossing the boundary in the opposite direction—reaching into the customers' activity chain and providing customers with tools to do their own traditionally defined jobs much more efficiently. Examples include Polymerland's design support tools (which help customers of GE's plastics supply division design their own products more quickly and easily), GE Fleet's economic analysis tools (which help customers monitor the costs of running their own vehicle fleets), and GE Medical's calculate-your-own-productivity tools.

GE's momentum is toward the customer's system. GE is trying to do all it can in response to one simple question: *How can I provide information and analysis tools to make my customers significantly more productive in performing their traditional tasks?*

ENHANCING THE CUSTOMER'S
DIGITAL READINESS

There is a second important aspect to GE's efforts to enhance its customers' productivity. GE is leading its customers to become more digital—

and therefore more active, and a source of greater levels of revenue and profit for GE. Each new digital productivity tool introduced by GE encourages more GE customers to adopt digital technologies. The customers' economics improve as a result, and the customers become more closely wedded to GE as the supplier of choice.

Cemex is moving in the same direction. It has done an excellent job of eliminating one of its customers' major headaches (i.e., "Will the ready-mix concrete get to my construction site on time?"). But beyond the concrete-delivery part of the equation are hundreds of other headaches endemic to the construction process—problems of scheduling, sequencing, and coordinating; people management; financial and legal hassles. The vast majority of these problems are bits problems. They are based on access to and transmission of accurate information.

Having created one of the world's great bit factories and applied it to one aspect of the construction equation, Cemex is now working on extending its systems to bring the capabilities and benefits of its approach to its customers. It will be trying to help its customers do their own tasks more efficiently—for example, by developing systems whereby handheld digital assistants provided to Cemex customers can be enabled to monitor and report changes in construction schedules and supply data, as tracked by Cemex's intranet.

Both GE and Cemex, then, are deliberately gearing up to produce more active customers for the system. Their goal is to be engines of digitization in their spheres of economic activity. The result will be financial benefits for the suppliers and their customers, and enhanced customer allegiance for GE and Cemex.

The emergence of the active customer isn't simply a challenge to old ways of providing service or responding to problems. It's an enormous opportunity to change the landscape of business by redefining the customer relationship in ways that will help both suppliers and their customers.

Make your customers active co-conspirators in your success.

OBSTACLES TO GOING DIGITAL: BEATING THE ODDS

INSIGHT AND COURAGE

Many business leaders get excited as they learn about the potential benefits of going digital, but then become discouraged when they consider the practical difficulties of shifting a traditional company to the digital way of doing business. We don't intend to minimize those difficulties. The reality is, many members of the Fortune 500 will *not* succeed in making a timely transition to digital. As a result, many companies will stagnate or be absorbed.

Nonetheless, we strongly believe that virtually any company can overcome the obstacles to going digital if only two crucial ingredients are present: *insight* and *courage*.

Insight distinguishes the issues that are most important to the business, identifies what's possible, and determines the right sequence of attack. Where is value migrating in your industry? How are your customers' priorities changing? To make a successful transition to digital, a company needs to do the hard work required to create accurate insights into these and other fundamental business questions.

Equally important is *Courage*—transforming your insights into actions, in spite of the inevitable pain of implementation. Think about the companies this book describes. They had the courage to act in spite of lost revenues due to commission compression (Schwab); to risk making what Wall Street considered overpriced acquisitions (Cisco); to endure the fear of moving too quickly for their customers (Cemex); and, as we'll see in later chapters, to tackle the huge internal marketing challenges posed by an entrenched workforce (IBM and GE).

Obstacles to going digital come in many flavors, but they all boil down, in the end, to either a shortage of insight or a lack of courage. We'll detail several of the most frequently encountered obstacles later in this chapter. For now, study the Digital Obstacles Checklist on pages 191 to 193, and indicate the obstacles that you recognize in your own business situation. If your company is like most, you'll discover at least ten to twelve obstacles that are perceived as standing in the way of a shift to digital.

The Digital Obstacles Checklist

Our company won't shift from conventional to Digital Business Design because:

_____ We're doing too well financially (there is no sense of urgency).
_____ Change is too difficult, and no one has the appetite for this much change.
_____ We have too many other priorities.
_____ We're in the midst of a turnaround and can't focus on digital.
_____ We don't know how to do it.
_____ It's not in our current business plan.
_____ It's not in our budget.
_____ It's not part of our vision.
_____ We don't want to alienate our existing customers.
_____ We don't want to upset our sales and distribution channels.
_____ Our customers aren't digital-ready.
_____ Our employees aren't digital-ready.
_____ We can't afford to spend money on the digital infrastructure.
_____ Our management team isn't digital-savvy.
_____ We're already too late.
_____ _____
(Add your own reason here.)

(continued)

Consider the set of obstacles you checked. Which is the most powerful? Which is second? In the spaces below, list the five most powerful obstacles you face, in the order of their stopping power or drag effect.

Our Most Powerful Obstacles

1. _____

2. _____

3. _____

4. _____

5. _____

Debate this list with your colleagues. Do you all agree about the relative importance of the obstacles you face? Do you consider any of the obstacles potentially fatal? Or can all of them be overcome? What will it take for your company to remove the obstacles that stand in the way of business-centric digitization?

Use the following Obstacles and Countermeasures analysis to begin mapping a strategy for overcoming the obstacles you face. If you're not sure how to devise effective countermeasures, return to this analysis after you've finished reading the rest of the book. The profiles of other digital innovators may suggest countermeasures that your company can try.

Obstacles and Countermeasures

Most Powerful Obstacles		*Most Effective Countermeasures*
1. _____	→	1. _____
2. _____	→	2. _____
3. _____	→	3. _____
4. _____	→	4. _____
5. _____	→	5. _____

Obstacles and Countermeasures *(continued)*

What are the key investments (especially of management time and emotional energy) required to implement the most effective countermeasures?

_____

_____

_____

_____

_____

_____

_____

_____

_____

_____

THE THINGS PEOPLE SAY

We've mentioned the importance of hearing your customers' stream of consciousness. The stream of consciousness of your own talent is equally important. The things people say about change—and specifically, about the need to go digital—aren't always to be taken literally. But they offer clues to the pressure points that exist in an organization: the places where resistance to digitization is likely to be high, as well as the soft spots where, at a push, the walls will quickly collapse.

Which of these seven comments have you been hearing in the elevator, in the washroom, or even, if you're very lucky, in the conference room?

1. **"What do you mean, 'Go digital'? We just spent $2 million on laptops!"** As we've discussed, Digital Business Design is not about wiring

your company; it's about identifying opportunities to serve your customers better through digital options. If your company has just spent $2 million on laptops but has no plan for how or why the laptops will be used to improve service or increase productivity, then the idea of going digital may seem pointless. Retooling people's thinking around *the customer benefits* of digitization (rather than gee-whiz technology) is the key first step.

2. **"Our customers aren't ready."** There may be truth in this objection. The degree of digital readiness in specific markets varies widely. But change is coming faster than most businesspeople think. The Internet has reached a wider segment of the U.S. marketplace more quickly than the telephone, the automobile, radio, television, or any other earlier major technology. Changes in customers' digital readiness are occurring in monthly, not annual, increments. Furthermore, to make digitization strategically and financially attractive, it's not necessary for a majority of your customers to be digitally ready. If you move now to seize the high digital ground, you'll be there to welcome your customers as they migrate to join you.

3. **"But none of our competitors are digital."** Bear in mind that (a) a traditional competitor may be about to announce a major digital redesign that could instantly upend the competitive landscape; (b) a company you've never heard of may be on the verge of entering your industry; and (c) a company from some neighboring industry may be about to move into your space. Even if none of the above is true, can you be certain that none of your competitors will be digital next year? And even if *that* is true, isn't the lack of digital competition an opportunity you can take advantage of—rather than a reason for inaction?

4. **"Going digital may be fine for other industries, but our business is different."** Every business is unique, and it may be tempting to use the uniqueness of your industry as a reason to ignore changes elsewhere. But the walls between markets are disintegrating. The changes wrought by digitization affect many of the most fundamental business activities, from sales and service to talent recruitment and financial management. The potential for 10X Productivity improvements may exist in many of these areas.

5. **"But our profits [stock price, sales growth, margins, XYZ] are pretty good—what's the problem?"** The human tendency is to relax in

good times—to regard them as proof that a business design is sound and there is little or nothing to fear. But if the 1980s and 1990s didn't obliterate that attitude, the 2000s surely will. Digitization lowers barriers to entry and creates strategic opportunities that competitors will take advantage of, unless you act first. History shows that once a new winning team takes the field, a reversal of fortune for other teams is likely to happen very swiftly. One quarter's handsome bottom line can still turn into a year of losses—perhaps faster than could have been expected.

6. **"Our people aren't ready, and change is very hard."** Don't be so sure. Readiness to change is often far greater at the *lower* levels of organizations, where the talent tends to be younger, hungrier, more ambitious, and less wedded to traditional systems and ways of thinking. Change does complicate our lives. But it also poses fresh challenges for business leaders; it requires them to communicate, coach, train, and inspire their talent in new ways. Digitization is unlike some previous managerial revolutions in that it offers major benefits to individual working people as well as to the organizations that employ them and the customers they serve. If your plan for going digital emphasizes these objectives (*internal* marketing is essential), the benefits to your talent will be obvious and highly motivating.

7. **"We're still knee-deep in Six Sigma [cost reductions, reengineering, globalization, XYZ]."** This is true in every company. Any large organization needs to reinvent itself continually— and usually on more than one level. Digitization doesn't compete with these other initiatives; it supports and enhances them. Remember why you designed the current five-year plan as you did. You wanted to attack and solve your crucial business issues. Digital Business Design opens up new and more powerful solutions to these issues.

A MARATHON, NOT A SPRINT

Although the obstacles to going digital *can* be overcome, it's important to begin the process with a clear-eyed recognition of the realities involved. One reality made clear by the experience of the digital innovators is the fact that transforming a traditional business into a digital one takes *at least four years.* (All those profiled in this book launched their digital transitions in the mid-1990s.)

Why so long? There are several reasons. First, it takes serious time to develop a smart plan for going digital: to focus on your key business issues, to figure out how your customers can benefit most powerfully from digitization, to ascertain the optimal mix of atoms and bits in your business processes, and to decide what kinds of bit engines you'll need. Most companies will require six to twelve months just to work through these questions.

Second, the effects of going digital are so sweeping, and the changes required so pervasive, that every division, department, and individual in your company will have to become involved. The internal marketing effort this demands is enormous. (As we'll explain in Chapter 15, it is easy to vastly underestimate the investment required.) And it simply takes time for a complex set of ideas like those involved in business-centric digitization to percolate through all levels of an organization.

Think also of the time required to make sure that everyone genuinely, viscerally understands and accepts the importance of going digital. Only *then* can the heart of the process—the difficult, often painful rewiring of personal and organizational habits—really begin.

So four years is a fair estimate of the time required to transform an incumbent business into a digital one. If your company today sets a target date four years in the future for being a fully operating digital organization, don't imagine for a moment that this provides a comfortable window for the transition. *Going digital can be accomplished in four years if you start working at it immediately—and like banshees, just as the digital innovators did.*

INVESTING IN GOING DIGITAL

Whatever amount of money and time you spend on going digital, think of it as an investment. Like any worthwhile investment, it will pay dividends—in money *and* time. Intelligent digitization will leverage your own talents, enabling you to spend more time doing the creative personal work only a human mind can do. Your real priorities can only benefit.

Every company's combination of obstacles is unique. At the start of any major change effort, obstacles will appear greater than rewards. Can they really be overcome? We've studied a group of digital innovators that *have* overcome them. Others are in the process of doing so. The chapters that follow explore some companies that are in transition. They are finding creative ways to defeat the obstacles that stand between them and the Northeast quadrant.

INCUMBENT ON
THE MOVE: GE

WORKS IN PROGRESS

Only a handful of businesses today clearly inhabit the Northeast quadrant—the sector where both business-driven digitization and business design have evolved to a high level.

Two of these companies, Dell Computer and Cisco Systems, are artifacts of the digital age that are dealing in information-age products and services. As young companies, they had few if any legacy systems to dismantle or reinvent when their push to digital was launched.

Two others, Cemex and Schwab, represent pioneering efforts to transform traditional industries through Digital Business Design. Because of their early insights, both are well ahead of their competitors in realizing the customer benefits and internal gains that DBD enables.

Most other companies remain below the digital divide. Many incumbents have yet to viscerally recognize the necessity of going digital, or are in the earliest stages of the process. Some may not successfully complete the transition in time to prosper. A relative handful are currently leading what will soon become a broad migration from the Southeast to the Northeast quadrant.

Two of the world's largest and most complex companies are in the vanguard of the digital migration: GE and IBM. Thanks to exceptionally insightful CEOs, these two organizations are already in the middle stages of reinventing themselves as digital businesses. It remains to be seen how successful they will be and, especially, whether smaller, nimbler competitors will arrive first in the Northeast quadrant spaces they intend to occupy. But examining how these very large and very complex incumbents have launched their digital transformations offers lessons for the leaders of the thousands of other companies that are hanging back or just getting started.

In this chapter, we'll track GE's migration toward the Northeast. As you'll see, it's the story of how an incumbent with innovative leadership is finding ways to make a potentially lethal enemy—the power of the Internet—into its strongest ally.

JACK WELCH'S EPIPHANY

In October 1994, Jack Welch, the CEO of General Electric Company, was quoted as saying, "I don't need a personal computer." He admitted, "I don't know what I'd do with it." What Welch said honestly reflected what many other CEOs thought but didn't dare to say.

Today, the transformation to DBD has no more committed advocate than Jack Welch: "I don't think there's been anything more important or more widespread in all my years at GE," he has said. "Where does the Internet rank in priority? It's number one, two, three, and four" (*Business Week,* June 18, 1999).

In Welch's new view, the Web completely changes business:

> It will change relationships with customers. . . . Nothing will be hidden in paperwork. . . . Execution is very important. Every error you make is transparent on the Web.
>
> It will change relationships with employees. We will never again have discussions where knowledge is hidden in somebody's pocket. You will have to lead with ideas, not by controlling information.
>
> It will change relationships with suppliers. Within eighteen months, all our suppliers will supply us on the Internet or they won't do business with us.

Obviously, Welch's attitudes have shifted dramatically—and quickly. He traces his own digital epiphany to the holiday season of 1998. The Welch family was immersed in Christmas shopping, but Jack noticed that they hadn't set foot outdoors. Instead, they were doing all their shopping on-line. Suddenly, the practical power of the Internet, and the role it could play in GE's businesses, became clear. What had changed between 1994 and 1998? In 1994, the PC was a *computer*. By 1998, it had become something different: a *communicator* and a *transactor*. As such, it could and would have a much greater impact on how GE and its customers did business.

Welch acted quickly to translate understanding into action. In January 1999, at GE's annual managers' meeting in Boca Raton, Florida, Welch sketched the future of GE in terms of four initiatives, ranked as follows:

1. The Internet and e-commerce.
2. Globalization.
3. Services.
4. Six Sigma.

Globalization, an emphasis on the service component of GE's businesses, and the quality control system known as Six Sigma had actually been high on the company's agenda for years. The Internet and e-commerce represented a new focus—one so important that it leapfrogged immediately to the top of Welch's list.

"THE GREATEST OPPORTUNITY YET"

Under the leadership of Jack Welch, GE had long been the world's most innovative large company in terms of its business design. Welch had already led the company through at least three major reinventions before his digital epiphany occurred:

1. In 1981, when Welch took the helm at GE, he saw that market-share leadership had become the surest way to increase profit per product sold. So Welch decreed that GE operating units must be either Number One or Number Two in their businesses. Otherwise, they'd be sold or shut.

2. Later in the decade, when it became clear that market share no longer guaranteed success, Welch initiated Work-Out—literally, take unnecessary work out of the process—which anticipated the reengineering wave by nearly half a decade. He insisted that GE's Number One market share philosophy be translated into a Number One productivity position in every business.

3. When Welch recognized that productivity leadership was no longer enough because profit was migrating downstream—from making and selling products to offering product-based solutions and services—he led the way again.

Thus, GE has consistently been ahead of the curve whenever the source of competitive advantage was going to shift. This is why it has captured a disproportionate share of its industries' profit and shareholder value. Now GE faces what Welch has called "the greatest opportunity yet": the advent of Digital Business Design. (Read "greatest threat" also.) It's a challenge that will test GE's adaptive capabilities as never before.

Welch has announced that he will step down as CEO in April 2001. The digital transformation he is pushing at GE will have to be completed under new leadership. But even if Jack Welch had chosen to stay at GE for another decade, he would have had to hire a successor: a reinvented, digital Jack Welch.

GE'S BUSINESS ISSUES

Because GE has been one of the world's most persistent reinventors, it is moving to a Digital Business Design from a position of strength. GE's sales, its market positions and mindshare, its profitability, and its company value are all at historic highs. GE's many businesses—ranging from plastics and appliances to broadcasting and insurance, from locomotives and aircraft engines to medical equipment and mortgage lending—all face various specific business issues. But, in essence only one key business issue challenges GE as a whole: *Where will the threats to GE's future strategic control arise?*

This is a key issue faced by any successful business. But Digital Business Design complicates the issue and magnifies the potential threats enormously. By reducing or eliminating barriers of space, time, and money, DBD enables the entry of unexpected competitors and creates new business design options, and new openings in the value chain, that others can exploit.

> **In a digital universe, the radar screen you scan in search of threats to your business must be many times wider, and more sensitive, than in the conventional world.**

It's easy to imagine Jack Welch, sometime during the fourth quarter of 1998 or the first quarter of 1999 (or perhaps just after his fateful Christmas shopping epiphany), waking up in the middle of a business nightmare and thinking:

I've been working for eighteen years building the most adaptive, robust, and competitive big enterprise in history, and where are we? *Nowhere.*

The Internet will make all prices at all levels, for all products and services, absolutely transparent. Margins will compress. Over the next two years, if our selling prices go down much faster than our purchasing prices, our profits will plummet.

And we already know that services and financing are where our real profits come from. But those are pure bits businesses, with lower barriers to entry in a digital world. If digital players start grabbing pieces of those businesses, our profitability will disappear.

And new middlemen are suddenly multiplying on the Internet—online marketplaces, auctioneers, and networkers pushing themselves between us and our customers. If they succeed, we'll lose control of our key relationships with the customer.

And now there are dozens of new players on the edges of the radar screen—whose economics we don't understand—taking aim at each of our businesses. If we don't move fast, they will destroy our economics before we can stop them or preempt them.

So *now* what do we do?

To identify the future threats to GE's businesses, it was no longer enough to monitor the traditional competitors or to think in traditional terms. The GE team had to consider such questions as:

- ☐ Will digitization reduce or destroy the value of GE's role in the value chain, enabling customers to bypass GE while saving time, money, or energy?
- ☐ Will companies from neighboring industries make use of new digital options to move into the business spaces GE currently occupies?
- ☐ Will new digital middlemen begin outcompeting GE as suppliers of GE products and services (*reintermediation*)?
- ☐ As the use and importance of Choiceboards expands, will GE be able to control the Choiceboards in its industries?
- ☐ Will digital companies use their advantages in speed, accuracy, productivity, and cost to challenge GE's highly profitable, bits-only service and finance businesses?

GE's position of strength *complicated* the challenge. Any successful organization tends to become complacent, or at least comfortable. And a superficial glance at the digital landscape, especially prior to 1998, might have suggested that a behemoth like GE had little to fear from the fledgling world of e-commerce. Even Welch has commented, "Look at the size of these Internet companies. They're all popcorn stands!" But Welch understood that some of these "popcorn stands" owned keys to the future of business. He took the threat and the potential of the Internet and DBD seriously, and set out to spread the same attitude throughout the company.

FROM DESTROY YOUR BUSINESS TO GROW YOUR BUSINESS

In early May 1999, Welch unveiled to a group of analysts the digital strategy that would guide GE into the new century. He called it "Destroyyour-business.com." It was a typically brilliant internal marketing move by Welch: Devise a simple, unforgettable formula to summarize a crucial message, and then repeat it at every opportunity. "Destroyyour-business.com" (or DYB) soon took its place beside "Number One or Number Two," "Work-Out," and "Services" as GE terms that were known throughout the company and throughout the business world.

It also became the topic of Welch's first-ever E-mail message to his top managers. In the memo, he urged his unit heads to deploy under-25-year-olds whose sole task would be to figure out how the Internet could be used to destroy GE's existing businesses. For an executive whose hand-written notes are famous, Welch's choice of E-mail as the medium sent a compelling signal: If Jack Welch is using digital technology to convey his most important message of the year, those who work for him had better use it, too.

In accordance with Welch's directive, each GE company recruited a team of three to seven e-commerce experts who reported directly to the president. They set about examining all the business models in their field to determine which ones posed a threat to GE and to begin developing competing models.

Only an initiative like DYB could simultaneously address all the dimensions of Jack Welch's nightmare: price transparency, challenges to GE's pure-bits business, reintermediation, and the appearance of off-the-radar-screen competitors. Driven by the rise of the Internet, he initiated a systematic attempt to map the new digital space and to identify the threats and opportunities it created for GE.

Within six months—by November 1999—the DYB teams had identi-fied most of the major threats GE faced, and had begun crafting potential responses to them. DYB thus evolved into "Growyourbusiness.com" (GYB). GE was no longer on the defensive. It was proactively seeking ways to grow in the digital space.

Empowered to violate every GE rule except the company's core values, the GYB teams were now assigned to push forward the company's digital transformation by expanding e-commerce on the Internet, establishing customer-specific extranets to enhance service and sales, and exploiting intranet capabilities to streamline internal processes—for starters. Today, many of these initiatives have already produced important benefits.

GOING DIGITAL ACROSS GE'S BUSINESSES

GE began by applying digital technology to improve its internal processes, from Six Sigma quality control to human resources management, knowledge transfer, and so on. Costs and cycle time were removed from the system, and the processes were made more accurate and productive.

An example of GE's early initiatives is its Trading Partner Network (TPN), which extensively digitized the procurement process. It allows customers, including GE's own business divisions, to request price quotes for products and services on the Web; it then manages the bids from potential suppliers digitally, and yields drastic cuts in the time and energy required to make purchases. GE Lighting, for example, which uses TPN to purchase parts and supplies, has trimmed the average cycle time from 20 days to nine. The digital process also eliminates paper flow, reduces errors, and expands the competition among suppliers by drawing on a global network of companies, thereby saving GE even more money. (Among non-GE companies, Consolidated Edison, the New York electrical utility, is now using TPN to streamline its procurement processes.)

More importantly, GE recognized the potential impact of digitization on other elements of its business design. Welch saw that digital technologies could transform the company's customer relationships, value proposition, and strategic control. As all the GE businesses moved to rapidly prototype new Internet business models, four key DBD themes emerged:

1. **Digital selling.** The Internet provides a powerful medium to interact with customers interested in buying GE products and services.
2. **Customer productivity tools.** GE can use the Internet to deliver free analytical, design, and modeling tools to customers, saving them time and money and solidifying their relationships with GE.
3. **Information destination sites.** GE's Internet sites deliver so much value-added information for the benefit of customers' businesses that the GE sites are the first sites they turn to.
4. **Remote diagnostics.** Using the Internet and various sensory technologies, GE can capture real-time information on a customer's

systems, enabling the delivery of cost-effective, fix-before-fail services.

These ideas, now accelerated across multiple businesses and geographies at GE, are leveraging the company's culture of collaboration and teamwork. The next four sections illustrate how these key DBD themes are contributing to the transformation in progress at GE. In reviewing them, ask yourself: Are these simply smart individual initiatives, or do they add up to something larger?

DIGITAL SELLING

GE Polymerland

GE is a major supplier of plastics used in manufacturing thousands of consumer and industrial products. The Polymerland Web site provides customers with digital tools that make choosing, ordering, and tracking plastics products easy, fast, and cost-effective. The Order Center lets customers check product prices and availability, place and monitor orders, and create reports for their own financial records. The IDES Prospector Web provides information on resins from *every* major manufacturer, based on whatever product criteria the customer specifies. The Custom Compounding page lets customers choose from an extensive selection of custom-compounded and custom-colored products without having to work with a sales rep.

GE Appliances

This consumer Web site includes an on-line guide for buying GE small appliances, parts, and accessories. (Major appliances will be added to the Web site in time.) Following the hybrid model, GE offers a choice of sales channels: on-line, by phone, or through a dealer. If customers provide their zip code and their product preferences, the GE Appliances Web site offers them recommendations for nearby stores as well as data on local contractors, kitchen remodelers, and other service suppliers. The Web site also offers access to GE financing services, extended warranties and other service plans, on-line order tracking, and frequently asked questions about GE products.

CUSTOMER PRODUCTIVITY TOOLS

GE Plastics

The GE Plastics Design Solutions Center lets customers use design tools to develop unique, customized products that can then be purchased on-line. It includes a collection of Engineering Design Tools (troubleshooting charts, technical tips and case studies, a glossary, and a calculator), a Visualizer (visitors can view actual engineering multipoint data on-line, compare the characteristics of various resins, and download models), and Color Xpress service, which responds to customers' queries with nine options of plastics colors that closely match their needs. (The customer selects one or a few color options and receives a business-card-sized sample in less than two days—down from two weeks under the old, nondigital system.)

GE Capital Fleet Services

For managers of commercial truck, van, and auto fleets, this site offers access to a comprehensive array of information: current expense, usage, and problem reports for a particular fleet; daily news on the fleet industry from sources like the *Kelley Blue Book* and the American Trucking Association; and the latest updates on federal and state regulations. A fleet manager can use the site to view and audit the most recent expense report, drill down for details on specific costs, and even check odometer readings on specific vehicles to analyze and fix usage anomalies.

INFORMATION DESTINATION SITES

GE Financial Network

This collection of personal finance Web sites offers a wide range of information, services, and tools drawn from many reputable sources. For example, the GE Home Mortgage site offers Mortgage Tour, an interactive guide to the mortgage–loan process (visitors can ask questions along the way). The Mortgage Library can be researched for relevant articles from many sources, including the Mortgage Bankers Association. Smart Quote provides tools to search for loan programs customized to particular financial needs. Visitors can calculate the interest rates, payments, and fees most likely to fit their profile.

GE Medical Systems Learning Solutions

This complex of Internet information sites currently offers GE customers over 750 hours of on-line training on a huge array of health care/technology topics, from diagnostic imaging—X-ray, magnetic resonance imaging (MRI), computer tomography—to a range of clinical topics—cardiology, internal medicine, pediatrics, and so on. An on-line Guidance Counselor is available to offer advice on training needs, and Internet learning may be supplemented by programs offered on the GE TiP-TV broadcast network, including seminars and interviews on topics of current concern in health care.

REMOTE DIAGNOSTICS

GE Aircraft Engines

By electronically uploading specific data from airlines and other aircraft users, GE can monitor up to 1,000 parameters for each of its aircraft engines. Early detection of problems permits prompt corrective action. Daily and weekly fault reports, trend summaries, maintenance recommendations, and troubleshooting are provided, and service personnel can be dispatched quickly if necessary. GE estimates that an airline using GE Remote Diagnostics may be able to save up to $70,000 per aircraft per year, and will experience reduced service delays and downtime.

GE Power Systems

GE power systems are used in everything from ocean-going vessels to giant manufacturing plants. GE's Remote Monitoring & Diagnostics system (RM&D) lets the company track the performance of GE turbines and generators around the world, twenty-four hours a day. The system eliminates needless maintenance visits, improves fuel efficiency, and increases safety. If necessary, GE engineers can start and stop machines, increase or decrease loads, and perform other tasks—all remotely. It's a powerful shift from fixing errors to preventing them.

In many cases, the service provided by GE's Remote Monitoring & Diagnostics system is mission-critical. Richard Holmes, who runs GE Energy's RM&D program, cites an example:

> Royal Caribbean Cruises runs each ship with two gas turbine engines. They rely on us to monitor and diagnose their units every twelve hours. It would be disastrous if they had a problem out in the middle of the ocean. We prevent them both from having problems and from having to worry about it.

A GE customer in charge of a power plant in southern England compares remote diagnostics to business as usual:

> Last week, we had a problem with a different technology company. An engine needed to be diagnosed by someone in the States. We had to download the data and send it via E-mail to the American specialist. Then, because of the time difference, we had to wait until both we in the UK and the guys in the States were in their offices to have a conference call. Then they asked for different data, and we had to wait another day to get the information, send it to them, and so on. All the while, we just wanted to get our engine fixed.

By contrast, the GE specialist in the office in the U.S. instantly sees an exact reproduction of the computer screen at the site—pages and pages of readings with temperatures, pressures, and so on. In addition, he sees diagrams and pictures of the engine, which allow him to watch what happens as various remedies are tested. RM&D essentially allows the specialist to be at every customer's site at once.

GE'S NEW VALUE PROPOSITION: ITA

If we step back and consider the entire array of GE's digital customer options, it's clear that GE is evolving an entirely new value proposition for its customers (and prospects). Having analyzed a customer's activity chain, GE is moving to make the customer's job easier and more productive at every link in that chain. Although all GE customers are different, they perform most of the following activities: getting and analyzing general and specific data, making comparisons, purchasing, checking orders' status, requesting technical service, scheduling maintenance, writing reports, signing up for training, requesting updates, maintaining records, and tracking performance.

GE is increasingly enabling its customers to perform these activities digitally. This would eliminate hundreds of hours of low-value activities: searching for data, placing phone calls, correcting errors, updating calendars, editing documents, and so on. Using Internet-based technologies, GE businesses are enabling customers to execute digitally. By managing bits rather than atoms, they can improve productivity on specific aspects of their operations by up to ten times.

Whether through digital selling, customer productivity tools, information destination sites, or remote diagnostics, GE is essentially providing its customers with three powerful new benefits labeled ITA:

1. **Information** (both general and specific).
2. **Tools** (to analyze, compare, and make choices).
3. **Actions** (that are easy to take via GE).

Together, these benefits amount to a new type of customer value proposition that could not exist without digital technology.

> *ITA*—Information, Tools, and Actions—is a new, digitally enabled value proposition. It goes beyond products and services and brings the benefits of DBD directly into the heart of customers' operations. This direct pathway ties customers more closely to the provider.

ITA is the value proposition provided to customers by Dell, with its on-line Configurator; by Cisco, with its Cisco Connection Online; and by Schwab, with its OneSource, MySchwab, and other customized investing tools. ITA helps *customers* move from managing atoms to managing bits; it shifts their data acquisition from lag time to real time; and it helps them move from guessing to knowing. It leverages the talent of the company *and* the customer.

The more customers work with GE's digital technologies, the more digital *they* become—and the more closely they are tied to the GE system. Thus, besides enhancing the unique value proposition for the customer, ITA strengthens the company's bond with its most important customers.

HOW DO YOU GET THERE? THE POWER OF INTERNAL MARKETING

Don't think about GE's move to DBD as if it were a simple matter of Jack Welch's handing down orders. Changing the mental habits and behaviors of more than 200,000 employees is an enormous task. The fact that GE is a highly successful, 122-year-old company makes change even harder to implement. Welch worried recently, in an interview with *Fortune:* "Do we have the right gene pool? Do people who join big companies want to break glass?"

Working in GE's favor is the history of Welch's previous management revolutions. At a glance, these may appear anarchic—change for change's sake—but Welch has launched relatively few campaigns (one every three years, on average). They have been managed with great care and intelligence, and have applied the most important principles of internal marketing:

- ☐ **Simplify the message.**
- ☐ **Repeat the message seven hundred times.**
- ☐ **Use multiple media for communication.**
- ☐ **Communicate the strategy and business design continually.**

GE's talent is almost universally on the same page as its CEO. Employees share the same set of values, sense of mission, strategic focus, and even a unique language. People whose businesses have little in common trade GE war stories in the same vernacular.

Many of the tools that brought about GE's past revolutions are being used to market digitization internally. They include training at Crotonville, GE's corporate university, and close linking of pay and promotion to "boundaryless behaviors." Jack Welch remains a tireless communicator. He frequently sends notes to employees (especially the 3,000 managers he personally mentors) and reinforces his messages through news articles, speeches, memos, interviews, and so on.

Some unique internal marketing initiatives have been developed for the drive to digital. In the fourth quarter of 1999, GE sponsored a company-wide ninety-day *digital* Work-Out on the company intranet. It focused on using the Web to eliminate bureaucracy and move toward e-commerce. Welch has ordered the top brass in each of GE's global divisions to find "e-business mentors" among their junior staff. Now, the gray-haired bosses—including Welch himself—spend a minimum of two hours a week with their digital whiz-kids, surfing the Net and learning the ropes of e-commerce.

For most companies that have yet to embark on the transition from conventional to Digital Business Design, the hardest questions will be: "How do you get there? How do you move the organization from point A to point B?" In reality, the most critical elements in managing the transition to Digital Business Design are the care, energy, and skill required to do the internal marketing that will create commitment to the transition. That task is particularly challenging in organizations where commitment has to be inspired in the hearts and minds of thousands of employees.

The most important lessons from the GE experience are not just about customers' new value-added. They illustrate how internal marketing has to (and can) move an entire organization to embrace and propel the transition.

> **Digital Business Design *minus* internal marketing = 0.**

Any attempt to move to a Digital Business Design without the right investment in internal marketing to fuel the transition will not work.

GE'S BUSINESS DESIGN

Table 12–1 summarizes the emerging Digital Business Design toward which GE is moving.

GE's customer selection has been quite broad and will remain so. Its value proposition for customers, however, is becoming much more compelling. It now includes customer choice, convenience, and productivity, and new types of value such as remote diagnosis.

The company has long offered a strong value proposition for its talent—the Crotonville learning facility, the Jack Welch mentoring program for GE's 3,000 top managers, and a culture that rewards values as well as performance. The shift to DBD is further strengthening the talent value proposition to include digital mentoring, digital information and decision tools, and a rapidly evolving digital culture.

GE's profit model will become stronger as digital improvements widen the productivity gap with GE's competitors, and as new sources of profit are created from GE's digital businesses and programs. Strategic control

TABLE 12-1   GE's Emerging Digital Business Design

Customer Selection	☐ Broad cross-section across industries and consumers
Unique Value Proposition for Customers	☐ Solutions ☐ **Choice** ☐ **Ease of interaction** ☐ **Customer productivity** ☐ **ITA (Information, Tools, and Actions)**
Unique Value Proposition for Talent	☐ Crotonville ☐ Jack Welch's mentoring (for top 3,000 managers) ☐ Leveraging of ideas and tools across the company
Value Capture/ Profit Model	☐ Multicomponent: product, service, solution, and financing ☐ Recurring service revenues ☐ **Digital productivity improvements**
Strategic Control/ Differentiation	☐ GE Social Architecture ☐ Close customer–CEO relationships ☐ **Network to tie partners to GE** ☐ Six Sigma quality
Scope	☐ Relationship company ☐ Comprehensive customer solutions ☐ **Information services** ☐ Investments (GE Capital)
Organizational System	☐ Culture of collaboration and teamwork ☐ Internal marketing system ☐ Willingness to constantly change and reinvent
Bit Engines	☐ **Electronic links to customers and supply chain** ☐ **Remote diagnostics** ☐ **Electronic marketplace**

Boldface = digitally enabled.

will also benefit from (1) much stronger links to customers, and (2) fewer openings for off-the-radar-screen competitors to establish positions in the economic spaces that are important to GE.

Most of the crucial elements of GE's evolving business design are not yet digital. Look for this to change within the next two years—assuming that GE is successful in completing its transition to DBD.

FROM NIGHTMARE TO OPPORTUNITY

Jack Welch's Internet nightmare had two key elements: *margin compression* and *intrusion*. Welch realized that if the Internet drove down GE's selling prices faster than its purchase prices, the company's margins would crumble. And if new intermediaries got into the game, they would attack GE's downstream positions, inserting themselves between GE and its customers.

The GE digital initiatives born out of the Destroyyourbusiness crusade *reversed* this nightmare.

Creation of the Trading Partner Network (TPN) drove down purchase prices for GE and its partners. Meanwhile, GE's Web sites decommoditized the buying process for GE's customers, placing the focus on value, not just price. They also made GE's customers more productive, and they provided information destinations so rich in value-added information that the customer could say, "I go to the GE site first, and it's so comprehensive I have no reason to go anywhere else." Through programs such as Remote Diagnostics, GE delivered information (and solutions) no one else could provide. The cumulative effect of all these initiatives was to preempt new intermediaries and build a much stronger bond with the customer.

Jack Welch's two-decade tenure at GE has been marked by the evolution of the customer relationship from *transactional* (selling products) to *continuous* (multiyear service relationships) to *unique*. In this latest reinvention, GE is putting the Internet to work to create a unique relationship with its best customers. GE provides a portfolio of products, services, solutions, information, analytical tools, and action support that no other provider can match.

GE'S NEXT BUSINESS ISSUES

GE has made great strides toward becoming a digital business. But the process is far from complete, and the company faces important challenges in the near future.

One challenge is the ability to achieve a growth rate that is attractive to investors in the new economy. Despite its size ($112 billion in revenues in 1999) and age, GE has been able to show double-digit increases in sales (11 percent over 1998) and profits (15 percent). Its profits stand today at a record $10 billion, and its shareholders, including thousands of employees and retirees, enjoyed a total return of 54 percent last year. But GE will have a hard time growing as fast as many smaller, well-managed companies with Digital Business Designs. Can GE remain a first choice for investors?

The more time one spends visiting GE's Web sites and talking to GE's customers, the more likely it appears that the answer will be *Yes*. Two factors will be crucial: (1) How rapidly will GE execute? and (2) How quickly will its rivals take steps to reduce GE's uniqueness and to offer alternatives that are even more attractive to customers?

When Jack Welch steps down in 2001, GE will face the inevitable challenge of any company with a powerful CEO: maintaining positive momentum after his departure. The next several years will test whether the DNA of GE has been permanently and successfully changed by the digital transformation Welch initiated.

Examples of effective successions after the departure of a great leader are rare. More commonly, we see the opposite. When very strong leaders leave, companies often struggle for years before resuming a period of value growth.

Is such a decline inevitable for GE? Can Welch prevent it? Will GE's rapid progress in shifting to DBD create such a large and secure base of unique customer relationships that the company's performance will not suffer when the leadership changes? The next three years will tell the tale.

GE may have an important factor working in its favor: Its shift to a Digital Business Design is not happening at a constant rate; it is accelerating. The process started on a defensive note: "Destroyyourbusiness" before the competitors do. In 1999, it shifted to "growyourbusiness.com." Anyone who follows the evolution and rapid changes in the whole array of GE's Web sites can feel the pace picking up: better sites, easier navigation, more value-added information, sales of non-GE products, and so on.

In some GE businesses, this momentum may be blunted by strong competitors. In others, the momentum will gather even greater force in 2001. "Destroyyourbusiness" grew into "growyourbusiness" and is now moving to "destroy*their*business."

The acceleration effect, if strong enough, might well carry GE through the transition period unscathed.

To get a firsthand sense of GE's transition, take the GE tour (Appendix E). Then spend an hour on the Internet visiting the actual GE sites. Consider these questions: What does GE enable its customers to do? How much of GE's content is unique? How do GE's sites compare to its customers' other best experiences on the Internet?

GE's challenge has been to shift a large, complex, and extremely successful collection of businesses to DBD in order to head off potential challenges to its leadership. As we'll see in the next chapter, IBM, another powerful incumbent, faces a very different challenge.

INCUMBENT ON
THE MOVE: IBM

THE CHALLENGE OF BUSINESS REDESIGN

As we've seen, GE is the preeminent example of a company that is moving to a Digital Business Design from a position of strength. IBM's "near-death experience" in the early 1990s created an entirely different challenge for the company.

The outlines of the story are familiar: After posting record profits in 1990, IBM lost $2.9 billion in 1991, $5 billion in 1992, and $8.1 billion in 1993. Revenues from the highly profitable mainframe business were stalling, and, a decade after essentially inventing the concept of the personal computer, IBM was losing PC customers to Compaq, Dell, Hewlett-Packard, and other players. Microsoft was becoming the computer industry's mindshare leader. Network-centric companies like Cisco, and startups like AOL and Netscape, were stealing the Internet spotlight. While still critical to large, established back-office processing operations, IBM was losing its relevance to new growth-oriented customers—always a life-threatening condition. The value of the company declined dramatically (See Figure 13–1).

In reality, IBM hit the wall in the mid 80s. Many of its losses in the early 90s were related to the downsizing from 406,000 to fewer than 250,000 employees. IBM was facing the same challenge that many other businesses have faced during the past decade and a half: How to transform itself from a product seller into something else—a services provider, a

FIGURE 13–1   From 1987 to 1993, IBM Lost 75 Percent of Its Value

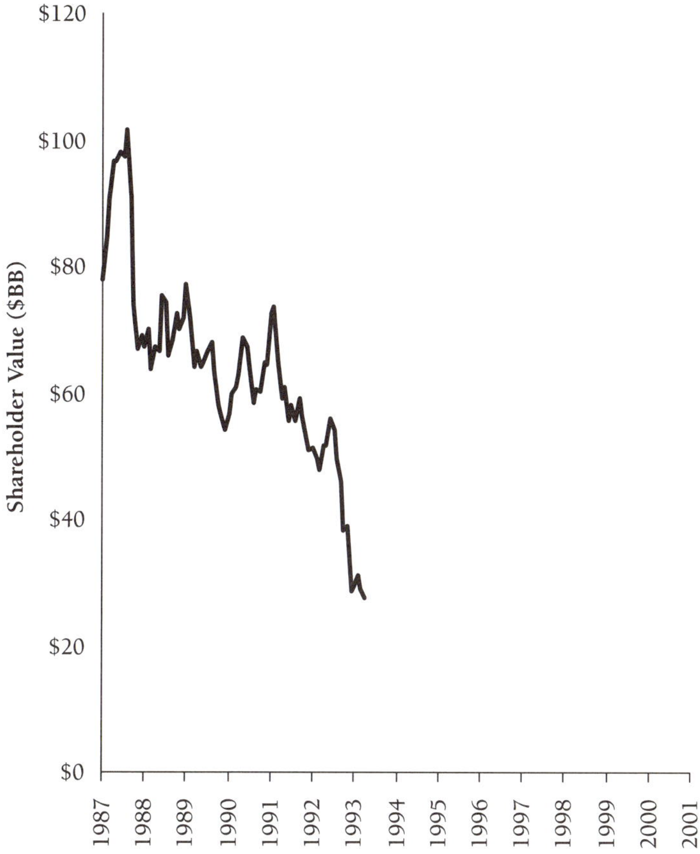

Source: Compustat, 7/00.

systems provider, an infrastructure manager, or a solutions seller. So many product markets were becoming no-profit zones during those years that scores of companies had no choice but to change their business designs or face stagnation. IBM began the process of building a new business design foundation in the late 1980s by creating initiatives for several new businesses, embracing open architecture, and starting OEM components and services businesses.

The drive toward Digital Business Design (DBD) is reinforcing the same message with new urgency. In a digital world, where every customer can access product offerings from every supplier anywhere in the world, merely offering a competitive product at a competitive price provides no assurance of profitability.

> As the Internet takes hold, the worst place to be stuck is in the old product-centric business design. The Internet exposes price positions and commoditizes offerings in the minds of customers. Companies that *didn't* reinvent their product-centric business during the 1990s are now heading into a period of maximum vulnerability, and the Internet is causing the clock to tick just a little bit faster.

IBM is still working on that reinvention—while striving to move to a Digital Business Design at the same time. Its portfolio is scattered across the quadrants of the DBD matrix. For the last decade, it has been a case of parallel tracks with a vengeance, demanding what amounts to three major changes at once: (1) a business turnaround; (2) an overhaul and repair of many of IBM's product-centric business designs; and (3) a shift from conventional to digital.

GE is moving into the Northeast quadrant from a relatively strong position in the Southeast quadrant (great business design/low digitization). IBM is trying to move diagonally, from the Southwest quadrant to the Northeast quadrant. Having to migrate across an east/west border at the same time as a north/south border makes IBM's challenge at least twice as difficult. It's the kind of challenge most established businesses will face in the next five years. Will IBM succeed? It's too soon to tell. What follows is a progress report with some tentative lessons.

IBM'S BUSINESS ISSUES, AND
THE CUSTOMERS' ANSWERS

As we've suggested, an effective way to begin the process of rethinking a company's strategy is by identifying the five top business issues facing the company. When Lou Gerstner arrived at IBM in 1993, he had a talented team that had initiated a number of turnaround and new business efforts. But the company's portfolio was scattered across numerous technologies and markets. There were probably twenty candidates for his top-five issues list. Three steps were essential: first, establish financial stability; second, fix the portfolio of business designs; and third, create platforms for growth.

Prior to Gerstner's arrival, IBM had begun the process of rationalizing its portfolio, the process that GE had aggressively executed from 1981 to 1984. In those early years under Jack Welch, GE cleaned up its act; it sold companies, fired excess employees, and fixed its systems. (This is the period when Welch became known as "Neutron Jack." His task then was largely negative: clearing away the weeds and underbrush before new planting could begin.) IBM had to decide what businesses it wanted to be in, make sense of its basic business design, and rationalize its processes.

At the risk of simplifying a very complex picture, IBM's biggest business issues at the start of the Gerstner era were:

- ☐ A flawed, product-centric business design; fundamental economics were bad and getting worse.
- ☐ Excessively complicated, mutually incompatible internal systems and processes that made customer service slow and inaccurate and thwarted the creative potential of IBM's talent.
- ☐ A corporate culture of entitlement and turf-protecting.
- ☐ Perhaps worst of all, a sense that IBM had become less and less relevant to its most important customers, especially those who were defining the structure of network-centric computing.

These issues raised a host of questions. What were Gerstner's business design options for fixing these problems? What new focus could be developed to replace the old focus on IBM's "big iron" hardware products? Would it make sense to break up the vast and unwieldy company and create a collection of more manageable, faster-moving "Baby Blues," as John Akers, Gerstner's predecessor, had planned? Or should Gerstner strive somehow to keep IBM together? Could the massive IBM bureaucracy be simplified and unified? Could the company's warring factions be united and energized around one or a few simple and compelling themes? How could IBM's ingrown corporate culture, once the envy of the business world but now increasingly dysfunctional, be revitalized?

Happily, the single most important question—whether to split up the company—was one on which Gerstner had a clear insight. He had been an IBM customer during his previous careers at American Express and Nabisco. Now, as the new CEO, he assumed the role of IBM's chief customer service representative. (Compare this to Doug Allred's title at Cisco: Vice President for Customer Advocacy. The title is important. Even more important is inculcating this mindset throughout the business.) Soon after his arrival, Gerstner hosted, in Chantilly, Virginia, a conference of the company's 200 biggest corporate clients. These large enterprises had traditionally been IBM's most profitable customers, but during the previous decade and a half, their loyalty had eroded.

Gerstner asked these customers what *they* wanted from IBM. Their response was surprisingly unanimous. They recognized the chaos caused by IBM's internal confusion and conflicting bureaucracies; after all, they had had to live with its effects, such as dueling data platforms that didn't share information. But a company breakup, they said, was no solution. They didn't want to deal with half a dozen Baby Blues, no matter how entrepreneurial and fast-moving each one might be. Instead, they wanted IBM to get its act together and develop the capability of offering unified solutions to their information management problems.

This customer demand was driven by the increasing complexity of information systems. Mainframes, PCs, servers, routers, internal and external networks, software, databases—somehow these had to be made to work together, *especially* in the large enterprises that were IBM's most important customers. IBM's huge size and scope could position it uniquely as a supplier of solutions for information management—*if* Gerstner could clean up the company's own systems and redeploy its resources with a focus on customer value.

For several years now, Gerstner and IBM have been pushing to respond to this customer demand in three ways: (1) by fixing the company's business design; (2) by rationalizing its internal processes; and (3) by moving (especially since 1996) toward a fully Digital Business Design.

FIXING THE BUSINESS DESIGN

Lou Gerstner likes to diagram the computer industry in the year 2000 as a "vertical barbell." He describes it this way:

> The big weight at the bottom is components. At the top end is software and services. The skinny bar in the middle is everything else: PCs, servers, network gear. Profits are moving to the ends of the barbell. The value is being pulled down to the people who have the real underlying assets.

The same pattern, which we call the Collapse of the Middle, has happened in many industries in recent years:

> **The Collapse of the Middle pattern occurs when value migrates away from middle positions and toward the extremes.**

Retailing is a simple example. Profits and shareholder value have migrated to the price discounters and superstores (at one end of the spectrum) and the high-end specialists (at the other), leaving department stores (which offer a little bit of everything but not enough of anything) floundering in the middle. (For more information on this pattern, visit http://www.profitpatterns.com.)

During the early 1990s, the Collapse of the Middle hit the computer business with a vengeance, as the proliferation of IBM clones turned the PC into a commodity to be purchased on price alone. That trend shows no sign of abating; witness the recent advent of the *free* PC (given away to attract sales of Internet access and other services). In such a world, being the premier maker of high-quality hardware—IBM's longtime, once-proud position—is a no-profit, no-win situation.

In response, IBM is in the process of shifting to a dual value-growth strategy, focusing on the extreme ends of the computer technology spectrum: components (i.e., pure technology) at one end, and software and services at the other end.

At the components end of the spectrum, IBM is changing its customer selection and selling technology to other companies—even to those once considered mortal enemies. That strategy was unthinkable in the pre-1985 IBM, but Gerstner believes it can help kickstart IBM's growth. The company is now selling some of the world's best technology—tiny disk drives, speedy new chips, and more—to some of its fiercest rivals, including Apple, Hitachi, and Sun. During 1999, for instance, IBM announced a five-year, $2 billion contract to sell networking chips to Cisco Systems, against whom it used to compete, and a $16 billion contract to sell computer parts to Dell. IBM will even design other companies' new products, build in the latest breakthroughs, and provide a peek at product plans and research secrets in its labs.

As Gerstner explains, hoarding technology was fine in the 1960s, when IBM captured two of every three dollars spent on computing. Today, when IBM gets one dollar in ten, such hoarding would be "really dumb."

Meanwhile, at the solutions end of the spectrum, IBM is continuing to serve its traditional enterprise customers, but with a new emphasis on selling a wide range of sophisticated computer services, as a kind of "general contractor" for the wired world (in the words of *Business Week*). IBM's Global Services division helps companies create and run IT infrastructures using equipment from many manufacturers—not just IBM. It's a marked departure from the old IBM, where service was, at best, an add-on to product sales whose main role was to drive more hardware sales.

Since 1995, IBM has become the world's largest computer-services business, with current revenues of $32 billion. Service sales are now about 37 percent of IBM's revenues and are expected to rise to 46 percent by 2003.

FIXING THE PROCESSES AND THE CULTURE

In the late 1980s and early 1990s, John Akers had built a loose federation of businesses within IBM. As its earlier sense of teamwork and community degenerated into turf-protecting, the company's divisions hardened into self-perpetuating fiefdoms. Systems proliferated, unnecessary staff multiplied, and communication became defensive and ritualized. To change all this, Gerstner had to act on several fronts: forcing concrete changes in the bureaucracy while making both symbolic and substantive gestures to encourage cultural renewal. Early on, he gave a now-famous speech saying that the last thing IBM needed was a vision. What they needed, he insisted, was focus and execution.

When Gerstner joined IBM, the company was maintaining 120 different general ledgers and a dozen different information networks. Only in the past five years have all these disparate systems been reduced into one—a process that removed billions of dollars of cost. Gradually, IBM is moving in the direction of real-time rather than lag-time information and from separate silos to an integrated system, developing the capabilities needed to be customer-responsive in a digital business era.

Gerstner has pushed to change corporate patterns of thought and communication. He started at the top, with his direct reporting relationships. Soon after his arrival, Gerstner asked each of his twenty top executives to write a short paper, answering several simple questions: What is your business? Who are your customers? What is your marketplace? What are your strengths and weaknesses? Who are your main competitors? The executives were forbidden to use slides, formerly the hallmark and organizing focus of every IBM presentation; instead, they had to communicate in plain English. Gerstner set a two-week deadline, and he met personally with each executive to discuss the results. In a small way, it was a revolutionary act. "People weren't used to writing in sentences," Gerstner later observed.

Based on the results of this process, Gerstner and his team focused on four initiatives: (1) the reintegration of IBM; (2) global industry (for example, financial services, healthcare, retail); (3) growth through technology, software, and services; and (4) network computing (which eventually evolved into an entire range of e-business efforts).

Gerstner introduced a new mantra at the company: "Win (in the marketplace), Execute (with quality), Team (across functions and units)." And Gerstner made it real through concrete steps, such as encouraging IBM scientists to meet regularly with customers rather than remaining cloistered in labs.

Gerstner personally set an example of open communication. He went on tour and hosted "town meetings" at dozens of IBM sites. Instead of broadcasting a message via satellite or making a canned presentation (as many employees expected), he spoke for an hour without notes, then answered any and all questions with surprising candor. He spoke out against the "good news only" syndrome, which had discouraged IBM talent from telling the boss the truth; he insisted that business reports run no longer than ten pages; he eliminated the reliance on elaborate visual aids; and he reduced the size, number, and formality of meetings.

Several "public hangings" (i.e., well-merited dismissals of prominent antichange managers) were held during the first few months, to illustrate vividly that the days of entitlement were over. Perhaps most important, Gerstner insisted that the company peg a significant portion of bonus pay to overall company performance rather than the performance of individual business units. This decree reversed the pernicious incentive that had encouraged the various divisions to compete with, rather than support, one another. Since 1994, IBM's variable pay pool has increased by more than 60 percent. Stock options are also being emphasized: the number of employees granted options doubled in 1996, doubled again in 1997, and tripled in 1998.

Thus, the value proposition for IBM's talent is being realigned with the company's strategic focus. As the company's turnaround gains momentum, IBM's strengths in R&D, plus its worldwide reach and great brand name, are regaining their power—another good reason for many of the brightest technology minds to want to work there.

GOING DIGITAL: FIRST FRUITS

Even as Gerstner and IBM tackle reinventing the company's business design and reforming its business processes (and the dysfunctional culture that went with them), they have also been pursuing a third parallel line of major change: moving IBM toward a Digital Business Design.

Early on, IBM understood the importance of the Internet. Soon after his arrival, Gerstner began pushing the company toward using the Net as a crucial business tool. In 1995, he initiated an internal Internet and e-commerce task force led by John Landry, Chief Technology Officer at Lotus; Doug Sweeney, Vice President for Strategy; and Buzz Waterhouse. This led to the installation of Irving Wladawsky-Berger as head of all Internet initiatives and the decision to spend hundreds of millions of dollars on an e-business advertising campaign. The campaign became the basis for the growth platform and the repositioning of IBM as one of the companies that will lead the new economy. Gerstner puts it this way:

> The Internet is ultimately about innovation and integration. Innovation is what your objective is—in cost structures, selling, marketing, sales, supply chain. But you don't get the innovation unless you integrate Web technology into the processes by which you run your business.

The context of Gerstner's comments was a description of what IBM's customers need to do to realize the advantages of digital business, but the vision applies to IBM itself. The company has been moving to make Gerstner's ideal into a reality. Here are some examples:

☐ **Digital procurement:** IBM's internal e-procurement team won the "Chairman's Award" in 1999 for saving the company hundreds of millions in the purchasing of nonmanufacturing supplies (paper, pens, corporate services, and so on). In that year alone, IBM bought over $11 billion worth of goods and services over the Internet and generated cost savings of $240 million. More than 6,700 suppliers are plugged into the electronic procurement system, which now permits more efficient control of purchase approvals.

☐ **Digital training:** IBM is rapidly shifting its employee training online. Analysts forecast that for every 1,000 classroom days converted to electronic courses delivered via the Web, more than $400,000 can be saved. Estimates indicate that IBM will save $120 million by delivering 30 percent of its internal training on-line. The expansion and improvement of training that this saving makes possible further enhances the value proposition for IBM's talent.

☐ **Digital sales and services:** IBM's on-line business-to-business (B2B) revenues are skyrocketing. The 1998 figure of $3.3 billion grew past $12 billion in 1999—an increase of almost 300 percent. The company expects some 35 million service requests in 2000; by handling such calls on-line, the saving is estimated to be 70 to 90 percent. Savings expected in 2000: some $750 million in customer support costs.

☐ **Digital R&D:** Linking IBM's global network of research facilities has enabled the company's technical minds—among the best in the world—to work on the Internet, greatly increasing productivity. Software developers now electronically transfer code from offices in Germany to suburban New York to Silicon Valley and then to Tokyo, so that experts in each time zone can add their own improvements. What would have been at least four full days' work in the old IBM is now completed within twenty-four hours.

The productivity gains IBM is realizing from digitization are important. But the most significant aspect of IBM's shift to Digital Business Design—which Gerstner views as a "bet-the-company decision" is its move to make e-commerce its central source of future revenue and profit growth.

E-COMMERCE: WHERE'S THE "PAY" BUTTON?

At an internal meeting, IBM's new Internet division demonstrated the prototype for the first IBM Web page. It offered reams of information about the company and its products plus attractive graphics, useful links, and other state-of-the-art features. Lou Gerstner's first question was: "Where's the page's 'Pay' button?"

Gerstner's intuition that the Internet was destined to become a major source of revenues was prescient. John Patrick recalls, "E-commerce didn't exist yet. [Gerstner] was asking questions in '94 that other people didn't ask until years later." This was fortunate for IBM. It has taken years for the company to overcome the skepticism of customers, suppliers, the media, and others who doubted that the giant among old-fashioned hardware companies was serious about e-commerce. The breakthrough in public perception finally arrived in 1999, two full years after IBM became the first big hardware company to pitch its software and services for the Internet Age.

Today, IBM invests fully half of its $5.6 billion R&D budget in Internet projects, up from 25 percent in 1996. The emphasis is on finding ways to help IBM customers transform themselves into effective e-businesses. IBM estimates that, by 2003, companies around the world will spend $600 billion on e-business: 29 percent of that total on hardware, 9 percent on software, *and 62 percent on consulting services.* IBM is positioning itself to win a large slice of that business, particularly for consulting services. Its army of 130,000 consultants is already doing $5.7 billion worth of Internet work—more than competitors Andersen, EDS, and Computer Sciences combined.

IBM currently offers an array of some thirty e-commerce services, including Web site design, Web hosting, security consulting, and the delivery of enterprise software over the Web. The breadth of its service offerings and its strengths in hardware and software have positioned IBM to claim a unique ability to help businesses manage the complex shift to an e-commerce model. The company's 21,000 e-commerce customers include many of the giant businesses that represent IBM's traditional customer base—for example, Ford, Prudential, and the New York Stock Exchange. But IBM is also going after smaller businesses and offering them, for as little as $99 per month, a package that includes all the hardware, software, and services they need to go on-line.

In the process, Gerstner's IBM is striving to develop the nimbleness and speed of response associated with an entrepreneurial startup. For example, IBM helps Charles Schwab manage its on-line customer systems, which are among the world's busiest (up to 76 million hits/day). In December 1999, Federal Reserve Chairman Alan Greenspan was preparing to address Congress—an event that drew intense anticipation throughout the investment community. If Greenspan announced something that would move the markets, the Schwab Web sites might be overwhelmed with hits. In response to a last-minute request from nervous managers at

Schwab, IBM shipped and installed a phalanx of additional computer equipment in less than three days (as compared to the thirty to ninety days typically required). Schwab's CIO commented, "IBM understands what it means to support an enterprise 24/7."

SURVIVAL VIA DIGITAL BUSINESS DESIGN

It's obvious that IBM is moving to a digital business model as quickly as possible and on several fronts, both internal and external. However, the importance of DBD for IBM runs deeper than the obvious impact of any single initiative. Lou Gerstner's most crucial business design choice—the decision to scrap John Akers's plan to break up IBM—may well have been impossible without DBD.

> Digital Business Design and the productivity improvements it generates are making it possible to manage organizations of greater scale and complexity than ever before.

Gerstner himself has commented on the revolutionary business design impact that digitization can have:

Consider that every one of the commonly accepted conventions of business—things like manufacturing, distribution chains, stock exchanges, and retail sales—are all a function of time, space, and distance in a physical world. And every one of those limitations is affected, if not dismantled, in a digital, information-based economy.

We can see the power of DBD to enable operations of unprecedented complexity in areas beyond business. For example, NATO forces were able to wage war in Kosovo for three months with *no* Allied casualties because of the armies' electronic information capabilities, such as digital target acquisition. (One much-publicized error from that campaign—the accidental bombing of a Chinese embassy—was caused by a human mistake in reading a map. The fact that such a mishap, the likes of which would have been a daily occurrence in the Vietnam War and other predigital wars, generated international controversy for a full year indicates the degree to which digital efficiencies have already become routine.)

If you are involved in running a large business, consider the complexity of the information you need to control. In many firms, that complexity is overwhelming the ability of the internal talent to master it. There are just too many product lines, departments, branch offices, countries, customers, competitors, suppliers, cost fluctuations, and so on. Certain levels of complexity simply can't be managed without Digital Business Design.

This is true partly because the sheer amount of information is so massive that only digital systems can capture and manage it all, and partly because only digital systems can engage the intelligence of *everyone* in your company.

> It's no longer enough for the person in the corner office to have access to all the latest information. Everyone in your company needs it now, so that *all* of your company's brain power can be leveraged to solve business problems.

Only Digital Business Design makes this possible. If Gerstner succeeds in shepherding IBM through the most complicated and ambitious reinvention in corporate annals, it will be due, in large part, to the *power* of DBD—its ability to transform a large enterprise from a collection of disconnected silos into a linked and mutually reinforcing system.

IBM'S EMERGING BUSINESS DESIGN

Table 13–1 summarizes the Digital Business Design toward which IBM is moving. Its customer selection has evolved to include competitors as well as its traditional enterprise accounts. The value proposition for the traditional accounts offers end-to-end IT solutions, world-leading expertise to "help your company move to e-business," and risk reduction

TABLE 13–1   IBM's Emerging Digital Business Design

Customer Selection	☐ Enterprise accounts with heterogeneous, complex systems ☐ Technology OEMs (e.g., Apple, Dell, Cisco) ☐ Global small and medium businesses ☐ Net-generation firms
Unique Value Proposition for Customers	☐ **"Help you move to e-business"** ☐ End-to-end solutions ☐ State-of-the-art component and software technology ☐ Brand/Risk reduction
Unique Value Proposition for Talent	☐ **Digital training** ☐ **Systems rationalization/Information flow (idea and knowledge management)** ☐ **Intellectual Capital Management (ICM) System**
Value Capture/ Profit Model	☐ Product, service, software, and component margins ☐ Licensing fees ☐ Investment returns ☐ **e-Care, e-Learning, e-Procurement**
Strategic Control/ Differentiation	☐ **"Only IBM has the depth and breadth to help you manage your complexity"** ☐ Industry-leading R&D, two-year lead
Scope	☐ Hardware, software, components ☐ Services ☐ Consulting ☐ Strategic application partnerships (Siebel, Ariba, SAP, Peoplesoft)
Organizational System	☐ Evolving from product silos to single-company culture ☐ Server business, software business, service business, technology business
Bit Engines	☐ **Electronic marketplace**

Boldface = digitally enabled.

through the powerful promise of quality and reliability inherent in the IBM brand. For the former competitors, IBM's value proposition is state-of-the-art technology.

IBM's value proposition for talent was a real question mark in the early 1990s. Today, it includes participation in a genuine large-scale turnaround as well as multiple sources of leverage and growth—intellectual capital management, e-training, and so on.

The company's profit model has also been transformed. Margins on hardware and services have been expanded to include margins on components, an enormous flow of licensing revenues ($1.5 billion in 1999), and rapidly increasing profit contributions from digital productivity and digital business partnerships. For example, in May 2000, IBM announced the launch of a new company (in partnership with an e-business incubator, Internet Capital Group) to buy, sell, and license patents and other forms of intellectual property on an Internet exchange.

IBM's strategic control now derives from several sources: a two-year lead in technology, deep and powerful customer relationships, and a B2B brand that, in the minds of major customers, is rapidly recapturing its former selling power and leadership position. The organization is evolving from a collection of distinct and warring product silos into a single, well-integrated company, and a bit engine is being built around an electronic marketplace through which an increasing portion of IBM's sales are conducted.

IBM'S NEXT BUSINESS ISSUES

IBM is still in the middle stages of its reinvention (see Figure 13–2). Will it succeed? As IBM's old business model fades, can its new business model evolve quickly enough to take its place? The jury is still out. Here are some of the challenges ahead:

☐ **Increasing the corporate growth rate.** In recent years, IBM's revenue growth has averaged 7 percent; for 1999, it rose to about 9 percent (still not fast enough for investors in the new economy),

FIGURE 13–2   From 1993–2000, IBM's Value Grew Eight-Fold

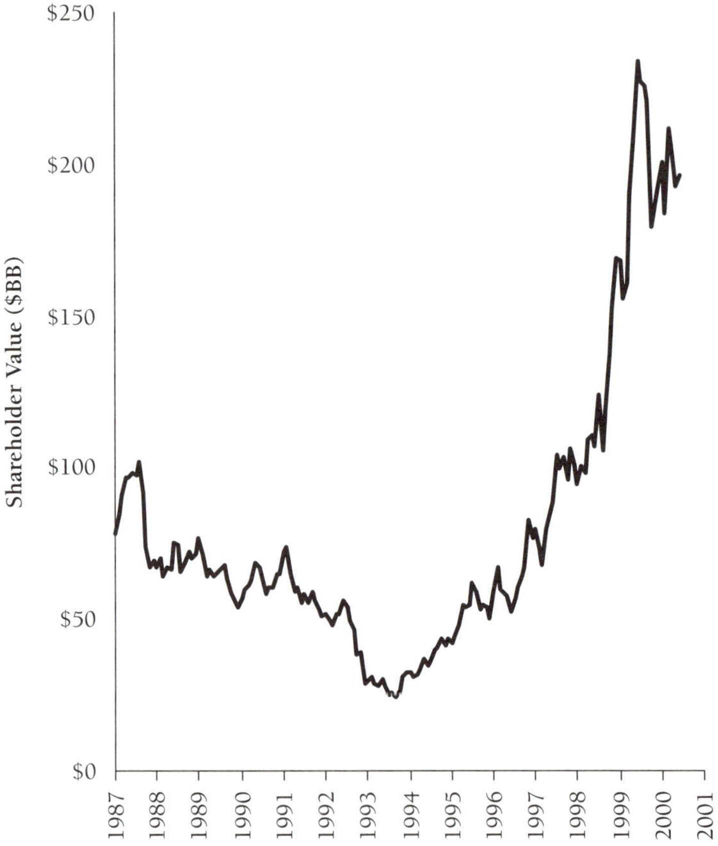

Source: Compustat, 7/00.

then fell back below 3 percent during the first quarter of 2000. The shift to services and e-commerce should help, but can IBM make the transition quickly enough to satisfy the demands of Wall Street?

☐ **Fending off aggressive new competitors.** IBM was among the first to focus on e-business services, and its large, traditional customer base and huge array of resources enabled it to grab an early lead. Now a host of smart, agile computer-industry competitors—including Sun, Microsoft, Hewlett-Packard, and Intel—are leaping into the fray. IBM will also be increasingly competing with businesses from other arenas—companies like Andersen (in consulting) and Federal Express (in e-logistics). Will IBM's size and scope suffice to stave off focused competitors eager to steal slices of its business?

☐ **Growing the customer base.** Can IBM maintain its strength among its traditional customers—large enterprises—while attracting newer, smaller customers?

☐ **Continuing the process of cultural change.** Six years into IBM's turnaround, the company is highly vulnerable to a letdown, a return to complacency. As Gerstner puts it, "We have to guard against any tendency to take our foot off the accelerator." IBM's talent pool of 300,000 employees is a potentially huge asset. How successfully can they leverage it?

LESSONS FROM THE INCUMBENTS

As we've seen, the GE and IBM stories have many differences. Operating from a position of strategic strength, GE has been able to focus on identifying and preempting the competitive challenges that digital technologies might pose to its core businesses. IBM has had to juggle several levels of reinvention at the same time: fixing its business design, streamlining its internal processes, and reforming its corporate culture, while also focusing on the shift from a conventional to a Digital Business Design. GE is well advanced in its migration from the Southeast to the Northeast quadrant. IBM continues to struggle with the much more difficult trek from the wastelands of the Southwest quadrant.

Nonetheless, some common lessons for other incumbents emerge from the GE and IBM experiences:

☐ **Start with the customer.** Most large organizations have a powerful tendency to focus internally, particularly in staff divisions such as human resources and information technology. Thus, it's easy for incumbent firms to pursue digitization in ways that reinforce an internal focus rather than a customer orientation. At GE, Jack Welch used the deliberate "glass-breaking" focus of Destroyyourbusiness.com to combat this tendency. At IBM, Lou Gerstner, the former customer and now chief customer advocate, has played a similar role. *If you are an incumbent planning a migration to the Northeast quadrant, don't start by focusing on how Digital Business Design can help you. Instead, look first for the benefits it can bring your customers.*

☐ **Identify and address the few truly crucial issues for your business.** At many incumbent firms, CEOs can be heard yelling, "Get us on the Internet—I don't care how, just do it!" The sense of urgency is appropriate; the lack of focus is not. Start, as GE and IBM did, by identifying your key business issues, especially the evolving needs of your customers and changing sources of profitability. Then examine how Digital Business Design can help you address them. *Digitizing a bad business design is worse than useless; it drains time, energy, and money from your real needs while creating an illusion of progress. It ends up saddling your company with legacy systems that will only hamper future movement in the right directions.*

☐ **Emphasize internal marketing.** Changing the thoughts and behaviors of 100,000+ people is never easy. It requires massive, constant communication, through all channels, around a very few consistent themes. Jack Welch is a past master of internal marketing; Lou Gerstner's introduction of the customer mantra and his adroit hosting of IBM town meetings illustrate his understanding of the same dynamics. *If you are an incumbent ready to shift your company toward Digital Business Design, try to* overestimate *your internal marketing requirements. This may enable you to do enough.*

If GE and IBM, two of the world's largest and most complex businesses in rapidly changing technological industries, can launch and sustain highly focused programs to move to Digital Business Designs, so can any other business, whatever its size, industry, legacy systems, or geographic location. This is the single most important—and most positive—lesson from the GE and IBM stories.

14

DOT-COMS ON THE MOVE

MIGRATING FROM WEST TO EAST

In the previous two chapters, we examined major incumbents—GE and IBM—that are in the process of transforming their traditional business designs into Digital Business Designs so that they can eventually move into the Northeast quadrant.

How do the lessons of going digital apply to the Internet world, where everyone already thinks digital?

Our research suggests that, in today's dot-com world, where digital technologies are ubiquitous, few companies have learned that true Digital Business Design requires the integration of digital technology with sound business design. The challenge for the vast majority of today's dot-com businesses is not to keep up with the latest changes in technology but to develop a viable and sustainable business design—to migrate from the Northwest to the Northeast quadrant.

In this chapter, we'll survey the Internet landscape to understand how dot-coms can avoid perishing in the wasteland of the Northwest quadrant, and we'll profile three companies that have already successfully migrated to the Northeast: AOL, Yahoo!, and eBay.

THE INTERNET LANDSCAPE

There's no doubt that the Internet is exploding as a medium for communication, information, advertising, and commerce, as well as an instrument (albeit an unreliable one) for wealth creation. Reliable statistics are elusive, but the following data are at least of the correct order of magnitude:

- Internet users currently number approximately 170 million (about 2.5 percent of the world's population); that figure is expected to double by 2002.
- Both business-to-business (B2B) and business-to-consumer (B2C) e-commerce are booming. B2B revenues are expected to total $295 billion in 2000 and nearly $2 trillion by 2004; B2C sales are estimated at $44 billion in 2000 and about $200 billion by 2004.
- Web advertising sales are projected to total $4.4 billion in 2000 and to increase to $7.7 billion in 2002.
- During 1999, there were 107 e-commerce initial public offerings (IPOs) by B2B, B2C, and portal companies.
- By year end 1999, B2B, B2C, and portal companies had a market capitalization of $503 billion.

No wonder the hype surrounding e-commerce has been so intense. No other new business medium has ever generated comparable customer traffic, sales revenues, and company value so quickly. The huge scope of the Internet revolution is now familiar to everyone in business.

REALITY CHECK

During the first half of the year 2000, the fact that the bloom is off the rose became equally apparent. The stock market boom, largely driven by Internet speculation, has turned into a roller-coaster ride. The share prices of many high-profile dot-coms are down from their all-time highs by eighty percent or more. And nearly all of the dot-coms are losing money. During 1999, B2B, B2C, and portal businesses had average profit margins of minus 63 percent. What does it all mean? Is the business potential of the Internet space a cruel illusion?

The short answer is *No*. As a powerful new environment that has already attracted hundreds of millions of users and many of today's best entrepreneurial minds, the Internet is producing a genuine business revolution. There are enormous fortunes to be made in e-commerce. But that doesn't translate into easy or automatic profits for the first companies to stake claims on the Internet.

As in any business, *sustainable* shareholder value is key. In the Internet space, this will be produced by the same forces that govern traditional businesses: growth, stability, customer allegiance, and, above all, profitability. These won't come automatically, even to companies that succeed in claiming significant market share on the Internet. Consider the auto and airline industries. Both revolutionized modern life and created huge economic powerhouses. Yet very few companies have realized sustainable value in these industries, as the ongoing travails of the major automakers and the entire airline sector attest.

In any explosive new industry, a shakeout that decimates the majority of start-up businesses is inevitable. In his book, *Managing the Dynamics of Innovation,* James M. Utterback notes a repeated historical pattern in new industries: A boom in which dozens of companies are founded is followed by a period of consolidation with only a few survivors. In the auto industry, for example, within a few years, the number of U.S. manufacturers went from 180 to twelve. Similarly, 160 makers of televisions were reduced to ten; 300 personal computer makers dwindled to twenty.

We can expect a similar pattern in the dot-com world. Of the 125 Web sites for B2B e-commerce in the furniture business alone (in 1999), just five to ten are likely to survive in a few years. Many of today's dot-coms will be sold or will fold in the near future.

Some of the money-losing dot-coms are still in the investment or "land-grab" phase. They are spending heavily on marketing and advertising, in an effort to capture a customer base that will one day yield the holy grail of scale. In the recent dot-com IPO frenzy, many companies went public during the investment phase rather than waiting until they could show a profit, as was traditional. Their current unprofitability is now publicly exposed, and their investors and analysts are becoming nervous and impatient. Historically, most businesses have required three to five years before reaching the break-even point. Some dot-coms will probably attain profitability in time—if they get the chance.

But many others are unlikely ever to achieve profitability. They are simply bad businesses put on-line—businesses with weak, ill-considered, or unsustainable business designs. Some will never attract the eyeballs they need. Others will attract them but fail to retain them. And still others will attract and retain eyeballs but will have no idea how to monetize them—that is, gain a profit from them. Hundreds of dot-com businesses face this predicament.

How could so many smart people go so far wrong? Some fundamental misunderstandings contributed to many of the dot-com mistakes. Barriers to entry on the Internet are low. Anyone can create a Web site. With a little effort, a start-up team of a half dozen twenty-somethings can create a site as impressive as those built by some *Fortune* 500 companies. This fact makes brand-building on the Internet appear deceptively simple, inexpensive, and fast. But the same ease of entry that facilitates the launch of a dot-com start-up guarantees lots of competing Web sites, often with little or no differentiation in their customer value propositions. And the same technology that makes it fast and easy for customers to click onto a site makes it fast and easy for them to click on the exit button the instant they get bored, confused, or annoyed.

Some e-commerce contenders have lured eyeballs with free or no-profit products and services, in the belief that advertising revenues will support the business. This will rarely work. Only two advertising models make sense in today's economy. One is advertising to a small, intensely loyal, deeply interested niche market (readers of *Field & Stream* magazine, for example). The other is advertising to a very large (10 million+) general audience (like the viewers of *Friends* on NBC). Most dot-coms have attracted a mushy midsize audience that's somewhere in between—a market of little use to either the makers of high-end fishing gear (who want to reach the *Field & Stream* readers) or the makers of cola, soap, cars, or beer (who want to reach the millions of sitcom fans). Advertisers who experimented with banners on some of the popular Web sites are already beginning to abandon them.

Is the Internet, then, a no-profit zone? Not at all. As our three profitable role models demonstrate, there is money to be made on the Web even today. But remember: Digital Business Design is about business first, design second, and digital third. The Internet landscape is littered with companies that are 80 to 90 percent digital, yet have business designs that would score one or two on a scale of ten. The founders and managers of these companies are well aware of the power of digital, but they know little of the power of smart business design.

They inhabit the Northwest quadrant. To survive, they must begin to migrate east. They need to focus on business design to create the type of enduring profitability and customer allegiance that long-term investors will reward.

LESSONS FROM THE NORTHWEST GRAVEYARD

It's not surprising that the Internet space has proven to be a wasteland—potentially, a graveyard—for hundreds of seemingly promising business start-ups. As we've seen, the factors that make the Internet an attractive business venue are the same factors that make it treacherous: low barriers to entry, low switching costs for customers, volatile revenue, and no "moat around the castle" to protect profitability. Add the fact that both the technologies and the economics of the Internet are still undergoing rapid and continuous change, and it's easy to see why success has eluded most dot-coms.

How can an Internet business avoid burial in the graveyard of the Northwest quadrant? Here are the key overall lessons we've extracted from our study of the dot-com space.

> **A unique and robust on-line value proposition for your customers is essential.**

Because barriers to entry are few, competing sites will proliferate. (Witness the over 100 on-line brokerage sites currently competing with eSchwab.) The companies that win are those that regularly deliver outstanding value to customers and thus create sticky on-line relationships. Later, we'll discuss in detail how America Online (AOL), Yahoo!, and eBay have made this happen.

> **A customer you cannot monetize = 0.**

The Internet has created new customer value propositions that provide access to new tools, new sources of information, and new communities that can make life more entertaining, enriching, and productive. But value for the customer is only half of the business equation. The other half is value capture. Many dot-coms have no idea how they will monetize their customers to pay for the costs of customer acquisition—to say nothing of creating an ongoing stream of shareholder value.

> **Advertising offers a sustainable value mechanism only if you can deliver either a well-defined niche audience or a true mass audience.**

As we've discussed previously, advertisers love either a very focused niche or a mass audience. It's very difficult to survive if you're at neither end of the spectrum. Many dot-coms are attempting to be mass media players, but as the history of network television demonstrates, only very few will emerge.

> **The business fundamentals are more important than ever.**

Many dot-coms have created cool and enticing on-line interfaces while neglecting key off-line links in the customer activity chain, such as service and fulfillment. On-line customers quickly become frustrated over long hold times, delivery failures, billing errors, and the like, and, given the information transparency of the Internet, stories about poor service circulate quickly.

> **Evolve fast or fail.**

In the digital world, business models can be commoditized overnight. Because today's hot new concept will be quickly imitated and surpassed, resting on one's laurels is even more dangerous than in traditional business. Prodigy and CompuServe faded, in large part, because upstart competitor AOL has been a relentless innovator. It continually evolves its customer offerings to remain one step ahead of its rivals.

Dot-coms that pay attention to these business issues and master the discipline of business design have a better chance of migrating toward the Northeast quadrant than their technology-centric competitors. A very few companies have shown the way.

THE PROFITABLE DOT-COMS

To date, only three significant Internet-based companies—AOL, Yahoo!, and eBay—have managed to avoid the Northwest graveyard and turn a profit by creating truly superior Digital Business Designs. It pays to understand exactly what they've done.

Mass Media On-Line

AOL and Yahoo! have taken mass media business designs to the digital arena. The key ingredients for success in traditional mass media, which these companies applied to the Internet, include:

☐ An intense focus on the customer.
☐ Ubiquitous brand-name promotion, to attract eyeballs.
☐ Continual refinement and addition of content, to retain eyeballs.
☐ Value capture through monetizing users.

As we'll see, AOL and Yahoo! have developed unique variations on this path, but the results have been similar: highly developed customer value propositions with profitable revenue streams and self-reinforcing strategic control.

The Exchange On-Line

eBay has avoided the Northwest graveyard by taking a different traditional business design—the exchange—and bringing it on-line. It has worked well so far, but eBay faces significant challenges if it hopes to continue to grow rapidly in the years ahead.

DOT-COM ON THE MOVE: AOL

On-Line Survivor

In 1991, when predecessor company Quantum Computer Services was officially reborn as America Online (AOL), the World Wide Web was still in the future. But, for a reasonable monthly fee, several on-line computer companies were providing users with access to information and services no single source could otherwise provide. Prodigy and CompuServe were the established, dominant players; AOL had fewer than 150,000 users, revenues of about $20 million, and small profits.

Today, AOL rules the space. It boasts 22 million subscribers, a spot in the S&P 500, a stock valuation of over $250 billion, and 1999 profits of $762 million on revenues of $4.7 billion. After its pending acquisition of Time Warner is completed, AOL will control a media empire that includes movie studios, book publishers, record labels, and cable TV networks.

How did this happen? AOL's business design has evolved through several distinct phases, but it always focused on a central goal: To make the benefits of on-line services available to all, not just technophiles. The result has been the first true mass media enterprise in the digital world.

Customer Focus

From the beginning, AOL's customer selection was a broad spectrum of computer users—people more interested in the information, personal connections, and interactive services they could enjoy on-line than in the underlying technology. As AOL founder Steve Case has put it, "It's not about technology. It's about making this a mass medium and becoming part of the everyday habits of ordinary consumers."

His customer selection dictated the Web site's look, feel, style, and content: AOL was to be simple and friendly for even novice computer users (who were, of course, the vast majority of computer users in the early 1990s). AOL offered such features as seamless dial-up access, speedy and powerful search capabilities, an easy-to-understand and customizable interface that users could quickly navigate by clicking on buttons, and plenty of available help, both on-line and via a telephone.

Here is just one telling example of the difference between AOL and its rivals. When E-mail became popular, all the major on-line services provided E-mail addresses to their members. These were typical addresses found on the three top contenders:

Prodigy	tbpk80c@prodigy.com
CompuServe	84375.2945@compuserve.com
AOL	JimR@aol.com

Which address would you rather use?

Although "power users" and members of the "digerati" disdained AOL's folksy style, it was crucial to the company's value proposition for customers. AOL was one of the few companies to make it easy, and even fun, for people to use their computers.

AOL has continued to upgrade its user interface. Each new version has added features and options, improved speed, and expanded the range of supported technologies.

Brand Ubiquity

By December 1993, AOL had attracted over half a million subscribers to its on-line service—a respectable number, but only third best in the industry. More ominous, digital giant Microsoft was primed to enter the arena with its own service, MSN, deliberately designed as "an AOL killer." To compete, AOL had to build its subscriber base—fast. "It is a land grab," Steve Case declared, "and it is never going to be cheaper or easier to own that territory."

Ted Leonsis, AOL's "chief evangelist," said AOL must become a great brand name, like Coca-Cola:

> I took a trip to Florida . . . and in the first day of any trip, I always have to go shopping. I went to Publix, Blockbuster, CVS, the local pizza parlor, and in every place, they were selling or advertising Coke. There is literally always a Coke everywhere you are. It should be the same with AOL: You should always see us. Great marketers can do that.

To achieve brand ubiquity, AOL offered easy-to-install free software and free trial periods (costly software was required to use Prodigy or CompuServe). AOL signed bundling deals with major computer makers (AOL software was then included in their units) and paid a bounty fee for each new subscriber gained (AOL's rivals charged manufacturers for their software). AOL made sure its service was seamlessly integrated with *both* Windows and the Apple operating system. CompuServe and Prodigy were slow to integrate.

AOL capped the effort by mailing millions of free disks to computer users. To this day, you can probably recognize an AOL disk in your mail after only a glance at the package. All told, AOL spent close to a *billion* dollars in marketing its brand name during the 1990s. The money was wisely invested. Today, AOL is one of a tiny handful of truly well-known Internet brands.

Content-Rich

AOL recognized that its service would only be as good as its content. In the early 1990s, AOL had already negotiated several content partnerships and licensing arrangements. In 1994, AOL created Greenhouse, its own content studio, to provide money and guidance for content sites dealing with health, fitness, and other popular topics. The biggest resulting hit: The Motley Fool Web site, which quickly became one of the most popular personal finance/investment sources in any medium and one of the first "killer apps" on the Internet.

AOL's content also derives from scores of media partnerships—magazines, newspapers, and TV networks—as well as on-line shopping partnerships with a huge array of retailers: Barnes & Noble, Lands' End, Sharper Image, and Delta Airlines, among many others. These partnerships give AOL users more reasons to visit the portal, and they generate revenues for AOL through slotting fees and sales commissions. In fact, so valuable has access to AOL's membership rolls become that most content providers now pay AOL rather than charging AOL licensing fees.

Some of the best content on AOL is created by its own members. (This is another example of the active customer at work.) From the start, AOL wanted to create a sense of community for its members. This was done initially through chat rooms, discussion groups, and E-mail. Today, the AOL community has expanded to include instant messaging and buddy lists.

The Dual Domain

In 1994, the game shifted to the Internet, which was just beginning to develop. Prodigy announced that it would provide access to the World Wide Web by the fall of that year—earlier than AOL and therefore a direct challenge to AOL's leadership status.

AOL was torn. It couldn't ignore the Internet, but it feared becoming irrelevant in a world where the unrestricted and rapidly growing Web offered more information and services than AOL—and at a lower cost. Internet service providers (ISPs) offering unlimited access to the Web at a single low monthly rate were blossoming. AOL's response was a unique business design—the Dual Domain. Following a series of investments and acquisitions designed to give it a stronger presence on the Internet, AOL continues to support its own proprietary environment while still offering the entire breadth of the Net.

AOL's new unique value proposition includes an internal and an external domain. The internal domain consists of AOL-owned or -licensed content and partner-owned areas, such as the Web sites of AOL retail partners. The external domain includes all other content on the World Wide Web, such as Yahoo!, eBay.com, and other sites. All can be accessed through the AOL portal.

This model combines the broad access of a traditional ISP with unique services and content available only on AOL. Think of AOL as a kind of value-added ISP, analogous to Schwab's model as a value-added on-line discount broker. This combination of offerings has proved highly popular. The AOL subscriber turnover rate dropped from 50 percent in 1995 to 25 percent in 1998. Customers are spending fully 60 percent of their AOL time in the internal (proprietary) domain.

As a result of AOL's intensive marketing efforts, content development, creation of an on-line community, and embrace of the Internet, AOL membership has grown enormously: from one million in August 1994 to five million (February 1996), ten million (November 1997), and fifteen million (December 1998). In July 2000, the enrollment was 22 million and counting.

By way of comparison, an average prime-time network TV show may garner twenty share points, equivalent to about 12 million viewers. When AOL passed the 10-million-member mark, it morphed into a true mass communications medium, with huge implications for its profit model.

Monetizing Customers

AOL's rapid pace of subscriber growth and the "stickiness" of its content (i.e., its ability to attract and retain eyeballs) would mean little if AOL were unable to monetize those customers. But, compared to other dot-coms, AOL has done a better job of developing a powerful profit model and maintaining strategic control of those profits.

In December 1996, with its customers becoming increasingly restless over per-minute service charges, AOL introduced a monthly unlimited usage fee of $19.95 (now $21.95 per month). These subscription charges remain AOL's largest revenue source (over $3.3 billion in 1999). However, other revenue sources are growing rapidly, especially advertising revenues, and fees and commissions from on-line commerce. These totaled over $1 billion in 1999—twice as much as advertising revenues on the Warner Brothers (WB) television network, and more than the ad revenues of ESPN and ESPN2 combined. Media analyst Tom Wolzien predicts that, by 2003, AOL will generate more ad revenues than either ABC or CBS.

Next Business Issues

Today, at any given moment in prime time, about 1.1 million people are logged onto AOL. That's more viewers than tune in to CNN, CNBC, or The History Channel. To maintain and grow this audience base, AOL must find ways to keep adding value to its customers. Content expansion is the most obvious way.

AOL had basically three options for acquiring content: (1) build its own; (2) "rent" content from partners; or (3) buy content through company acquisitions. The first option would require large in-house investments; the second would risk having to pay ever-increasing prices for the choicest content (think of the spiraling price NBC must pay to renew hit shows like *ER* and *Friends*). Consequently, much like Cisco Systems, AOL has chosen to use acquisitions as its primary technique of R&D.

Recent acquisitions have included former rival CompuServe, Internet browser Netscape, community guide provider Digital City, and music sites Spinner.com and Winamp MovieFone. The largest deal is the agreement to acquire the media empire of Time Warner for $183 billion, which positions AOL to become the world's largest entertainment and media corporation. The deal strengthens AOL's unique value proposition by giving customers access to branded content from Warner Music, Warner Brothers movies, the Turner cable networks, Time, Inc., and so on.

A key tool for distributing AOL's services in the future will be Time Warner's large cable network system, the nation's second-largest (after AT&T) with 13 million subscribers. This will help ensure that AOL does not get locked out of the broadband game. It has also made agreements with Motorola, Sprint, Nokia, and other companies in the wireless market, to further its newest initiative, "AOL Anywhere."

On June 19, 2000, AOL launched AOLTV, a television service that will allow subscribers to send and receive E-mail, surf the Web, and use interactive TV content through set-top boxes and wireless keyboards. AOLTV will be competing with powerful rivals, including AT&T and Microsoft, for the interactive TV market, which some expect will grow to 25 million U.S. households by 2003.

AOL is also expanding internationally, with a 50 percent stake in AOL Europe, AOL Australia, and AOL Japan, as well as partnerships with the major telecom companies in Asia and Latin America. Steve Case's future vision: "To build a global medium as central to people's lives as the telephone or television . . . and even more valuable."

DOT-COM ON THE MOVE: YAHOO!

On-Line Platform

Yahoo! has attained its position as one of the world's best known, most popular, and most profitable Internet players by doing two things exceedingly well: (1) relentlessly focusing on satisfying the needs of its customers, and (2) aggressively promoting its brand name.

The result has been a self-reinforcing business model. Outstanding customer-focused content and great brand recognition generate a large audience, which attracts top-flight advertisers and merchants. Their presence generates more audience members, and *they* continue to build the brand, increase the audience, attract advertisers . . . and so on.

Yahoo! started in 1994 as a free Internet directory created by Jerry Yang and Dave Filo, Stanford grad students who decided to categorize Web sites mainly as a service to the on-line community (though, admittedly, they were motivated in part by dissertation procrastination). Tim Koogle joined the company as CEO in 1995. Revenues from advertising on the Yahoo! site enabled the company to turn a profit in the fourth quarter of 1996, a year ahead of expectations.

Today, Yahoo! boasts the Web's single largest audience (120 million unique users worldwide), the largest directly owned base of registered user profiles (over 100 million), and 465 million average daily page views. Forty million Yahoo! users live in twenty-one countries outside the United States. In December 1999, Yahoo! joined AOL as the second dot-com to be listed in the S&P 500.

Yahoo!s vision: To be the world's largest digital intermediary, or "on-line platform," linking advertisers, merchants, and content providers with a global on-line audience. Here's how they're pursuing that vision.

Customer Focus

Yahoo! has always been surrounded by competitors—initially, Web intermediaries offering tools for searching the Internet that are at least as powerful as Yahoo!s search engine. Yet Yahoo! has managed to out-compete such rivals as Infoseek, Excite, Altavista, and Lycos because of the *quality* of the hits it offers (as opposed to their quantity). As *Fortune* magazine put it, "Yahoo! had the best name, the worst technology, and a quaint belief that while other companies' machines surveyed Web site addresses by the thousand every second, the human touch could somehow win out."

A telling anecdote illustrates the difference in mindset. Once, at an industry conference, then-new Yahoo! CEO Tim Koogle ran into Steve Kirsch, the engineer who headed rival Infoseek. Kirsch bragged that Infoseek's searches "are five seconds faster than yours." Alarmed, Koogle ran back to Jerry Yang, asking, "Is he right?"

He was. But, as Yang explained to Koogle, *it didn't matter.* Yahoo! wasn't in a search-engine contest. It was about helping Web users find what they really wanted—simply, quickly, and reliably. Yahoo!'s indexing feature makes it easier for users to track down the information they want; sites are organized into fourteen categories and dozens of subcategories, which users can navigate at will. And Yahoo! keyword searches tend to turn up fewer irrelevant and useless matches than other portals.

Yahoo! almost lost its way in 1995 when it got caught up in an "arms race" with other Internet portals. "We had [categorized] 5,000 sites, and we were getting into this ridiculous measuring game with other companies." Yahoo! "won" the race by pulling out—it stopped listing the number of sites available. Instead, it challenged customers with the number of useful, relevant hits it provided. This focus on customers' needs helped catapult Yahoo! to the top of its category.

The success of Yahoo! despite its failure to deploy *the* most powerful search engine illustrates a crucial point.

> **The power of your technology is unimportant in itself; what matters is the degree of relevance of your technology to customers' needs.**

Jerry Yang puts it this way: "Technology can be leap-frogged. Brands cannot." Thus, Yahoo! was able to treat technology as a commodity, to be used for a time, then discarded and replaced as necessary. In fact, Yahoo! outsourced technology R&D to Inktomi and chose to focus its own energies on customer service and brand building—the truly crucial aspects of its business scope.

Brand Ubiquity

Yahoo! became the first Internet company to exploit the product-to-brand pattern. Legend has it that the company name was derived from a programmer's jokey acronym: "Yet Another Hierarchical Officious Oracle." True or not, the brand suggests a company and a service that are fun, irreverent, and cool. Marketing analyst Owen Shapiro says, "The name contains the promise of the product. It reinforces the idea that when I go to Yahoo!, I'll be so pleased, I'll be Yahooing afterward."

Yahoo! has tirelessly built the brand name, not by spending hundreds of millions of dollars (like AOL) but through word of mouth and effective public relations programs supported by strategically placed advertising. The Yahoo! logo has been deployed on tins of breath mints, on Slinky spring toys, on parachutes, skateboards, sailboats, surfboards, yo-yos, kazoos, and the Zamboni ice-grooming machine that patrols the San Jose Sharks' hockey arena.

The brand is further reinforced by Yahoo!'s strong commitment to mono-branding: All Yahoo! services must bear the company name: Yahoo! Shopping, Yahoo! Auctions, Yahoo! Finance, and so on.

Content-Rich

To attract and retain customers, Yahoo! has continually refined, expanded, and enhanced its Web site offerings, without losing its emphasis on quick and reliable Internet access. "Every time users returned to Yahoo! for a search, the site seemed to offer some new, cool, and free feature. Stock quotes, maps, chat rooms, news, weather, sports, Yellow Pages, classified ads . . ." (*Fortune* magazine).

Yahoo!'s ever-expanding content array has often come from strategic acquisitions. Among them are:

- ☐ Viaweb Inc. (1998), the foundation for Yahoo!'s on-line shopping initiatives (Yahoo! Store).
- ☐ GeoCities (1999), a Web community brand and the fifth most frequently visited Internet site.
- ☐ Broadcast.com (1999), an audio/video Internet broadcaster.

Another content source has been Yahoo!'s 1,000-plus partnerships with content providers, ranging from ESPN and Reuters to The Street.com and infoUSA.com. These form the basis for such services as Yahoo! Finance, Yahoo! News, Yahoo! Sports, Yahoo! Music, Yahoo! Politics, Yahoo! Pets, and many more.

Yahoo!'s customers are themselves content providers who create on-line information using message boards, chat rooms, E-mail, and such specialized services as Yahoo! Calendar, Yahoo! Clubs, Yahoo! Invites, and Yahoo! Photos.

Monetizing Customers

Advertising generates 70 percent of Yahoo!'s revenues, which totaled $589 million in 1999. Banner ad rates currently range from $6-per-thousand impressions for run-of-network ads to $90-per-thousand impressions for highly targeted audiences. Yahoo! has some 3,675 advertising customers and gleaned an average of $73,500 in revenues from each during the second quarter of 2000 (60% higher than the figure for the previous year).

E-commerce is an increasingly important part of Yahoo!'s business model. Yahoo! Shopping, launched in 1998, now features 10,500 merchants who pay the portal a percentage of the sales generated on-site. For the 1999 holiday season, Yahoo! Wallet and Yahoo! Express Checkout were launched. They enabled quick and simple purchasing across thousands of participating merchants. Yahoo! Auctions lists 2.5 million items across over 3,700 product categories, and Yahoo! Classifieds has grown to several million listings.

Having attracted millions of Internet users through the ease and reliability of its services, Yahoo! retains them, in part, through the customization it offers and through the sheer power of its brand name. One Yahoo! customer explains:

> I've invested a lot of time to set up my Yahoo! services the way I like them. I have no interest in setting all that up again on another site. Not to mention that tons of my friends know my Yahoo! E-mail address. The second reason I stay with Yahoo! is that I'm confident that, as the market leader, it's always going to be ahead of the curve in terms of services offered and the overall scope of the site. Every day I see them coming out with new things. As the site with the deepest pockets and best brand name recognition, they're in the best position to offer premium service and to still be around in ten years, which is comforting to know.

Breaking through to the number-one brand-name position in a rapidly evolving business arena like the Internet can be in itself a powerful source of strategic control.

Next Business Issues

Yahoo! is clearly an Internet success story, with 1999 sales of $589 million (up 189 percent over the previous year) and profits of $61 million (up 139 percent). But the challenges ahead are substantial.

Yahoo!'s business model has evolved rapidly. It used to compete only with other free-service search engines such as Excite, Lycos, and Infoseek. Yahoo! now competes against portals like AOL, MSN, Go.com, and such specialized players as eBay and iVillage.

This is a challenging arena in which to play. A recent Media Metrix report ranked Yahoo! fifteenth in user loyalty among the Internet's top Web sites—not a comfortable standing. AOL users spend an average of fifty-six minutes each time they visit; the figure for Yahoo! is just twelve minutes, and it *must* improve to prevent advertising revenues from deteriorating. But how? Yahoo! currently strives to offer "all things to all people"—a difficult position to maintain. It's not yet clear how Yahoo! will effectively specialize so as to become a true destination site (and an e-commerce venue) for millions of Internet users.

Pressure on Yahoo!'s advertising revenues is likely to increase in the near term. Ad rates per 1,000 hits are already falling, and some industry analysts predict that, by 2003, half of all on-line advertising will be sold on a performance-based system rather than the current flat-rate system.

Yahoo! has one of the strongest positions of any Internet-based company, but maintaining this advantage during the next five years will take at least one major reinvention of its business design.

DOT-COM ON THE MOVE: eBAY

Accidental Empire

Pierre Omidyar launched eBay as a result of a conversation with his wife, an avid collector of Pez candy dispensers. She remarked how great it would be if she had some easy way to talk and trade at a distance with other collectors. An early Internet enthusiast, Omidyar launched eBay on Labor Day, 1995, in response to this wish. Six months later, to cover his costs and pay for his time, he began charging a small listing fee and receiving a small percentage of each sale as a commission.

Essentially, eBay developed a great business design by accident. Acting as an auction switchboard, and incurring no manufacturing, distribution, or marketing costs, eBay became very profitable very quickly. Today, eBay is the world's largest personal on-line trading community and has created a new marketplace; it offers efficient one-to-one trading in an auction format on the Web. Individuals and a growing number of small businesses use eBay to buy and sell items in thousands of categories: antiques, sports memorabilia, computers, toys, dolls, coins, stamps, books, music, photography, jewelry, paintings, and much more. Because eBay is the leading consumer-to-consumer (C2C) trading site, collectors are compelled to trade on eBay because that's where the great bulk of desirable items is available. Each day, over 400,000 new items are offered, and more than 3.5 million auctions are in progress on eBay.

Strategic Control

As the pioneer of on-line C2C auctions, eBay had definite first-mover advantages: critical mass efficiencies, economies of scale, and some degree of strategic control. But (particularly on the Internet), being a first mover doesn't guarantee any sustained advantage. By 1996, any of a number of fast followers—Ubid, Ebid, 4Utobid, Mybid!, Atozbid—could have become today's eBay. But eBay invented a means of strategic control by recognizing and implementing a potential solution to a crucial problem of the on-line auction marketplace.

The problem: How to establish the *credibility* of on-line buyers, sellers, and products. Without face-to-face contact and the time- and labor-intensive authenticating process used by traditional off-line auction houses, eBayers (as they call themselves) worried about how to avoid fraud or simple sloppiness when buying on-line. The eBayers themselves (in their role as active customers) provided the solution. In 1996, in messages posted to Omidyar, they began proposing a system whereby buyers and sellers could rate one another.

The system was duly launched and has evolved into the Feedback Forum, which has been compared to a "peer-review credit-rating system." Every eBay buyer and seller develops a Feedback Profile, including a numerical score, that reflects the experience of other eBayers in doing business with that person. High-scoring individuals attract more business; low-scoring individuals are shunned.

The system itself is a huge value creator for both eBay and its customers. Peter Kollack, a UCLA sociology professor who has been studying eBay, says early findings suggest that buyers are willing to pay up to 30 percent more for items sold by individuals with high feedback ratings. As we'll see, the system is not foolproof and is currently facing a significant public relations challenge, but it has been largely reliable and is one of eBay's major sources of strategic control.

The Feedback Forum solution solidified eBay's position as the leading on-line auction house and one of the few profitable dot-coms. The individual reliability ratings help people feel comfortable doing business on eBay and encourage repeat business. As a result, eBay blossomed. Satisfied buyers and sellers brought friends. Over time, a collection of hundreds of on-line communities developed, each centered around a particular obsession: Beanie Babies, rock 'n' roll memorabilia, Appalachian folk art, antique teddy bears—whatever. Supported by message boards and chat-rooms, a newsletter, and an on-line library of informational articles, eBay communities have become *the* home base for millions of aficionados in hundreds of subject fields. As one eBayer, a collector of antique wood-working tools, puts it, "I wouldn't mind buying and selling tools some-where else—on the Web or off-line—but everyone I do business with is *here* now. Why would I go elsewhere?"

Customer Self-Service

The eBay community of communities has become a self-sustaining business design in which customers do most of their own marketing and customer service. The auctions themselves are run by the eBayers with minimal oversight and control by the company, and the feedback system, which creates "eBay reputations" for millions of users, encourages loyalty to the company. The word-of-mouth communication fosters further growth for eBay. Each auction page has a link that allows users to E-mail the auction to a friend (and thereby spread more awareness).

eBayers comment on the self-perpetuating nature of the eBay system. One toy collector with the on-line moniker Frantic-city says, "As a seller, you know that the number of hits [on eBay] is extensive. If you place an item for sale on a lesser known site, the chance of getting the best price is less." Hence, Frantic-city is unlikely to want to sell any item elsewhere. Another collector known as Trixie00 comments:

> I trade on eBay because they are the biggest auction site on the Web. I collect Snoopy, and I have found so many things on eBay that my Snoopy collection is now over 2,000 pieces and growing every week. As for selling, everyone I know has heard of eBay. I know when I put something up for sale it is going to be seen by a lot of people, thus giving me the chance to make more profits.

eBay customers also service themselves; for example, experienced members coach novices on the eBay message boards. The opportunities offered to active customers to serve and market themselves and one another are so attractive that eBay grew rapidly with no national advertising campaign until October 1998.

Ever-Widening Scope

Recognizing the power and potential value of the business design its originators stumbled onto, eBay is moving to establish an infrastructure that can serve as a global platform for trading almost anything anywhere. The expansion of eBay's business scope includes the following shifts:

☐ **Rapid expansion of product categories.** In 1995, eBay offered products in ten categories. By 1998, the number had expanded to 1,500. In 2000, the number is over 4,300 and continues to grow.

- **From collectibles-only to practical everyday goods.** Today, 60 percent of the merchandise sales on eBay involve noncollectible items like cars, computers, and sports equipment.
- **From casual sellers to power sellers.** It's estimated that at least 20,000 Americans now make selling on eBay a full-time job, accounting for up to 80 percent of eBay's total business. Some sell tens of thousands of dollars of merchandise every month.
- **From C2C-only to B2C.** As part of its Power Seller Program, eBay works with small businesses to create virtual storefronts within eBay Web sites. Information about these businesses, their products, and current auctions is provided.
- **Moving into the B2B market.** Launched in March 2000, the eBay Business Exchange auctions more than 60,000 products (computer gear, office equipment, tools, electronics) in thirty-four business-related categories.
- **Globalization.** eBay now has more than 200,000 registered users in ninety countries outside of the United States. It has launched home pages in the UK, Canada, Australia, Germany, and Japan.
- **Localization.** In 1999, eBay launched Local Trading, a network of fifty-three regional sites around the United States, to encourage the sale of: items that are too bulky or fragile to ship, items of purely local interest (concert tickets), and items people prefer to view before buying.

Partnerships and Acquisitions

Growth has also come through relationships with other companies. eBay now has over 200 on-line partnerships, including a $75-million deal with AOL, a four-year joint promotional agreement with Go.com, and a joint venture with Autotrade.com that aims to create the Internet's largest auction-style marketplace for used cars.

Acquisitions have enabled eBay to move into specific vertical markets. In 1999, eBay acquired Krause International, one of the largest off-line auctioneers of collectible cars. The acquisition led to the launch of eBay's Motors site, which sells collectible cars.

In the same year, eBay bought Butterfield & Butterfield, the world's fourth largest off-line auctioneer of fine arts and collectibles. This permitted the launch of eBay Great Collections, which showcases high-quality items from dealers and auction houses around the world. eBay hopes to make inroads into the high-end auction world, where the economics differ greatly from those of eBay's traditional business. The average eBay auction results in a $47 sale price (of which $3 goes to eBay). The average Butterfield auction closes at $1,400 (of which $400 goes to Butterfield).

Flexibility and Opportunism

The key to eBay's success may be its flexibility—its readiness to move opportunistically to identify and solve problems and to morph its business design in response to customers' concerns. Like its quick response to the credentialing issue, which resulted in the Feedback Forum solution, eBay has taken other steps to strengthen its business design. Among them are:

- □ An eBay **escrow service** (with partner I-Escrow) provides added security by holding merchandise for buyers to inspect and approve before closing the deal.
- □ Partner SquareTrade provides a **dispute resolution service.** A trained mediator works with buyers and sellers to settle any differences.
- □ Partner Lloyd's of London provides **insurance for sellers.**
- □ Partner Equifax provides **identity verification.**
- □ Billpoint service, initially provided to 5,000 power sellers, facilitates secure on-line **credit card acceptance** by eBay sellers.

Next Business Issues

eBay's 1999 net income was almost $11 million on revenues of $225 million. Astoundingly, after going public in September 1998, at an offering price of $18 per share, the company now trades at over $200 per share and has a total market cap of over $15 billion. (Both figures have been quite volatile during the first half of 2000.) But eBay's enormous valuation poses one of the key business issues it faces: What can the company do to grow into its outsized market cap? As we've seen, the company is widening its scope in many ways—e.g., through the B2B initiative, the Butterfield acquisition, and the provision of other services—but will all this be enough to produce the rapid growth that the stock price requires?

eBay faces a number of potentially powerful competitors in the on-line auction business. Amazon and Yahoo!, for example, which have huge audiences, are aggressively promoting their auction sites, and Amazon is currently offering free product listings as a customer lure. A new twist is the so-called "mega auction sites," where potential customers can name items they seek and then search *all* on-line auctions for availability. Such sites could eventually break down the loyalty of eBayers.

So far, the competition has made little headway; eBay currently retains fully 88 percent of the on-line auction market. But can the company continue to evolve fast enough to retain its customer base?

Continued growth poses its own problems. At the core of eBay's success is its on-line community, which makes both buyers and sellers feel at home there. Can eBay retain this close-knit feeling as the size and complexity of the system increase? There may already be rumblings of dissatisfaction among some eBayers. Barry Goldberg, who collects antique pocket watches, had these comments:

> What drew me to eBay in the first place was that it was all about people with unique items finding buyers with unique needs. That's all changing now. eBay is giving people incentives to become retailers on the site and to sell brand-new retail merchandise. It's turning into a more impersonal site. When I do a search now, I'll get hundreds of identical retail items. It clutters things up.

The Valuation Issue

The bottom line may be that eBay is a nice *small* business—quite profitable, but unlikely to grow into its current inflated stock price value unless it is *dramatically* reinvented. The moves it has been making will not suffice to justify a $15 to $20 billion valuation. Can eBay find a way to develop a huge new source of value from the networks of relationships, customer communities, and buyer–seller information it has built?

THE DOT-COM CHALLENGE

Remember cold fusion? It was a scientific breakthrough, announced with much fanfare, that supposedly overturned the laws of physics and ushered in a new age of virtually cost-free, unlimited energy. Unfortunately, in the years since its inventors held their first press conference, no one has been able to replicate their work, and the scientific and technical communities have returned to other pursuits.

We're writing in mid-2000, a time of stock market turmoil that has severely buffeted many of the dot-com superstars of 1998 and 1999. There is no way to predict with precision the future gyrations of the market, but one conclusion seems increasingly clear: The era of cold fusion in business is over.

> **Dot-com valuations will no longer remain at astronomical levels in the absence of sustainable profit models, strategic control, and the other elements of sound business design.**

This doesn't doom the Internet to being a business graveyard. The successes of AOL, Yahoo!, and eBay demonstrate that it's possible for Internet businesses to be profitable, as long as they have:

- ☐ A clearly-thought-out selection of customers.
- ☐ A unique value proposition with which to attract those customers.
- ☐ A value capture/profit model that makes sense and is sustainable.
- ☐ A basis for maintaining strategic control over their profits and customer relationships.

- □ Willingness, ability, and courage to evolve quickly in response to new competitive challenges, customer changes, technological innovations, and market shifts.

The last element listed is a special challenge for many of the dot-coms. Often headed by youthful executives who have never lived through (let alone managed their way through) a major recession or stock market downturn, and who may be technologically oriented rather than customer-focused and business-focused, hundreds of dot-coms will be facing their greatest challenge in the next one to three years. Can they withstand adversity? Will they respond effectively to tumbling share prices, invigorated assaults by industry incumbents, unexpected demands from customers, regulatory and legal challenges, and public relations missteps? In short, do they have the smarts, flexibility, integrity, and instincts needed to enable them to evolve sound business designs as a foundation for their technological prowess?

One shared characteristic of AOL, Yahoo!, and eBay has been their ability to establish brands and to evolve in response to external change:

- □ AOL faced down challenges from competitors such as Prodigy, CompuServe, and Microsoft; developed a strategy for embracing the Internet without being rendered irrelevant; and morphed into a mass media company fueled by sales of great content and advertising revenues.
- □ Yahoo! outperformed a host of competing (often superior) technologies. In the process, it evolved from an Internet search engine to a portal and to a brand and a content provider, and is now engaged in a new evolution into an e-commerce service provider and merchant.
- □ eBay moved opportunistically to expand its services in response to consumer demands, and to devise an unfolding series of solutions to customers' concerns about the reliability, security, and safety of its offerings.

eBay currently faces one of its most serious challenges. The press is trumpeting charges that rings of "shill bidders" are abetting fraud on eBay by jacking up auction prices on one another's offerings. Some say that rings of sellers also fraudulently enhance each other's feedback ratings with phony cross-endorsements. In response, eBay has launched investigations and suspended or expelled some members. There's no evidence that fraud in on-line auctions is more widespread or serious than in traditional off-line auctions. But because of the relative newness of the Internet, it will be important for eBay, as the industry leader, to be seen as moving decisively to lay the legal and ethical issues to rest.

This isn't the first time the dot-coms have faced such problems. AOL successfully navigated a similar challenge in 1996, when the Communications Decency Act (CDA) was passed by Congress in response to a perceived crisis of on-line pornography. (AOL defended free speech on the Internet, and the CDA was declared unconstitutional by the U.S. Supreme Court the following year.) Similar problems can be expected in the future—perhaps over state and federal taxation of e-commerce, for example.

Internet-based businesses must be prepared to address the same kinds of unexpected, unpredictable, often seemingly unfair business challenges that traditional companies have always faced. Responding to these challenges successfully will be a matter not so much of technology as of foresight, flexibility, integrity, and courage. Today's dot-com leaders will be tested on all these fronts in the years ahead.

15

THE DIGITAL ORGANIZATION

THE ORGANIZATION OF THE FUTURE:
A PRELIMINARY SKETCH

The development of the digital organization is still in its early stages. Its state of evolution might be compared with that of the twentieth-century corporation in 1920–1921, when Pierre S. DuPont was designing DuPont as one of the first modern corporations. Today, a host of individual changes fostered by digitization in every area of business activity, from sales and marketing to recruiting and management, from design and manufacturing to customer service and finance, are accumulating, interacting, and catalyzing one another so as to produce broader changes that are fundamental. Early forms of the digital organization of the future can be seen in companies like those profiled in this book. They predict a different *kind* of organization than the now-traditional corporation pioneered in the early years of the twentieth century.

In this chapter, we are not attempting a finished portrait of this new digital organization. Instead, we offer a series of sketches to suggest some key aspects of its emergence, including how it is taking shape and some of the qualities that will distinguish it from organizations of the past.

PARTNERING AT THE TOP

How does a new form of business design emerge from an older model? In a world where businesses designed along traditional lines have been successful, and where business schools, books and magazines, corporate mentors, cultures, and histories all combine to reinforce the "tried and true," how do design innovations occur?

Our examination of the digital innovators as well as of exceptionally innovative incumbents, like GE, that are rapidly following them into the Northeast quadrant, suggests a pattern.

> **Companies that are innovators of Digital Business Design are generally headed by a CEO who is *business-centric* rather than *technology-centric,* and who is working in close partnership with a CIO who understands the principles of good business design.**

The backgrounds of the CEOs who head the digital innovators we've profiled in this book illustrate that, for a company eager to migrate to the Northeast quadrant, the most effective leader is someone steeped in the importance of customer needs and business imperatives rather than someone focused on technology alone.

But digitizing a large organization—building bit engines to leverage talent and serve customers; reinventing internal and external processes around bits rather than atoms; and so on—requires a powerful fund of technological understanding. This is why a strong partnership with a forward-looking CIO is so crucial. Such a partnership exists in virtually every digital (or digitizing) organization we've studied·

Organization	CEO	CIO Partner
Cemex	Lorenzo Zambrano	Gelacio Iniguez
Cisco	John Chambers	Peter Solvik
Dell	Michael Dell	Randy Mott
GE	Jack Welch	Gary Reiner
IBM	Lou Gerstner	Stephen Ward
Schwab	David Pottruck	Dawn Lepore

Similar partnerships exist in the handful of profitable dot-coms operating in the Northeast quadrant. For example, AOL's Steve Case is supported by technology maven Bill Raduchel, and Yahoo!'s Tim Koogle has Farzad Nazem.

What makes such a partnership possible, and what must a business leader do to make it effective? There are several key requirements:

☐ The CEO *and* the CIO must focus on the customer and the elements of **good business design** first, technology second. They must understand that digitization is valuable *only* if it enhances the value proposition for the customer and the talent, the company's profit model and strategic control, and the other crucial factors of DBD.

☐ The CEO and the CIO must share **a clear vision and focus** as to the company's key business issues and how its business design needs to change to address those issues.

☐ The CEO and the CIO must communicate in **a common language** when they discuss their concerns, problems, needs, plans, and vision for their company's internal and external development.

The requirement for a common language may seem obvious, but it can be surprisingly difficult to achieve. Because CEOs and CIOs generally come from such different educational backgrounds and business cultures, finding ways to avoid subtle misunderstandings, confusion, resentment, and conflicts can be a significant challenge. (This difficulty reflects a problem endemic to technological society, as described decades ago in C.P. Snow's seminal essay about the "Two Cultures" of the modern world—the culture of science and that of the humanities—which relatively few people can successfully bridge.)

Schwab's David Pottruck has analyzed this problem thoughtfully. In his book *Clicks and Mortar,* he has suggested a vocabulary for the different languages spoken by technical and nontechnical managers. Technologists, he has found, tend to communicate in terms that are *literal* and *granular;* nontechnical businesspeople tend to be *metaphorical* and *general.* Partly as a result, technologists will tend to think in terms of developing processes and solutions that are *complete* and *complex,* where a generalist might opt for *sufficient* and *simple.*

Such differences in outlook may be inevitable, but misunderstandings arise when the two managers are *unaware* that they are speaking different languages. The technologist responds to a request for a new business solution by saying, "That can't be done" (taking the outline of the idea more literally than intended), and the generalist replies, "Well, just find a way to do it!" (thinking, perhaps, that the technologist is stonewalling or protecting proprietary turf). With such conflicts at the outset, head butting and mutual antagonism tend to snowball. The project may eventually get done, but at twice the budgeted cost and in three times the acceptable time.

By contrast, when both sides work together toward sharing information, putting the technological needs into business and customer contexts, and analyzing what's really wanted rather than making assumptions, they often discover that most of their needs can be met in much less time and at a fraction of the cost. For this huge payoff, the price is the time invested upfront to create a common language and a common focus on the business issues that will define the company's future.

Creating a successful CEO–CIO partnership, then, requires leaders who are willing to learn, grow, and adapt to achieve their common goal. What is *not* required is a detailed preliminary roadmap for the process. Companies that have successfully reinvented their business designs generally have *not* known from the start exactly how their organization would change. Instead, they have launched the process with a broad direction in mind, kept in clear focus the specific business issues and general strategies they were addressing, and figured out the details as they went.

One key reality of business life is the fact that today's technology is changing so rapidly. A bit engine created today is almost certain to be obsolete tomorrow, and adaptations in tomorrow's technology will surely yield fresh opportunities to improve responses to customers' wants. Flexibility, openness, courage, and mutual trust are essential if this unavoidable learn-as-we-go process is to succeed.

For the pioneering companies that are now in the process of reinventing themselves along digital lines, our choice for an apt historical model for leadership would not be one of the great solitaries—a general like Grant or Lee, or a statesman like Washington or Lincoln. We would choose a partnership, like that of the great explorers Lewis and Clark. Historian Stephen Ambrose, in his classic narrative *Undaunted Courage,* shows how their expedition through the vast and unknown reaches of the American West succeeded—without losing a single team member—because the two leaders had complementary skills, an intuitive ability to communicate and share responsibility, and utter trust in one another.

INTERNAL MARKETING

The movement to Digital Business Design generally begins with a complementary team at the top of the organization, but it cannot succeed unless the entire organization is aligned behind it. How can the leadership communicate its energy and its commitment to digital business to hundreds, thousands, or tens of thousands people throughout the enterprise?

Making a shift from conventional to Digital Business Design is not easy. It's certainly no easier than, for example, introducing a dramatically new product into a market crowded with established competitors and quickly seizing the leadership position. No one would contemplate embarking on such an effort without a carefully planned, well-financed, creatively packaged, and intelligently honed marketing plan. And once launched, the effort would never be quietly abandoned after a few weeks or allowed to drift without energy and focus. It would rightly be a major focus of the CEO and the entire team for a matter of months, or even years. Whatever is necessary to make it work would be done.

Moving a company to digitization demands a marketing effort that is as thoroughly planned, well-supported, and tenaciously pursued as a major new-product launch. Such an important and complete shift cannot succeed without *brilliant* internal marketing to the company's own people.

Unless a major change can be accomplished first in the minds of your people, it will never be accomplished in your business.

INTERNAL AND EXTERNAL MARKETING

What exactly is internal marketing?

Internal marketing, like external marketing, is a process of changing people's thinking, attitudes, and behaviors, but directed toward your own organization's talent base—your *internal customers.*

The guiding precepts behind *both* internal and external marketing are:

☐ Know your customers.
☐ Create the right message.
☐ Embody the message in a simple and compelling form that is meaningful to your customers.
☐ Repeat that message seven hundred times.

Every dollar and every hour you invest in internal marketing has a multiplied value for your external relationships. When one of your people, having accepted and mastered a new digital capability, uses it to develop a better way of resolving customer complaints, the new method may be applied fifty times during the next month, potentially saving and expanding fifty customer relationships. The dollar value of the attitudinal shift underlying the behavioral change is difficult to compute but potentially enormous.

Internal marketing is more than just training. Both activities involve communication with your own people, and both aim to change thinking, attitudes, and behaviors in specific ways. But training is focused essentially on *making people better able to do their current job.* Thus, five hours spent in a seminar on how to conduct performance reviews, or thirty hours in a workshop on Six Sigma quality, constitute training. By contrast, internal marketing is designed to facilitate a major change in the business. The focus essentially is on *making people understand, accept, and devote their energies to changing how they do their job.*

The great internal marketers in business can be counted on the fingers of one hand: Jack Welch (GE), Steve Ballmer (Microsoft), Herb Kelleher (Southwest Airlines), Scott McNealy (Sun Microsystems), and Michael Dell (Dell Computer). They became spokespersons for their industries and for business in general because, despite the pressures of other business issues to which they could have easily devoted themselves, they recognized that communicating the heart of their company's strategy—internally and externally—is their most important work. And they insist tenaciously on living by that truth.

There are only a few great internal marketers because everyone in business has a day job (and usually a night job, too). The day job is the agenda of sales meetings, planning conferences, financial reviews, problem-solving sessions, client presentations, and so on, that more than fills the typical manager's day. "Internal marketing" is rarely even listed, much less defined, in anyone's job description. It's a task that easily gets overlooked altogether.

CREATING ORGANIZATIONAL MOMENTUM

Ignoring internal marketing is an incredibly costly mistake. Without it, two outputs essential to implementing any strategy—including going digital—simply won't exist. They are:

- ☐ Raw organizational energy and emotion.
- ☐ Organizational alignment behind the strategy.

> Together, *energy* and *alignment* create *Organizational Momentum* in the strategic direction toward which the company hopes to move.

This truth underlies successful change efforts of all kinds, in both traditional and digital businesses. Great organizations have always done a superlative job of generating enormous organizational energy and then focusing it toward strategic goals. The only way to do this is through communicating, listening, modifying the message based on what has been learned, and then reinforcing and repeating the message—in short, through internal marketing.

Southwest Airlines

Many of the great internal marketing stories grow out of one person's remarkable leadership instincts. Herb Kelleher of Southwest Airlines is an example. A great storyteller, Kelleher has helped to create and nurture a culture in which narratives of heroic service, employee creativity, and positive human connections between Southwest and its customers inspire employees and focus their energy toward the organization's strategic goals.

This much is not unusual. But in 1990, unwilling to leave this crucial element of the company's success to chance, Southwest created a Culture Committee, described (in *Nuts!* by Kevin and Jackie Freiberg) as "an inspired team of more than a hundred storytellers who are the company's cultural ambassadors and missionaries." It's one of the few standing committees tolerated at the famously antibureaucratic Southwest, and its members range from flight attendants to vice presidents. The Culture Committee represents Southwest's deliberate commitment *not* to allow internal marketing to be overlooked in the intense competition for time, energy, and resources that occurs within every organization.

Cemex

The digital pioneers have learned from the great internal marketers among nondigital businesses. We've already observed how Cemex is growing rapidly through acquisition of other cement companies. This requires a continual, ongoing process of digitizing formerly nondigital businesses—a process in which revolution is routine. To make this activity practical, Cemex invests significantly in communication and training for *all* employees, with a special focus on those at newly acquired companies. The education includes not only technical skills that are useful in their current jobs but also more general business knowledge: how to read a spreadsheet, how to analyze a P&L statement, how the investment markets influence business finance. Few companies consider these concepts important for rank-and-file employees, but they are essential for recognizing and acting on the profit potential in a digitized company.

Every employee in a newly acquired company must master the details of Cemex's Digital Business Design within sixty days of the acquisition.

Compare that with the glacial pace at which most merged companies integrate their systems and processes (if they ever do integrate them), let alone their corporate cultures. Cemex understands that the digital DNA of its business is at the heart of its productivity. Positive and decisive steps are taken to transmit that DNA quickly and accurately.

THE COMMUNICATION DISCONNECT

A reasonably successful company in the field of networked solutions consulted us for help in carrying out its business strategy. As formulated and communicated to us by the CEO and his top management team, the strategy appeared sound and even exciting. But the power of the idea had evaporated somewhere between conceptualization and implementation.

When we began talking with people around the organization, as well as key customers and suppliers, the explanation proved all too simple. The Communication Disconnect we discovered in this company was exactly similar to the one we've encountered in dozens of other companies:

- □ The CEO announces, "Our strategy is A."
- □ The sales force says, "Our strategy is B."
- □ The customers say, "Their strategy is C."

If your organization suffers from this kind of Communication Disconnect, then your business strategy is *not* Strategy A, no matter what your CEO may earnestly believe. It's not even Strategy B, despite the sincerity and eloquence of your sales force. In reality, your strategy is something between Strategy B and Strategy C. Strategy isn't what's announced; strategy is what actually happens.

By contrast, consider a story told by a senior executive from a leading national retailer. He happened to take an airline seat next to an administrative assistant from one of the many divisions of General Electric. He asked her, "What's new at GE?" and received in reply a clear explanation of the company's latest strategic direction—which turned out to be exactly as described by Jack Welch in an interview in the next issue of *Fortune*.

In this respect, every organization needs to emulate GE.

> **Invest time and energy to communicate your strategy and business design so clearly and so continuously that every member of your organization is on the same page as the CEO.**

THE INTERNAL MARKETING INVESTMENT

If internal marketing is an investment, then it must be possible to *underinvest* in it—just as it's possible to underinvest in equipment (hanging on to antiquated or inefficient machinery rather than replacing it), research (failing to explore ways of improving your products or services), quality (underreacting to customers' complaints about defects), or any other vital business function.

Almost all companies *do* underinvest in internal marketing—usually by a factor of ten. That's why most firms that attempt to move from conventional to digital in the next five years will fail: Right idea, right strategy, right program, but little or no internal marketing.

If you think your company may be an exception to this rule, consider the amount of organizational time, resources, and energy that it would devote to preparing a presentation for each of the following audiences:

1. Analysts who follow your company's stock for the half-dozen most influential Wall Street firms.
2. Your biggest customer or a major prospect that you hope to capture from your competition.
3. A group of highly-sought-after potential recruits—for example, MBAs about to graduate from one of the nation's top ten schools.
4. A gathering of current employees who are about to be introduced to the company's new strategy.

If your company is like many others, the relative allocation of available time, resources, and energy for these four presentations (with a maximum effort indexed at 100) would be roughly:

1. Wall Street analysts: 100
2. Biggest customer/Major prospect: 60
3. Potential recruits: 30
4. Current employees: 10

This distribution makes little sense. In the new digital age, the most important resource is the talent of your people. If you energize that talent and align it consistently in the direction of your organization's goals, there will be little that you can't accomplish. If you don't invest enough, there will be little that you *can* accomplish.

Smart companies moving from conventional practices to Digital Business Design invest ridiculous amounts of personal energy in marketing the ideas to the organization. Without that investment, they'd never get there, because their people wouldn't know:

☐ *Why* they have to change.
☐ *What* they must do, individually, to contribute to the change process.
☐ *What's in it for them.*

The last point is the most important. Remember that internal marketing and external marketing are *not* fundamentally different. You wouldn't dream of marketing a new product, service, or business concept to external customers with a message like, "Buy from us because we want you to," or "Buy from us so we can make lots of money." Yet, *most businesses* market change internally by delivering equivalent messages. Management explains the need for change by saying things like, "Going digital will enable us to compete more effectively," or " . . . will increase our profit margins." Messages like these will motivate only a fraction of the talent base. Why? Because the employee benefit—what's in it for them—is hidden rather than explicit.

Instead, you must spell out—explicitly and frequently—how change will directly benefit your internal customers as well as your external customers.

THE SIMPLE MESSAGE

One hallmark of a great marketer—whether external or internal marketing is being considered—is a focus on a single, extremely clear message, often encapsulated in a pithy but memorable phrase. Jack Welch is the preeminent example. Not only everyone at GE but almost everyone in the business world now knows the phrases that encapsulate Welch's internal marketing messages: "Number One or Number Two," "Work-Out," "Six Sigma," "Destroy your business." Welch has been so consistent and tenacious about repeating these themes that their wisdom has infiltrated (and been imitated by) scores of other organizations.

The late Sam Walton was equally effective at communicating a simple, clear business idea. Thanks to his decades of preaching the idea of "Customer advocacy," everyone at Wal-Mart, down to the most obscure clerk in a store in North Dakota, knew that the whole idea of the business was to get a lower price for the customer. Millions of Wal-Mart's customers came to know it, too.

Is there a danger in trying to reduce a major organizational initiative to a three- or four-word phrase? There can be. Albert Einstein once remarked, "Everything should be made as simple as possible, but not more so." Details are obviously lost when a complex idea is encapsulated in a few words. Yet Einstein's own ideas (which no one has complained are "too simple") are memorably evoked in the phrases "Relativity theory" and "$E = mc^2$." Even his characteristic intellectual technique is described in the simple and oft-used phrase, "Thought experiment."

The key is to devote time, energy, and creativity to crafting, honing, and simplifying the message. Like many companies, you may spend millions on consumer advertising or on designing a logo. Developing the right message for the internal marketing of a crucial change in your business is no less important.

REPEAT YOURSELF

A smart internal marketer learns to do what the most effective politicians do: Stay on the message, no matter what. Repetition of the same idea may become boring for the politician's staff (and for the reporters traveling with the politician and attending rally after rally, speech after speech), but it's the only way of ensuring that the vital theme has a chance of breaking through the clutter of other messages that inundate voters—including the opposing candidates' countercharges.

When you are marketing a new idea, sheer numbers matter.

> **Estimate how often you need to communicate your message; then multiply your estimate by ten.**

We sometimes say: Communicate your message not once or twice but 700 times. We promise you: The 700th time you make The Speech, use The Slogan, or hammer home The Idea, *someone in the room will grasp it for the first time.* It's virtually impossible to overrepeat your most important message.

> **Communicate any important message not for a few weeks or months, but for at least one to two years.**

If you are a key decision maker in your organization, you and the people you work with most closely will probably become bored with the message long before everyone in your organization understands, accepts, and lives by it. Don't allow your boredom to affect how you communicate. It's highly tempting to begin varying the message, changing the carefully crafted language, adding new wrinkles, throwing in related concepts, or even skipping the key idea altogether, simply because you find the basic message so mind-numbingly familiar that you assume everyone else does, too. *They don't.*

Real organizational communication—not just the sending of a memo but the understanding and absorption of the ideas it contains—is remarkably slow. It takes much longer than you'd expect for any idea, and especially a really new idea, to permeate every cell of an organization.

The pharmaceutical industry has developed a shrewd understanding of the importance of the time element in marketing any idea. When a new medication is approved for sale, marketers begin the "premarketing" process by preparing the ground *eighteen months in advance*. They disseminate information among physicians and other health care providers, members of hospital formulary boards, state regulators, pharmacists, insurance companies and HMOs, and others whose attitudes may impact the success of the drug.

The pharmaceutical firms have learned that it takes a long time and multiple exposures for a customer (of any kind) to (1) understand a new idea, (2) become accustomed to it, (3) recognize its implications for his or her situation, and then (4) become a supporter. Rather than fighting this truth, these firms accept it and work with it. The same time-dependent sequence applies to internal marketing.

THE IRREDUCIBLE MINIMUM

To summarize, internal marketing means:

- □ *Not* just the CEO . . . *but* the top 200 managers.
- □ *Not* just transmitting a message . . . *but* listening and adjusting as well.
- □ *Not* a complex message . . . *but* a simple, concise, and memorable one.
- □ *Not* communicating once or twice . . . *but* 700 times.
- □ *Not* ten or twenty messages . . . *but* one at a time.
- □ *Not* marketing for a few weeks or months . . . *but* for one to two years.

Of all the obstacles that prevent companies from successfully achieving the digital transformation, failure to market internally is surely the most pervasive. It's also the most readily fixable—if the will to fix it is there.

LEVERAGING YOUR TALENT

It's a truism of the Information Age that ideas, not physical assets, are now the driving force of growth and profit. Interestingly, at the moment in history when the economic system called capitalism has triumphantly swept aside competing systems and won the assent of virtually every nation on earth, a central premise of that system—the predominant role of capital as the source of wealth—has begun to crumble. At one time, the wealth of General Motors could be measured by the size of its factories; that of Standard Oil, by the value of its petroleum reserves; that of Sears, by the vastness of its real estate holdings. These are still great companies. But, as value creators, they have been surpassed by the likes of Microsoft, Dell, and Cisco, whose physical assets represent only a small fraction of their worth. The methods, systems, channels, and techniques they have developed for managing bits—in a word, their *ideas*—make today's digital innovators valuable.

Ideas reside in the minds of people. A Web page, a procedures manual, a communications satellite, a network of fiber optic cables—these are necessary transmitters and facilitators of ideas. But by themselves, they make nothing happen. The Dell Choiceboard is a source of value only because Dell's human talent has designed it to appeal to the needs, habits, and interests of customers, who, accordingly, are motivated to use the Choiceboard to set in motion the Dell system for manufacturing and shipping products. "Our assets go down in the elevator every day" is an old business saying. In the digital age, it's finally true.

Today, making the most of the intellectual capital in your company requires that you design all your systems—digital and nondigital—to leverage the time and energy of your talent.

BEYOND HEAD COUNT

The English word *capital* comes from the Latin *caput,* meaning "head." (Think "head of cattle," one of the world's most ancient measures of value.) In terms of its root meaning, the current phrase "intellectual capital" is actually redundant; both words refer to "head power," the creative and problem-solving potential of the human mind.

Unfortunately, we still tend to think of our companies' human assets in terms of head count. We pay lip service to the notion that people are the ultimate source of wealth, but we behave as if they are a liability—a cost to be reduced, or, at best, a "human factor" to be rationalized, controlled, and minimized. Hence the anxiety many employees experience when managers use phrases like "process re-engineering." They fear this is code for "firing people and making those who remain somehow do more with less." They're often correct. This fear, usually unexpressed by your talent, is a source of much resistance to going digital.

In a traditional nondigital business, the need to reduce the "human factor" is very real. It's caused by the fact that many employees are engaged in low-value work—taking orders, filling out forms, transmitting data, tracking procedures, responding to routine requests for the thousandth time, and so on. Under such circumstances, the best thing a worker can do is behave like a reliable machine. Any other action can only delay or derail the process.

No wonder business leaders have focused on human beings primarily as a cost; no wonder Wall Street rewards companies that announce reductions in head count.

Don't misunderstand: It's sometimes necessary to reduce the size of a workforce. Companies have a natural tendency to add people, and they often fail to ensure that their deployment of human resources shifts in sync with shifts in markets or changes in the value chain. Departments, divisions, and businesses then become overstaffed with old-economy skills (often while others are begging for talent). Turnarounds of lagging companies must often begin with intelligently managed layoffs or firings.

One of the ways Digital Business Design can generate 10X Productivity improvements is by reducing the amount of time that people must devote to specific processes—and sometimes eliminating processes altogether. Money is saved and some jobs become unnecessary. *But cutting the head count is not the purpose of Digital Business Design. Its purpose is to free people to devote their time to the most important tasks.*

THE TALENT PYRAMID

Think of the talent-leveraging effects of Digital Business Design as forming a pyramid. From the lowest level of the pyramid to the highest, going digital produces a range of specific benefits.

Cost Cutting

At the lowest and broadest level, shifting to DBD saves money by simplifying processes, moving information more quickly, and reducing or eliminating specific costs. There are countless examples: the millions that companies save in printing, shipping, and storage costs when they virtually eliminate traditional paper forms, for example; or the millions that companies like Cisco, Dell, and IBM have saved by substituting on-line consultations for in-person service calls. This is the level of 10X Productivity gains, where a growing volume of business and an expanding base of customer needs can be served with a stable or even shrinking pool of physical and human assets, thanks to the efficiencies made possible by digitization.

Reducing Drudgery

At the next higher level, going digital saves your talent's time and energy by removing low-value work: gathering and disseminating data, for instance, or responding to purely routine problems. When Microsoft shifted the process of managing its employees' 401(k) plans to the company intranet, a staffer who previously had been trapped in the full-time task of responding to questions about the program (usually the same questions, over and over again) was freed up. She now manages the Web page that handles frequently asked questions, and she spends the rest of her workdays helping employees with more complex or specialized problems that only a human expert can handle.

Adding Value for Customers

At the level above that, going digital permits your talent to focus more directly on activities that benefit your customers. When sales reps (at Cisco, for example) are freed by an on-line Choiceboard from the tasks of filling in, double checking, and transmitting a paper form to record an order, they can spend more time discussing how their customers' businesses are changing and how Cisco's products and services can help manage the transition.

When service reps (at Schwab, for example) have instant access to their customers' entire financial history, they can devote a conversation to helping their customers develop a more effective asset allocation strategy for their portfolios, without having to track down numbers.

When marketing executives (at Dell, for example) have up-to-the-minute information on which lines of products are selling best to customers and which ones are falling out of favor, they can spend a departmental meeting not gathering and comparing staffers' guesses as to where the market is heading, but brainstorming with them about how next season's products should be configured to stay two steps ahead of the competition.

Developing Your Talent Base

At the level above this, going digital creates opportunities for individual talents to grow and develop. A confluence of digital effects makes this possible. These effects include:

- ☐ Reduction in low-value work and a consequent freeing of employees to concentrate on higher-order thinking and acting.
- ☐ Availability of the information needed to stimulate questions about customers' needs and strategic opportunities, and to make it possible to search for the answers painlessly.
- ☐ Increased access, through digital communication systems, to training, research materials, and mentors, both inside and outside the company.

☐ A breakdown of information barriers between departments and divisions within the company, as well as between the company and its suppliers and customers. This encourages employees to think in terms of the entire value system rather than a single product or process.

Many business leaders lament their inability to get employees to "think like owners." In today's most digital businesses, more and more employees *do* think that way. This is true not only because of the use of stock options, which turn employees into owners, but also because access to digital information systems makes it possible for anyone, at any level of an organization, to take a 50,000-foot view of the operation, grasping the purposes of and the connections between the various parts of the system in a way that was once possible only for owners and top management.

Enabling Collaboration

At the level above this, going digital transforms an entire business into a unified, dynamic network of diverse, often geographically dispersed talents that operate together to create and multiply value for customers. Here are two examples.

☐ **Manufacturing teamwork at Saturn.** At GM's Saturn division, about 8,500 auto workers are divided into teams averaging twelve to fifteen members who collaborate on specific functions: building car engines, for example. Each is equipped with a PC using a software system known as CIMplicity, which can continually track operations throughout the plant and can give, for example, an instant analysis of that day's quality concerns. "Through a Web interface the worker can retrieve data from a database, automatically load the data into a spreadsheet, and pivot through the data to analyze it by part and type of problem—trim, door panels, power train, and so on; fit, paint, weld, assembly, installation, and so on" (Gates,

Business @ the Speed of Thought). Without this kind of information flow, there's no way Saturn's team-based manufacturing system could work. Each team hires, fires, and trains its own members, and 20 percent of its compensation is tied to quality, customer satisfaction, and sales.

☐ **Knowledge-sharing at Great Harvest Bread.** Founded in Great Falls, Montana, in 1976, Great Harvest Bread Company has 130 bakeries in thirty-four states and generates annual sales of over $60 million. Before 1999, the individual owner of each bakery operated more or less independently; interaction between the company and the owners was limited to standard training and a few paper documents. That spring, Great Harvest created a companywide intranet for recipes, management tips, and ideas about store decoration, promotions, and marketing. Today, 80 percent of Great Harvest owners communicate with one another regularly via E-mail, and a great idea that springs up in Illinois quickly spreads from coast to coast. "We think of this as an intellectual-property business," says Tom McMakin, the COO, "We're a bread company, but we're also a university."

At the highest level of all, digitization enables companies to transform themselves from silos organized around particular functions, regions, or products, into connected systems that share information and mutually reinforce one another's efforts on behalf of the customer. As Gelacio Iniguez explains, Cemex's IT infrastructure was designed to help create this capability:

> We always had in mind that we would not have islands of information. Even back in 1987, we really believed that the driver of management should be a process design and not a function design, so we could have integration and a single source of information. This would allow people across different geographies to have the same interface, so that if you move from one part of the company to another, you see the same thing. And we replicated the model in every acquisition we made.

Cemex's goal has been to create a single network that would permit knowledge to flow throughout the company, across geographies, and ultimately out to the customers. The shift from silos to systems is perhaps the most far-reaching and powerful of all the benefits your company, your talent, and your customers can enjoy from your shift to Digital Business Design.

A PLACE TO STAND

Digital Business Design produces not just greater efficiency, cost savings, and improved customer service, but also the *redefinition* of many jobs:

- ☐ **Sales reps** shift from being order takers to being customer problem solvers.
- ☐ **Marketers** shift from being data trackers to being opportunity pursuers.
- ☐ **Financial managers** shift from being number crunchers to being strategic analysts.
- ☐ **Service reps** shift from being complaint processors to being value creators.
- ☐ **Managers** shift from being troubleshooters to being coaches and mentors.

This is *leverage* in the original sense of the word. In an old economy driven by scarcity of assets, especially physical and financial capital, leverage came to mean debt—the multiplication of value through borrowing. In the new economy, leverage means increasing the power of your business by shifting your assumptions about how you work. When you adopt Digital Business Design, you greatly multiply the potential of what your talent can do for your customers.

Archimedes, the early Greek scientific theorist, famously commented, "Give me a lever and a place to stand, and I will move the world." Digital Business Design provides both.

KNOWLEDGE VELOCITY

Inventory velocity is a familiar concept. The rate at which inventory turns is an important financial measurement that significantly impacts the profitability of many companies. As we've discussed, Dell is a great example of the power of inventory velocity to enhance a company's bottom line. Dell's use of DBD has enabled it to increase its annual inventory turns from six to sixty.

What Dell does with inventory, digital organizations will do with knowledge.

> **Knowledge velocity** is the rate at which an organization generates, disseminates, reuses, and modifies knowledge among all its talent.

Digital organizations are developing systems for *reusing* the wheel rather than *reinventing* it. When a customer problem is solved once, these organizations capture the solution and make it readily accessible so that the next hundred customers with the same problem can be satisfied in minutes rather than days.

Few organizations today recognize the concept of knowledge velocity, and even fewer consciously pursue it as a goal. Consequently, most organizations are *knowledge sluggish*. Information gets trapped within organizational silos. In some cases, proud fiefdoms hoard their knowledge, hoping to use it as a means of retaining power. More often, people simply never share knowledge because *there is no fast and easy means for doing so.* When customer solutions, best practices, innovative methods, and other ideas do get shared, it's usually by accident. A chance conversation at the buffet table during an offsite meeting leads to the revelation: "Oh, hadn't you heard? We fixed that problem two months ago. . . ."

Good examples of knowledge velocity are few and far between. The digital innovators profiled in this book have all taken steps down this road.

Cisco's on-line customer-service systems capture answers to customers' questions and make them available for others to access at their convenience. A single solution is then reused hundreds of times. Dell's training system does much the same for the company's own talent: A video training module is created once and made available for reuse hundreds of times, at the trainee's convenience and at just the moment when the trainee is ready and able to use the knowledge effectively.

Cemex has one of the most powerful knowledge velocity engines in business today. Its decision-making models are part of that engine. Cemex knows the algorithm for efficiently rescheduling truck routes in response to particular patterns of customers' requests and cancellation flow. Having created the algorithm once, Cemex reapplies it a hundred times.

Cemex's information-sharing systems ensure that knowledge is disseminated as widely as possible within the organization. Thus, a Cemex executive negotiating a deal in the Philippines can post a question on-line and receive suggestions within minutes from colleagues in Venezuela, Spain, and Texas. Few ostensibly knowledge-based businesses (law partnerships, consultancies, accounting firms) have developed knowledge velocity engines as powerful as those at this cement company.

Knowledge velocity practices are beginning to spread to a wide range of companies. One example:

☐ **PIPSA (Producer and Importer of Paper, S.A.)** is a 62-year-old, government-owned paper manufacturer located in the small Mexican town of Tuxtepec. In 1990, the company's official monopoly in newsprint was abolished, which plunged the firm into a competitive environment for the first time. The Mexican government has now announced plans to privatize the firm. PIPSA's response has been to promote leading-edge change by generating and sharing knowledge and ideas among its employees. Employee teams called "learning cells" are structured around specific priorities. Each week, the teams record their newest ideas and findings in a *libro blanco* (white book). Instructors from the company's Center for the Development of Learning and Productive Knowledge collate the ideas and post them on the company's intranet. Partly as a result, and despite the loss of monopoly status, company revenues have mushroomed from $78 million (1994) to $179 million (1999), and capacity is expected to double in the next five years.

The pursuit of knowledge velocity as a business objective is still in its infancy, but, for many companies, it will ultimately prove to be the single greatest benefit of DBD.

FROM POINT A TO POINT B

The greatest challenge in shifting from conventional to Digital Business Design, in getting from point A to point B, is the organizational one. However, a process of change management that begins with partnering at the top, invests in internal marketing, and provides leverage to the talent significantly increases the odds of making the transition successfully. It also begins to create the type of organization that can compete successfully in tomorrow's economy.

EPILOGUE: BE UNIQUE

THE DIGITAL DIFFERENCE REDUX

The technical details involved in going digital are so complex, interesting, and important that it's easy to get lost in them. In this book, we've tried to avoid focusing on stories of gee-whiz technology for its own sake; instead, we broadened our scope to emphasize the customer benefits, strategic impact, and business design implications of digitization. As we've stressed, what matters isn't just selling more products via your Web site, keeping in touch using E-mail, or handling procurement over the Internet. What matters is: moving from getting information in lag time to getting it in real time; from guessing what customers want to knowing their needs; from burdening talent with low-value work to gaining high talent leverage; and from only hearing about to *realizing* all the other benefits of Digital Business Design discussed throughout this book.

In this Epilogue, we'll raise our sights a little higher and consider some even larger implications of DBD. In particular, we'll discuss how DBD has the potential to change some of the most fundamental characteristics of your business and the role DBD can play in your company's quest for the ultimate form of differentiation: *uniqueness.*

FAST, ACCURATE, MORPHABLE, EXTERNAL (FAME)

As digital technologies and the rewiring of old behaviors spread throughout your organization, indirect effects begin to accumulate. Ultimately, your corporate culture is bound to be modified by the spread of the digital virus into every division, department, and business process.

One way to think about the impact of Digital Business Design on your organization is by using the acronym FAME.

> **Digital Business Design can make your organization Fast, Accurate, Morphable, and External.**

Let's consider the significance of each of these advantages.

Fast

How fast is your organization today? How quickly can you make a decision? How rapidly can you act on a decision once it has been made?

Being fast isn't just a matter of shipping products on time, answering customer questions promptly, or making service calls quickly—though it includes all these things. Nor is it merely using digital technology to communicate information rapidly among your people, customers, and suppliers—though it includes this, too. Being fast is also a matter of your business mindset. A sense of speed comes to permeate every facet of an organization; it enhances the management of human resources, finances, internal systems, strategic planning, and every other business function.

We have found that the companies that are moving to a Digital Business Design have become unusually fast at assimilating and acting on knowledge. This earns them a crucial advantage in today's ultracompetitive environment.

For example, Capital One, a rapidly digitizing innovator in the credit-card business, recently had a dialogue with an entrepreneur. In the course of a Friday morning conversation, a new business idea was sparked. The entrepreneur wrote up a business plan for the idea by Saturday. He had the lawyers in on Sunday to work up the paperwork, started negotiating with potential partners on Monday, and had the business up and running within two weeks.

Could such speed be possible without the use of digital technology to assemble, analyze, replicate, and transmit information? Probably not.

More important than the bit engines themselves, however, is the real time mindset that underlies Capital One's responsiveness. It's a cultural shift made possible by digitization; in turn, it enables taking full advantage of the larger benefits of DBD.

Accurate

Being fast and wrong gains you nothing. Speed is important, but accuracy is far more important. Think about "smart bombs" like the ones used in Operation Desert Storm. Electronic target acquisition, not speed, makes them effective.

As we've seen, to an unsettling degree, traditional business is run on the basis of guesswork. Digital Business Design makes it practical to re-place much of that guesswork with information. Using digitization to cap-ture, retain, analyze, move, use, multiply, and reuse data allows you to build a file of your interactions with customers to track how their needs and priorities are changing over time. Digital systems also enable cus-tomers to service their own needs. In many cases, they can find answers to their own questions by accessing your company's databases and configur-ing and buying products themselves rather than through an intermediary. The result is marketing and customer service that is dead-on accurate rather than more-or-less in the ballpark.

Morphable

Rapid change has a simple logic. When the world changes more quickly, you have to change more quickly as well. That requires a business design that is flexible, not fixed; one built around managing bits, not atoms; and one that relies on external resources (outside suppliers, customer-gen-erated information, and so on) rather than costly internal ones. Digitization facilitates all three.

Like every principle, this one has its limits. If it's impossible for exter-nal suppliers to provide the level of performance your customers demand, you may have to build your own source: a factory, a distribution network, a service center. But take this step only as a last resort. When (not *if*) the market moves again and makes your assets irrelevant, your legacy systems will enmesh you, reducing your flexibility and slowing your reaction time. The factory must be reconfigured, rebuilt, or sold; the people who have built careers around running it must be redeployed; the systems that embraced them must be redesigned. All of these steps take time, cost money, and distract attention from moves that can benefit customers more directly. Thus, it's crucial to avoid being saddled with internal resources that aren't central to your business scope.

We see it happen in industry after industry, sometimes several times in a single generation. Barnes & Noble invests heavily in real estate, buying or building mall stores and superstores to create the world's largest book retailer. Amazon.com comes along, selling books on-line, offering an even wider product selection with equal or greater convenience at equal or lower prices—and with no costly real estate to finance and maintain. Not all customers like on-line shopping, especially at first, but Amazon siphons away an increasing share of the book marketplace, and its capital structure allows it to grow at a rate far outstripping any bricks-and-mortar rival. On-line selling enables Amazon to go from start-up to global in one move. To provide even faster global customer service, Amazon builds warehouses—hundreds of millions of dollars' worth.

Now imagine the next stage: The e-book emerges. (Experimental forms of the e-book have already been around for a decade, but a format that a significant number of readers want to embrace has not yet swept the market.) It allows readers to download complete book texts from the Internet in a matter of seconds and at a fraction of the cost of a paperback.

Most customers still prefer physical books—you can't yet loll in a bathtub with an e-book. But a significant and growing percentage of the market accepts the e-book. A new player emerges—let's call it GalaxE. It sells e-books only, offering multi-language fast downloads, with far better economics than even Amazon enjoys.

Today, people are wondering: Can B&N morph quickly enough to catch up with Amazon? Tomorrow, they'll ask: Can Amazon morph to match GalaxE? Digital Business Design puts a premium on the ability to change quickly. The fewer atoms you have to lug about, the more efficiently you can morph.

External

During the past generation, businesspeople have learned how deadly internal self-absorption can be. There's always a Next Big Thing waiting around the corner to make today's skills and today's business design obsolete. The smartest businesspeople are always looking for the Next Big Thing—when they're not busy developing it themselves.

We've found that the pioneers of Digital Business Design are extraordinarily external in their orientation. The typical executive of a digital company is outside his or her office 80 percent of the time, talking to customers, suppliers, distributors, and investors, watching the markets move, and searching for patterns of change. Other employees learn to think that way as well. They continually ask: What's next? What's out there? When and how will we have to change again?

THE ULTIMATE DIFFERENTIATION: BE UNIQUE

In an increasingly interconnected, globalized world, it's becoming more difficult than ever for businesses to achieve differentiation from one another—to give customers a good reason to buy from you rather than from your many rivals. Today, companies large and small, located almost anywhere on the globe, have access to the techniques for producing goods and services at competitive prices and world-class quality standards. These techniques enable them to compete on a level footing with the most powerful and seemingly entrenched incumbents.

Yet new opportunities for business differentiation have also emerged. In the 1960s, in what we might call the Era of Bruce Henderson (often considered the founder of modern strategy), cost was seen as the most important factor by which businesses could differentiate themselves: The low-cost provider almost always swept the field. Later, in the Era of Michael Porter, the options for business differentiation might be mapped onto a 3×3 grid. A business could choose from among three main strategies: to be the low-cost producer, to be a niche player, or to offer a differentiated product. Within this categorization, competitors tried to create advantages on the basis of quality, service, or speed. On this simple playing field the strategic battles of the 1970s and early 1980s were waged.

In the late 1980s and 1990s, new strategic options proliferated. Companies began to find ways of redefining their scope of activity, to reposition themselves as service and solution providers rather than product manufacturers, to seize the opportunities created by dramatic changes in the value chain, and so on. In what we might call the Era of Business Designl, the 3 × 3 grid expanded into something like a 5 × 5 grid; the strategic options available on the playing field more than doubled.

In the early years of the twenty-first century, as we enter a new phase in the evolution of business, Digital Business Design is making available a new array of strategic options. As the businesses we've analyzed and the stories we've told throughout this book illustrate, these options include contacts with entirely new customer sets, new ways of focusing on particular links in the value chain, new methods for creating and managing networks of suppliers and customers, new routes for realizing the value inherent in the information that flows through your business, new leveraging of the creativity and energy of your talent, and many other options that didn't exist even five years ago.

Suddenly, the options available to your company have expanded again. The 5 × 5 grid is now an 8 × 12 grid: the eight dimensions of business design multiplied by as many as a dozen choices in each (see Appendix B).

The new options, in the hands of today's business designers, bring within reach the ultimate goal of differentiation: *uniqueness,* the ability to offer your customers and your talent a set of value propositions that no other company can match. The flexibility and speed made possible by DBD enable you to respond to change and evolve along with your customers and markets, so as to maintain the edge your uniqueness provides. So, in the age of DBD, the most important question your company can ask is: *Are we unique in a way that matters to our customers and our talent?*

The last decades of the twentieth century were the era of the Reinventors: businesses with the insight and courage to redesign themselves as needed to achieve and sustain a special place in the minds of customers, as well as a growing share of sales and profits. The first decades of the twenty-first century will belong to the Digital Reinventors: businesses that know how to take advantage of both traditional and digital options to create and occupy unique and continually evolving positions in a rapidly changing economic universe.

Appendix A

THE BIT ENGINES TABLE AND TOUR

BIT ENGINES CAN BE USED to fix, improve, or strengthen a business design. The Bit Engines Table is a partial list of the bit engines that are available. As companies realize the benefits of a Digital Business Design, they will evolve and expand their technological tools and systems. For examples of some of the bit engines already in use, visit The Bit Engines Tour, available on the Web at http://www.howdigitalisyourbusiness.com.

Bit engines enable changes in the roles of customers and employees. They provide tools and information that do everything from allowing a customer to create a customized product to providing employees with real-time data and information.

This Bit Engine Table can guide you through the business activity chain. Companies use bit engines to bring together customers and suppliers; to supply tools that allow customers to configure a customized product; to recommend further products; to offer productivity tools that help customers use their products; and to enable remote monitoring and diagnostics. Digital businesses use bit engines to provide on-line learning tools, foster community among customers and employees, digitize supply chains and R&D, leverage existing talent, and attract new recruits.

As you use the table, note how different companies have incorporated a variety of bit engines into their businesses. Can you think of any others? Which bit engines could your business use?

Here are some examples from The Bit Engine Tour:

☐ Visit the GE Center for Financial Learning. This e-learning engine provides free interactive workshops and on-line courses on a variety of financial subjects, as well as planning tools such as the Child Expense Calculator.

☐ Take a look at Landsend.com's Personal Model. Lands' End now supplies its customers with several unique bit engines, including productivity tools such as "Your Personal Model," which allows visitors to create a customized 3-D model, receive style tips and fashion advice based on that model, and even try on clothing with a single click. Landsend.com's collection of bit engines provides catalog customers with a way to "test drive" products. It is currently the number-one apparel sales site on the Internet.

☐ Amazon.com's book recommendation engine fosters personalized relationships with customers. It suggests products based on previous purchase decisions. This cross-selling feature enhances the bond with the customer and leads to repeat purchases and increased profitability.

☐ Customers can find answers to their own product questions with Cisco's World Wide Technical Assistance Center (TAC). This bit engine provides registered users with on-line troubleshooting tools for solving complex problems themselves. A customer can type in a question and be immediately directed to the answer and to additional resources.

Take The Bit Engine Tour and see how a number of companies, perhaps with strategic issues similar to yours, addressed their business issues by going digital and incorporating bit engine tools into their business design.

The Bit Engines Table

1. **Choiceboards**
   - ☐ Cisco Configurator
   - ☐ Dell's Configurator
   - ☐ Schwab's Mutual Fund Screener
   - ☐ Frictionless.com
   - ☐ Mattel.com
   - ☐ Point.com
   - ☐ More.com Acumins

2. **Community Engines**
   - ☐ Yahoo! Clubs
   - ☐ Evite.com
   - ☐ AOL Instant Messenger
   - ☐ eBay Message Boards and Chat Rooms
   - ☐ Napster.com
   - ☐ Lands' End Live!

3. **E-Learning Engines**
   - ☐ Cisco E-Learning
   - ☐ GE FinancialLearning.com

4. **Productivity Tools**
   - ☐ Schwab's Retirement Planner
   - ☐ Schwab Asset Allocation Manager
   - ☐ GE's *MyOffice@Fleet*
   - ☐ Dell Premier Pages
   - ☐ Bidcom Services
   - ☐ Cisco's Technical Assistance Center

5. **R&D**
   - ☐ Autodesk Products
   - ☐ PTC Software Solutions

6. **Recommendation Engines**
   - ☐ MySimon.com
   - ☐ Amazon.com Recommendations
   - ☐ Collaborative Filtering
   - ☐ Landsend.com Style

7. **Recruiting**
   - ☐ Cisco's Profiler
   - ☐ Monster.com
   - ☐ Hotjobs.com

8. **Remote Diagnostics**
   - ☐ GE's RM&D
   - ☐ Honeywell Home & Building Controls

9. **Transaction Enablers**
   - ☐ GE's TPN
   - ☐ eBay Auctions
   - ☐ FreeMarkets
   - ☐ Mercata.com

10. **E-Business Enablers**
    - ☐ Siebel Systems
    - ☐ Broad Vision Solutions
    - ☐ Ariba B2B Commerce Platform
    - ☐ Commerce One Solutions
    - ☐ Oracle Databases

Appendix B

HOW DIGITAL BUSINESS DESIGN EXPANDS YOUR OPTIONS

THROUGHOUT THIS BOOK, we have demonstrated how digital opportunities significantly expand the range of business design options available for companies today. Digital technologies, such as the Internet and wireless, make it possible to target new sets of customers, to create new and unique value propositions for customers and employees, to capture new types of value, to develop new forms of scope, and to achieve new levels of strategic control. As a result, companies today can respond to their evolving business issues not only with traditional business design options but with an expanded list of powerful digital options.

In this appendix, we'll briefly describe some of the new Digital Business Design options that have been created in the digital world. The list isn't meant to be exhaustive. It's intended to help you think about how your own business can benefit from the power of Digital Business Design.

To get a quick sense of how fully your company has exploited digital options to move toward a unique business design, take the next two minutes to assess your company's position today, answering the questions on the pages that follow.

HOW DIGITAL IS YOUR BUSINESS DESIGN?

Customer Selection and Value Proposition for the Customer

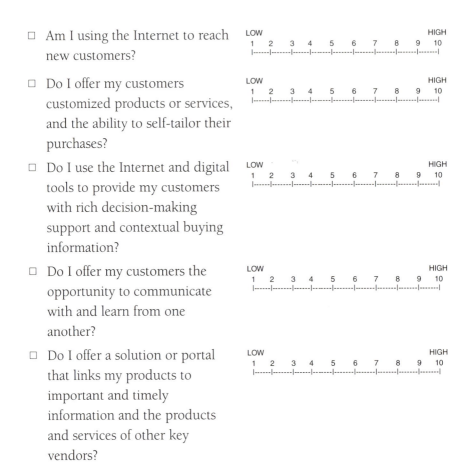

☐ Am I using the Internet to reach new customers?

LOW · · · · · · · · · HIGH · 1 · 2 · 3 · 4 · 5 · 6 · 7 · 8 · 9 · 10

☐ Do I offer my customers customized products or services, and the ability to self-tailor their purchases?

LOW · · · · · · · · · HIGH · 1 · 2 · 3 · 4 · 5 · 6 · 7 · 8 · 9 · 10

☐ Do I use the Internet and digital tools to provide my customers with rich decision-making support and contextual buying information?

LOW · · · · · · · · · HIGH · 1 · 2 · 3 · 4 · 5 · 6 · 7 · 8 · 9 · 10

☐ Do I offer my customers the opportunity to communicate with and learn from one another?

LOW · · · · · · · · · HIGH · 1 · 2 · 3 · 4 · 5 · 6 · 7 · 8 · 9 · 10

☐ Do I offer a solution or portal that links my products to important and timely information and the products and services of other key vendors?

LOW · · · · · · · · · HIGH · 1 · 2 · 3 · 4 · 5 · 6 · 7 · 8 · 9 · 10

Value Proposition for the Talent

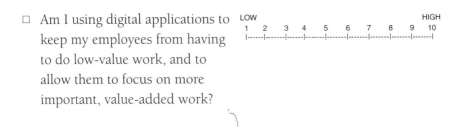

☐ Am I using digital applications to keep my employees from having to do low-value work, and to allow them to focus on more important, value-added work?

LOW · · · · · · · · · HIGH · 1 · 2 · 3 · 4 · 5 · 6 · 7 · 8 · 9 · 10

☐ Am I using digital applications to efficiently and optimally match my employees and recruits with job openings?

☐ Am I using digital applications to provide critical training conveniently and with uniformly high quality?

Profit Model/Value Capture

☐ Am I gaining upsell and add-on revenues through custom product configuration capabilities?

☐ Am I capturing ancillary related revenues by providing access to partners' products and relevant third-party service providers?

☐ Am I realizing higher pricing by delivering products more closely tailored to individual customers' needs or by bundling valuable information with my product?

☐ Have I gained inventory and production efficiencies through more accurate forecasting, faster production cycle times, and reduced inventory holding requirements?

Strategic Control

☐ Have I explicitly integrated
traditional assets with Internet
value-added to create
differentiated hybrid capabilities
relative to my competitors?

```
LOW                              HIGH
1   2   3   4   5   6   7   8   9   10
|-----|-----|-----|-----|-----|-----|-----|-----|-----|
```

☐ Have I created alliances or
licensing relationships that
provide exclusive access to
critical enabling technology in
my industry?

```
LOW                              HIGH
1   2   3   4   5   6   7   8   9   10
|-----|-----|-----|-----|-----|-----|-----|-----|-----|
```

☐ Does my strategy encourage
customer allegiance through
application hosting, creation of
customer-specific information
caches, and provision of
customized interfaces and
decision support that encourage
customers to spend their time
and dollars with me?

```
LOW                              HIGH
1   2   3   4   5   6   7   8   9   10
|-----|-----|-----|-----|-----|-----|-----|-----|-----|
```

☐ Does my business create and
profit from network advantages?
Does the overall utility of my
offering grow as the number of
customers rises? Is my business
constructed so as to encourage
customer growth?

```
LOW                              HIGH
1   2   3   4   5   6   7   8   9   10
|-----|-----|-----|-----|-----|-----|-----|-----|-----|
```

Scope and Activities

☐ Have I used the Internet to
dynamically reconfigure my
supply chain based on
customers' specific requirements?

☐ Have I used the Internet to expand the number and geographic scope of my suppliers?

LOW   HIGH
1   2   3   4   5   6   7   8   9   10
|------|------|------|------|------|------|------|------|------|

☐ Am I using the Internet to supplement traditional channels, to interact directly with customers, or to reach previously underserved customers?

LOW   HIGH
1   2   3   4   5   6   7   8   9   10
|------|------|------|------|------|------|------|------|------|

☐ Have I taken advantage of new digital options to greatly expand my product and service offering?

LOW   HIGH
1   2   3   4   5   6   7   8   9   10
|------|------|------|------|------|------|------|------|------|

WHAT HAVE OTHERS DONE TO DIGITALLY ENHANCE THEIR BUSINESS DESIGNS?

Where does your current business design lie on the Digital Business Design matrix? Where do you feel improvements could be made, to generate the highest possible return? Do new options provide potential quick hits with high short-term impact?

To help you answer these questions, consider the following list. These are common digitally enabled business design moves that many Northeast quadrant companies have implemented. The list is intended to stimulate your thinking so that you can exploit new options and create a truly unique business design for your company.

Customer Selection

☐ Cost-effective access to smaller customers.
☐ Specific niche segments and micro segments.
☐ New customers at different points in the value chain.
☐ New geographies.
☐ New digital-ready customers.
☐ Pre-buying-stage customers.
☐ Post-buying-stage customers.

Unique Value Proposition for the Customer

- ☐ Seamless and enjoyable on-line buying experience.
- ☐ On-line self-service:
    —Check status of order or account.
    —Answer questions.
    —Download software.
    —Check product information.
- ☐ Information destination:
    —Gain education and training.
    —Investigate pros and cons.
    —Do research.
    —Comparison shop.
- ☐ Definition and delivery of exactly what the customer wants.
- ☐ Greater breadth of products and services.
- ☐ Greater depth of products and services.
- ☐ Cost-effective products and services.
- ☐ Convenient purchase and service.
- ☐ Recommendations.
- ☐ More efficient markets.
- ☐ Community.
- ☐ Productivity tools.
- ☐ Maximized uptime.
- ☐ Benefits of a hybrid conventional/digital model.

Unique Value Proposition for the Talent

- ☐ Digital training:
    —Customized.
    —Just in time, just enough.
- ☐ Recruiting "Profiler" to optimally match job descriptions and talent.
- ☐ Convenient and accurate on-line application.
- ☐ Productivity tools.
- ☐ Access to real-time information for decision making.

Value Capture/Profit Model

☐ 10X Productivity improvement:
—Cost.
—Asset.
—Cycle.
☐ Up-sell and cross-sell.
☐ Negative working capital.
☐ No markdowns.
☐ New revenue and margin streams.
☐ Transaction facilitation commissions (from on-line auctions and marketplaces).
☐ On-line advertising.
☐ Referral fees.

Strategic Control

☐ Strong and more continuous bond with the customer:
—On-line destination.
—Premier Pages.
—Community.
—On-line "office."
—Remote monitoring.
☐ More precise knowledge of customers' buying patterns and profiles.
☐ Proprietary partnership networks.
☐ IT scale economies.
☐ Network advantages.
☐ Business redesign speed.

Scope

☐ Substitute bits for atoms.
☐ Empower the active customer:
—Build digital tools.
—Provide information.
☐ Let the customers do what they do best.

☐ Remotely monitor each customer's system.

☐ Interpret the customers' data.

☐ Let suppliers do what they do best.

☐ Migrate the talent base from low-value tasks to high-value tasks.

☐ Figure out what you do best, then do that better and do more of it.

☐ Create, leverage, and maximize external partnerships.

Organizational System/Culture

☐ Digital communication.

☐ From silos to system.

☐ From pyramid model to networked model.

☐ A flatter organization.

☐ Greater collaboration.

☐ Talent leverage systems.

Appendix C

THE CHOICEBOARDS TOUR

CHOICEBOARDS ARE CHANGING the way business is done. They enable customers to design the products they really want. They eliminate mark-downs, and they capture invaluable customer information in real time.

In Chapter 3, we discussed how Choiceboards can be created for products, services, or information, for use by end users or intermediaries. But the key business issues are: What are the most profitable Choiceboard opportunities in my business? How will I capture them first?

If you are interested in a deeper understanding of the concepts of the Choiceboard, we urge you to take The Choiceboards Tour at http://www.howdigitalisyourbusiness.com. It offers a visual investigation into the concept of the Choiceboard that is meant to provide additional insight into the ideas explored in Chapter 3.

After a brief introduction, the tour focuses on the integration of Choiceboards and business design and examines how companies have used Choiceboards to create unique new value propositions and new sources of value capture and strategic control. For example, companies like Point.com capture value through the sale of information; Dell achieves additional value capture from cross-selling and upselling.

Which Choiceboard strategy would be right for your company?

The tour then looks into the three main challenges in implementing a Choiceboard strategy: smart sequence, Value Nets, and differentiating against Choiceboard competitors. Not all Choiceboards need to be targeted at the end consumer. In the auto industry, consumer Choiceboards will not be important for the next two to three years, but dealer Choiceboards are important today. This section of the tour helps answer the question: Who is the key customer for your Choiceboard today: the end user, an intermediary, a supplier, or an internal customer—your employee?

The tour ends with thoughts about the future of Choiceboards, their evolution, and how Choiceboards can be used to help defend against commoditization and pricing transparancy.

Appendix D

THE CISCO TOUR

THE CISCO CONNECTION ONLINE (CCO) is at the forefront of Digital Business Design. It activates customers, enabling them to perform a broad spectrum of tasks by themselves. Cisco lets the customers drive the process by providing them with the advanced tools and features that allow them to download software, configure products, answer their own technical questions, and receive on-line training. The Cisco Tour, which you can take at http://www.howdigitalisyourbusiness.com, illustrates the key bit engines that turn the customer from a passive recipient to an active participant in the Cisco activity chain.

This shift has been made possible by Cisco's dynamic on-line Web site and the array of tools that support it.

☐ The Cisco Software Center not only offers physical fulfillment, but also enables customers to download upgrades and programs on-line. It is a full-service, one-stop-shopping location that can be accessed anywhere, at any time, from a single interface.

☐ Customers can design their own products by using the Configuration Tool. It provides up-to-date product literature, accurate configurations of models in Cisco's product line, and real-time lead times and list prices.

These dynamic features and information systems empower the customer with the knowledge and tools necessary to order products and configure complex systems on their own.

The CCO provides leverage to employees of Cisco:

☐ Prospective talent can apply for a job on-line via the Cisco Profiler, which tailors specific questions to each candidate, based on the background information provided.

311

☐ Customers and employees alike can access on-line learning and training tools such as The Cisco Partner E-Learning Connection, which provides interactive, Web-based courses.

☐ These courses, and other features such as the Technical Assistance Center, illustrate the hybrid structure of the CCO. It is not exclusively about self-service. It also provides the "human touch." Customer Support Engineers are available to work with customers and solve their specific problems.

This combination of individual control and guidance makes the CCO one of the leading Web sites on the Net. How can you leverage your bit engines to let your customers take control of the activity chain?

Appendix E

THE GE TOUR

GE.COM IS BUILDING one of the most advanced and complex Web sites on the Internet. It integrates all of GE's many business units into an extensive network that enables customers to achieve unprecedented levels of interactivity. It serves as a powerful model for organizations looking to move to a DBD, and it offers a great resource to analyze, understand, and emulate.

Given the breadth and depth of the GE site, which would take hours to fully navigate, we have created The GE Tour, available at http://www.howdigitalisyourbusiness.com. The tour leads you through parts of the GE Web site and highlights the next-generation value proposition being developed by the company. This new value proposition provides customers with three new things: Information (both general and unique), Tools (to analyze and decide) and Actions (that are easy to take via GE). Ultimately, GE's approach is designed to create a unique and stronger bond with its customers.

Most e-commerce sites on the Web allow you to purchase products on-line. But what about the ability to design your own products and interactively prevent or fix problems? The engineering design tools center at GE Plastics provides customers with an array of free tools and services, such as datasheets, a visualizer, a calculator, and a troubleshooter. These tools improve customer productivity (through information sharing) and create customer loyalty.

The following unique community builders and interactive tools and services are present throughout GE.com:

- □ GE Power Systems prevents problems before they happen by monitoring up to 1,000 parameters on each gas turbine.
- □ GE Aircraft Engines prevents delays by monitoring engine temperatures.

313

☐ GE Financial Services provides interactive on-line forums with financial experts.

These bit engines provide an extensive array of examples of what DBD can do for your customers and your organization.

ACKNOWLEDGMENTS

How Digital Is Your Business? is the product of the same organizational and intellectual energy that generates insights for the clients of Mercer Management Consulting. As we explored the concept of digital business, feedback from our clients challenged us to look beyond the excitement of new technology and to constantly focus on the underlying business issues. Their tough questions pushed us to gain a deeper understanding of this next phase in business evolution: how to think about it and how to take advantage of it. They provided us with the opportunity to work with them as they confronted their most pressing strategic issues. This constant challenge has helped us to form an understanding of the nature of Digital Business Design. We have come to recognize that it provides the foundation for creating uniqueness in an increasingly competitive business environment.

We would like to thank Karl Weber, who contributed enormously to the process of writing *How Digital Is Your Business?* In addition to sharing his own ideas and anecdotes, Karl's ability to communicate the concepts and potential of Digital Business Design, via analyses, narratives, and his professional observations, was crucial in our effort to present these important concepts to our readers.

We would also like to thank John Mahaney at Crown Business for his coaching, encouragement, guidance, and feedback as the manuscript was developed. His insights shaped our approach and helped us find the right balance among frameworks, case examples, and ideas.

The entire team at Mercer shared their research, their ideas, and their enthusiasm. Without the support of Peter Coster, President of the Mercer Consulting Group, and Jim Down, Vice Chairman of Mercer Management Consulting, we could never have collected the organization's ideas and insights nor integrated them into a useful framework and manuscript. Our partners at Mercer, including Rick Wise, Tim Byrne, Rich Christner, Simon Glynn, Bill Stevenson, Charlie Hoban, Steve Wolin, and John Kania, also contributed their diverse industry experience to validate and improve many of the concepts we have created.

A special thank-you goes to the Digital Business Design team at Mercer, led by Brian Caputo and Jack Kolodny, and including Chris Luo, Susan Sanders, Eric Buxton, Marc Copelovitch, Kang Ahn, and Matt Humbaugh. They gathered much of the research material and shaped many of the concepts included in the book. Helping us move from "guessing" to "knowing," their insights and energy were critical to propelling this project from start to finish.

ADRIAN SLYWOTZKY
DAVID MORRISON

Lexington, Massachusetts
August, 2000

INDEX

ABOUT THE AUTHORS

Adrian J. Slywotzky is the author of *Value Migration* and the coauthor of *The Profit Zone* and *Profit Patterns*. Mr. Slywotzky is a graduate of Harvard College and has an MBA from the Harvard Business School and a JD from Harvard Law School. He is vice president of Mercer Management Consulting and was recently selected by *Industry Week* as one of the six most influential thinkers in management.

David J. Morrison is the coauthor of *The Profit Zone* and *Profit Patterns*. A graduate of the U.S. Naval Academy, he also holds an engineering degree from Princeton and an MBA from Harvard Business School. Mr. Morrison is vice chairman of Mercer Management Consulting and head of Mercer-Digital, the firm's e-commerce practice.

Karl Weber is a writer and editor specializing in business and current affairs. He has worked with a distinguished list of authors that includes CEOs, leading consultants, and investment experts, as well as statesmen like ambassador Richard Butler, Representative Richard Gephardt, and former president Jimmy Carter.